JANUA LINGUARUM

STUDIA MEMORIAE
NICOLAI VAN WIJK DEDICATA

edenda curat

C.H. VAN SCHOONEVELD

Indiana University

Series Minor, 225/1

FOCUS ON MEANING

Volume I

EXPLORATIONS IN SEMANTIC SPACE

by

CHARLES E. OSGOOD
University of Illinois

MOUTON PUBLISHERS · THE HAGUE · PARIS · NEW YORK

ISBN 90 279 3114 3
First edition, second printing 1979
© Copyright 1976, Mouton Publishers, The Hague
Printed in the Netherlands

PREFACE

The common theme that links the three volumes of my psycholinguistic papers is *Focus on Meaning*, but each volume traces the development of a distinguishable strand in the small tapestry I've been trying to weave during my professional lifetime. This first volume takes the reader on an *Exploration of Semantic Space*; the second volume traces the evolution of my concern *From Words to Sentences*; and the third volume, subtitled *Cognizing and Sentencing*, represents my most recent efforts to forge at least the framework of a general psycholinguistic theory of how we understand and create sentences — an abstract performance grammar, if you will.

Chapter 1 of this first volume describes the development of semantic differential technique — from its origins in my own imaginings as a youngster to its maturation in *The Measurement of Meaning* (an obviously over-extended title!) in 1957. To the enduring amazement of its authors (Osgood, Suci and Tannenbaum), this little book became one of the best-sellers on the lists of the University of Illinois Press, and as of this date we can log some 3,000 books and articles which, in one way or another, utilize or refer to this technique. The latter pages of this chapter sample some of the diverse *ethnocentric* (American English) applications of SD technique.

Chapter 2 describes the extension of SD technique to what can very properly be called *anthropocentric* research. Beginning in 1960, and utilizing procedures designed to minimize dependence upon translation, it has been possible to demonstrate the universality of Evaluation, Potency and Activity as the dominant affective features of meaning for humans. Using pan-culturally comparable SD measuring instruments based on this universal semantic system, we are presently probing the affective dimension of subjective culture comparatively working in (now) 30 human communities around the world. This recent work is not covered in this volume, but those readers who are interested are referred to my "Explorations in Semantic Space: a Personal Diary" (1971) and to *Cross-cultural Universals of Affective Meaning* (Osgood. May and Miron, University of Illinois Press, 1975).

The intimate relation of these affective features of meaning to the well-attested dimensions of human emotions or feelings (Pleasantness, Tension-Control, and Activation) leads directly into Chapter 3 — an investigation into *the semantics of communication via facial expressions*. As indicated, this paper traces research that began when I was an Instructor at Yale in the mid-1940's, was toyed with in Information Theory terms in the mid-1950's, and was finally put together in the mid-1960's! The data as a whole point to this semantic system as having the structure of a truncated pyramid, with Activation-deactivation differentiating first into Pleasantness-unpleasantness and finally into Controlled-uncontrolled distinctions.

By virtue of the fact that semantic differential technique literally forces metaphorical usage of the terms defining the bipolar qualifiers scales, it amplifies affective features (apparently the common coin of metaphors) at the expense of those finer, more denotative, features with which linguists and philosophers are familiar. Chapter 4 describes more recent research on the development of *semantic interaction technique*. This is a semantic-feature discovery procedure that is based upon the rules of usage (appositeness, acceptability, anomaly) of words in syntactic combination — as judged by ordinary native speakers. I believe that this technique will prove to have much greater generality of application to semantic domains than the semantic differential technique — which, of course, does pull out affective aspects of meaning that still have great biological significance.

I would like to tell the reader something about how this three-volume collection of my psycholinguistic papers was prepared. As one who has had occasion to review several collections of papers by others in my field, I have developed certain rather intense biases. The nadir of such collections is characterized by (a) stringing papers in temporal sequence regardless of thematic content, (b) retaining the redundancies that inevitably result from writing for different audiences at different times, (c) having separate reference lists (often in quite different styles) for the separate papers, (d) being devoid of author or subject indexes, and (e) often being edited, not by the author of the collected papers, but by someone else. All of this makes such collections difficult to use — and even a bit unpleasant to read, independent of the value of the content.

I have spent a good bit of time in the editing of the three volumes that make up this collection, and the manuscripts have been completely re-typed for stylistic consistency (for which I must express my deep appreciation to Cathy Cappel, Shirley Watson and Stephanie Blackett, my personal secretaries over the several years involved). In the process of editing, I have (a) organized the papers in each volume in the logical order of their thematic content regardless of dates of publication (for example, in Volume II a very recent paper by Rumjahn Hoosain and myself on the "Salience of the Word as a Unit in the Perception of Language" (1973) follows a 1957 paper and in turn is followed by a paper dated 1960); I have (b) tried to reduce redundancies across papers as much as possible by deletions, always indicated by asterisks and footnotes stating "... added in 1974" or whatever was the appropriate date (for example, in Volume I large sections of Chapter 2, from my "Explorations in Semantic Space," which were covered in Chapter 1, are deleted); I have (c) arranged a single set of references, from all papers combined, for each of the three volumes; I plan to make indexes for each volume as I get the page-proofs in hand; and (e), in the process of editing these papers myself, I have added footnotes rather liberally (again, always indicated as added at the time of editing) to make certain up-dating comments and to orient the reader to relationships across papers, both within and between volumes.

I hope that these efforts will make these volumes of my psycholinguistic papers more readable than they otherwise might be — but, needless to say, the substance will have to speak for itself. Finally, I want to express my deepest gratitude to my wife, Cynthia — known by most as "Patty" (because, when we met back in 1938 in Hanover, New Hampshire, the only thing "Cynthia" made me think of was a brand of chocolates!) — without whose constant love and support none of what I've done would have been possible.

C. E. O.
Urbana, 1974

TABLE OF CONTENTS

Chapter 1

SEMANTIC DIFFERENTIAL TECHNIQUE: ETHNOCENTRICS

CONCEPTUAL ORIGINS: A PERSONAL DIARY[1]

My Grandfather Osgood — a graduate of Harvard University in the 1880's and a successful dentist in Boston — always felt frustrated because he had not become a college professor. As early as I can remember, he played all kinds of word games with me, teasing out subtle distinctions in meaning, giving me short lists of rare words to memorize, and rewarding me with penny candies when I used them spontaneously and correctly. I was thus one of the first M & M children, although the reinforcers were actually jelly-beans. Miss Grace Osgood — or Auntie Grae as I called her then and still do — was at that time a student at Wellesley College and soon to become a history teacher at Thayer School in Braintree; she was a participant-observer in these word games, giving me a helping hand from time to time behind the scenes, and on my tenth birthday (I believe it was) gave me Roget's *Thesaurus* — probably to even the odds a bit with Grampa O! I remember spending hours and hours exploring the Thesaurus — not then as a tool but as an object of aesthetic pleasure.

I also recall my visual representation of the *Thesaurus* — a vivid image of words as clusters of starlike points in an immense space. I have always been a visualizer, which may explain why I did well in geometry but miserably in algebra. It was soon after this that I began what I thought was to be a career as a writer. Since I was already devouring all of the fantasy, horror and science fiction I could lay my hands on — an appetite acquired from my father and appeased during long morning hours in the attic while everyone else was asleep — naturally my earliest efforts dealt with oozy monsters rising from the crypts of ancient castles, armies of giant ants sweeping the earth, and

[1] Excerpted from a version of "Exploration in Semantic Space: A Personal Diary" appearing in *The Psychologists* (T.S. Krawiec, Ed.), Oxford University Press, 1974.

such-like. At Brookline High (near Boston) I became editor of both the weekly newspaper and the monthly magazine, and soon became skilled at working reporter-style with a few fingers of each hand on a second-hand Royal #10 that my Grandfather Egerton had given me. And I turned to more psycho-dynamic stories about my family and my own budding romances. I collected my full share of rejection slips from editors of short-story magazines, a few of which I prize because they were intimate and encouraging.

Why I sub-title this paper "a personal diary" must now be obvious. But why do I title it "exploration" in semantic space? It is not just because I was for many years Director of an Institute of Communications Research organized within a College of Journalism — and "exploration in semantic space" *does* have a certain swing in an age of human exploration of outer space; it is rather because, for me, it *has* been an exploration — in time, in methods and in geographical space, as well as in the inner, subjective space of meaning.

The notion of a concept-studded semantic space — potentially quantifiable — lay dormant until I had been at Dartmouth College for a couple of years. I had gone there with the vague idea that I would get experience on the college newspaper while studying English literature and creative writing. And then I would support myself by newspaper work while writing The Great American Novel. But during my sophomore year I happened to take Introductory Psychology and then an advanced course with the late Professor Theodore Karwoski, affectionately known on campus as "The Count." I found what I had been, unknowingly, looking for all the time — the right combination of demand for rigor and room for creativity — and I forgot about writing The Great American Novel.

Ted Karwoski was a most remarkable person — quietly insightful, capable of thinking simultaneously on several levels and moving fluently among them, warmly supportive of students from whom he felt a returning spark, and thoroughly disorderly. My own father had died when I was thirteen, and in any case he had been a remote every-other-weekend-and-holidays figure since a divorce when I was only six. Although I did not realize it at the time, of course, Professor Karwoski became for me the intellectual goad that my Grandfather Osgood had been and the intimate confidant that my father had never been. If one could dedicate this report on my own explorations in semantic space to someone, it would certainly be Ted Karwoski. At the point when I moved into his life, he was doing casual experiments on color-music synesthesia and, more importantly, was thinking deeply about their implications for human cognition. He had the notion of "parallel polarity" among dimensions of human experience — the Yin and Yang of things — and conceived of synesthesia, not as a quirk of sensory neurology, but as a universal semantic process of translation across equivalent portions of dimensions thus made parallel. This, of course, is a complex and continuous case of what is called "metaphor" in language.

It would be hard to imagine an intellectual environment better suited to a young man with visions of semantic space in his head. Karwoski's associate in research was a younger man from Harvard, Henry Odbert, who had done his thesis research on the semantics of personality traits under Gordon Allport. Later Ross Stagner brought to Dartmouth his skills in attitude measurement and his intense concern with issues of peace and war — with World War II just over the horizon. Out of my apprenticeship with these men — an apprenticeship much more intimate and exciting than most graduate students in these crowded days are likely to enjoy — came studies of parallelism of visual and auditory dimensions, as observed both in complex synesthetes, and in the use of descriptive adjectives in ordinary language (Karwoski, Odbert and Osgood, 1942). Being a minor in Anthropology as an undergraduate at Dartmouth, I tried to determine the generality of such dimensional parallelisms across cultures, using firsthand ethnographic reports. With Ross Stagner, I studied the changing meanings of critical concepts as the United States moved closer to, and then, with Pearl Harbor, fully into World War II (Stagner and Osgood, 1941, 1946). The latter studies, along with research on occupational prestige with Professor Chauncy Allen (Osgood, Allen and Odbert, 1939), represented our first use of 7-step scales defined by adjectival opposites — which was later to be embodied in the Semantic Differential Technique — but the multidimensional concept was lacking, nearly all scales being Evaluative (attitudinal) in nature.

After an extra year at Dartmouth beyond my bachelor's degree — during which I served as everything from research associate to mimeograph operator — I went to Yale for graduate work. Like nearly everyone else there at the time, I got swept up into the monumental edifice of learning theory that Clark Hull was building. I had the heady feeling that here, with appropriate elaborations, lay the key to even the most complex of human behaviors, including language. Visions of semantic space receded, but the problem of dealing with meaning in learning theory terms came to the fore. My doctoral thesis (Osgood, 1946), among other things, was a test of a theory of meaning based upon sets of reciprocally antagonistic reaction systems – an extension and elaboration of Hull's notion of anticipatory goal reactions serving as mediators of overt behavior. I owe a debt of gratitude to Donald G. Marquis for keeping my interest in language alive, as well as to Charles Morris, who came to Yale as a Visiting Professor in time to help me defend my thesis. I am also grateful to the Powers that Be for seeing to it that I never became one of Hull's research assistants – else I almost certainly would have become, not a rat-pusher, but a clinician.

I wish more present-day students could have the experience I did of *independent* teaching while still in graduate school. This was during the war years while most of the faculty was in Washington as consultants, and as a third-year student I found myself teaching *all* of Introductory Psychology at Yale. I think that teaching is at its best when the ideas are being freshly molded by the instructor as well as the instructed, and there is no better way to discover what you really *don't* understand than to try to teach it to someone else. The same thing applied to writing textbooks – which is (or should be) a kind of teaching, too – as I discovered during three busy years at the University of Connecticut after the War, more or less simultaneously writing and teaching graduate experimental psychology.

Then, in the spring of 1949, came one of those academic bonanzas that all young scholars hope for – a chance for an associate professorship with tenure *and* a half-time research appointment for research of one's own devising to boot. (I must remind you that those were the days when we had bona fide Ph.D.'s as instructors.) From far away Illinois came a "feeler" about just such a position along with an invitation to pay them a visit. So onto the overnight sleeper and off to the cornfields, where I discovered that Ross Stagner, with whom I had worked at Dartmouth, and Hobart Mowrer, whom I had known at Yale, along with Wilbur Schramm, Director of a new Institute of Communications Research, were looking for a young man to develop research and teaching on the psychology of language – in short, *a psycholinguist* (although it would be several years before that title came into vogue).

THREE MODELS OF M

Needless to say, the people at Illinois were interested to know just what I might do by way of research in their new Institute – should I in fact be offered the position. So, back in Storrs, Connecticut, I began, for the first time, trying to put together, and down on paper, first a *behavioral theory of meaning* (based on Hullian learning theory, but with a more general representational twist), second a *measurement model* (based on the earlier attitude scaling studies with Stagner but tuned to the then new developments in multivariate statistics, in which I had discovered Illinois to be a hotbed of activity, what with Lee Cronbach, Ray Cattell and others on the scene), and third *an image of a semantic space* (based on my childhood explorations of Roget's *Thesaurus* and drawn from wherever one stores such things).

My original "vision" of a concept-studded space was refined to specify an *origin* or neutral point of the space, defined as "meaninglessness" (analogous to the neutral-grey of the color space), and to conceive of meaningful concepts as the end-points of *vectors* extending into this space, with lengths of the vectors indicating degrees of "meaningfulness" (like saturation in the color space) and their directions indicating the "quality of meaning" (analogous to both the brightness and hue dimensions of the color space). Thus two concepts might be similar in quality of meaning (same direction in the space) yet be quite different in intensity of meaning (distance from the origin), like HATRED and ANNOYANCE; or two concepts might be equally intense in meaning, yet be very different in quality of meaning, like GOD and DEVIL. And one could nicely specify adjectival opposites, like *hot* vs. *cold* or *hard* vs. *soft*, as points equidistant and in opposite directions from the origin of the space, connecting them with an imaginary line through the origin – thus analogous to complementary colors which, when mixed in roughly equal amounts, cancel each other out to neutral grey (or meaninglessness).

This spatial model lent itself directly to factor analysis as a mathematical means of bringing order out of the apparent chaos of lines (defined by adjectives or qualifiers) and points (defined by concepts or substantives). In semantic differential (SD) measurement operations a sample of concepts (e.g., TORNADO, SYMPATHY, MOTHER-IN-LAW, JUDGE) is rated against a sample of scales (e.g., *fair-unfair, hot-cold, tough-tender, quick-slow,* etc.) by a sample of native speakers of a given language — in our early work, American English speakers, of course. This generates a cube of data — Concepts X scales X subjects — and each cell in the cube contains the judgment of a particular subject about a particular concept on a particular scale, e.g.,

TORNADO

fair   :   :   :   :   :   :   X   unfair
_____

Thus each cell is a kind of implicit sentence produced by a particular speaker — here, John Jones "saying" that *a tornado is very unfair.* (I use deliberately this example of a "sentence" which would not ordinarily be said in English; we shall return to the methodological and theoretical implications). This cube of data is correlated (each scale against every other scale, across both concepts and subjects) and factor analysed, to determine the smallest number of underlying factors, or semantic features, which will account for the largest amount of the variance in judgments.

My behavior theory attributes the meaning (M) of all signs, both linguistic and non-linguistic (or perceptual), to *representational mediation processes* or r_M's. These mediating processes are developed via the association of signs (words, perceptual images) with significates (referents or things signified, the objects and events with which humans interact); some distinctive representation of the total behavior made to the Things comes to occur to the Signs of these things, and thereby the signs come to "mean" *these* things and not other things. Although such r_M (note that the subscript is a capital *M) as wholes* bear a unique one-to-one relation with the total behavior made to the things signified (R_T), they are analysable into sets of *component mediators* or r_m (note the lower case *m*), these components representing those aspects of behavior to things which have made a difference in adjustment to those things, and hence have been differentially reinforced. These meaningful mediation processes are (a) hypothetical constructs in total behavior theory, (b) have response-like functions in decoding (language understanding) and stimulus-like functions in encoding (language creating), and (c) render functionally equivalent both classes of signs and classes of behaviors — the "emic" principle of behavior theory.

By the time LAD (popular acronym for "Language Acquisition Device") is launching himself into linguistic sign learning, perceptual signs of most of the entities in his familiar environment (utensils, food objects, pets, toys, faces that smile and faces that frown) have been meaningfully differentiated in terms of distinctive mediators. Not only can such pre-linguistic processes serve as "pre-fabricated" mediators in the subsequent learning of linguistic signs, but even more importantly many of the distinctive features of meaning have already been established.

During the past decade there has been considerable debate — notable perhaps more for its heat than for its light — over the adequacy of *any* behavioristic theory, based on associative principles, for language and meaning. Beginning in 1959 with the brilliant critique of B.F. Skinner's *Verbal Behavior* by generative grammarian Noam Chomsky — to which Skinner has never replied — and continuing with attempts by philosopher-psychologist Jerry Fodor to show that representational mediation theory can be reduced to single-stage associationistic theories (Fodor, 1965, 1966) — to which I have replied (Osgood, 1966b, 1969) — this debate still goes on, the most recent contribution being a formidable, formal analysis by a young Finnish philosopher of science named Raimo Tuomela. I am happy to be able to say that Tuomela (1973) concludes that Fodor did fail to make his case! Further details of this debate would be out of place at this point.

I have been accused — by some of my close associates as well as by some of my dissociates — of being schizophrenic as far as my SD measurement model and my representational mediation theory of meaning are concerned. There is, they claim, no obvious relation between loadings on factors and little r_m's. This is, of course, disturbing to one who considers himself reasonably neat and internally consistent. My answer is that, the relation is not obvious simply because these critics have a feeble grasp of multivariate statistics, learning theory, or both. But this assertion — obviously — requires some elaboration.

Let us look first at the relation between spatial and measurement models. In the spatial model the meaning of a concept (it's M) is represented by a point in n-dimensional space. And, of course, since the psychological opposites which define each bi-polar scale are also concepts (albeit adjectives rather than nouns), they too are represented as points in the common semantic space, connected by an imaginary line running through the origin, and they therefore have their M's, too. Now, when a subject is asked to create a "sentence" of the specified type (*N is Quantifier Qualifier*), using a given noun concept and adjectival scale-pair, what he does, in effect, is to drop the shortest projection from the concept point to the adjective-pair line (which is necessarily at right-angles to that line and therefore the projection of the point onto the line), thereby generating the most nearly congruent judgment. If MOUNTAIN projects close to the *large* end of a *large-small* line, then *MOUNTAIN (is) very large* (checkmark on +3 of the scale) is the most congruent "sentence" for this item. If SYMPATHY projects just a little toward the *hot* side of a *hot-cold* line, then *SYMPATHY (is) slightly hot* is the most congruent "sentence."

As shown in Figure 1, application of the factor-analytic measurement model provides a framework of underlying dimensions *which is common to both concept-meanings and scale-meanings* and in terms of which both can be described in relation to each other. These underlying dimensions thus have the functional properties of semantic features. Anticipating our results for those who are unfamiliar with this research, SD technique typically yields three dominant affective factors (or features): Evaluation (Good/Bad), Potency (Strong/Weak) and Activity (Active/Passive).

We refer to scales as having *loadings* on these underlying factors; the scale *kind-cruel*, for example, has loadings of +.70 on E, −.35 on P (that is, *cruel* is more Potent than *kind*), and −.15 on A. From these loadings we can assign *kind* and *cruel* their reciprocal locations in the space. We can characterize *kind* as being Very Good, Quite Weak and Slightly Passive affectively, and *cruel* as being Very Bad, Quite Strong and Slightly Active. We refer to concepts as having *scores* on the same underlying factors; it the concept COWARD, for example, had scores of −.50 on E, −.70 on P and +.20 on A, its affectivity paraphrase would be a COWARD is Quite Bad, Very Weak and Slightly Active.

Fig. 1.

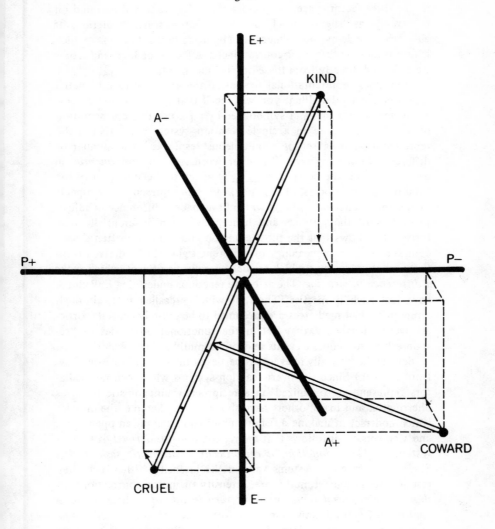

kind-cruel:　E+.70　P−.35　A−.15　loadings
COWARD:　E−.50　P−.70　A+.20　scores

Making the projection from the COWARD point to the *kind-cruel* line in the three-factor space, we predict that COWARD will be rated on the average as "slightly cruel" on the *kind-cruel* scale. Predictions of all concept/scale mean judgments can be made in this fashion — which is not at all remarkable, of course, since the factor loadings and scores were derived directly from these original judgments.

How does representational mediation theory relate to this spatial measurement model? First, you will recall that the mediation process associated with a sign and symbolized by r_M is *not* the representation of a simple response in a single reaction system but rather is the representation of a set of simultaneous responses in a number of different reaction systems. In other words, r_M is *componential* in nature. Second, the components (r_m's) which do become part of the total mediation process, or meaning, of a sign represent those aspects of the total behavior to things which have made a difference in adjustment toward these things and hence have been differentially reinforced. It follows that the most common and therefore often shared components of the meanings of different signs will be derived from those reaction systems which are behaviorally significant, which *make a difference in meaning*. The affective reactions underlying E, P and A have just such properties. Third, it will be recalled that, although representational mediators are presumed to be entirely central (cortical) events, in theory they retain the functional properties of "responses" as subsequent events and of "stimuli" as antecedent events.

Several theoretically relevant properties of mediation processes flow from this: (a) Since the overt reaction systems which central mediators represent are organized on a reciprocally antagonistic basis, as Sherrington and many others have shown — for example, the muscles which contract in making a fist are inhibited in making an open hand, and vice versa — it follows that *the r_m components derived from such systems will also function in reciprocally antagonistic fashion*. (b) Since overt reaction systems vary in the intensity with which they respond to various stimuli (here, intensity of motor contraction), *so should their central representations vary in intensity* (here, presumably rate of neutral activation). And (c), since the same reaction system cannot assume reciprocally antagonistic "postures" at the same time, but rather must display compromise between excitatory and inhibitory tendencies, it follows that *simultaneous tendencies toward* *antagonistic* r_m's (e.g., toward +E and −E) *must cancel each other toward neutrality or meaninglessness.* This last property of representational mediation processes is the entrée of behavior theory to cognitive dynamics generally (e.g., the "balance" theories of Heider, 1946, 1958; Festinger, 1957; and Osgood and Tannenbaum, 1955) and into semantic anomaly specifically.

Now, with the help of Figure 2 we can demonstrate the isomorphism of behavioral and measurement models. I chose this old figure from *The Measurement of Meaning* deliberately to show that way back in 1957 the componential notion of meaning was part of our thinking. I simply change the subscripts in the upper diagram to capital *M*s, and it comes up to date. *I identify the underlying semantic factors or features derived in the measurement model with the affective components* (r_m's) *of representational mediation processes.* That such features are characteristically bipolar in nature is consistent with the reciprocally antagonistic nature of the reaction systems from which such mediator components arise. That semantic features should be ordered in weight factor analytically and in productivity linguistically (frequency and diversity of usage as aspects of meaning) is consistent with the behavioristic notion of differential reinforcement of those mediating behaviors which make a difference in adjustment. Thus in the affective meaning system Evaluation (the Good vs. Bad of things) has more weight than Activity, just as Sex (the Masculine vs. Feminine of things) has more weight than Maritality in the semantics of kinship. *I identify the points in the measurement space which represent the meanings of concepts* (whether they be nominals like COWARD or adjectivals like *kind* and *cruel*) *with the total and unique mediation processes* (r_M's) *presumed in theory to be elicited by signs.* Such total representational processes, however, are analysable into simultaneous bundles of mediator components which vary in polarity and intensity (the directions and lenghts of vectors in Figure 2). But these components are *not* unique to particular signs; rather they are shared in different combinations by many signs.

I am not making the claim, of course, that representational mediation theory is the *only* theory appropriate to the SD spatial and measurement models; I am merely claiming that it is entirely consistent with these models. I must also point out that my semantic theory is not really inconsistent with many views held by linguists and philos-

Fig. 2.

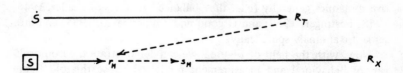

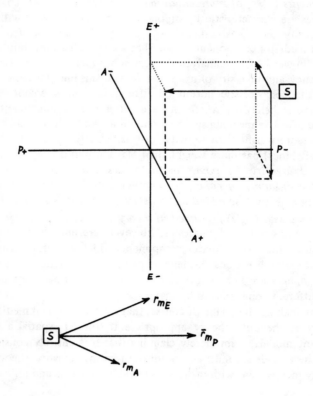

ophers, including as it does componential and polarity principles. It differs from most others, however, in its specification of continuous features as the general case (with discrete + or − codings presumably being a result of non-discriminate, high-frequency usage) and in its derivation of semantic features from actual behaviors toward things signified in the history of the organism. I would argue that derivation of semantic features from behaviors which have differential adaptive significance has the advantage of sharply constraining the proliferation of such features while enhancing the prospect of discovering ones that are universal in human languages.

Well, somehow I got the job at Illinois in 1949 and have been there ever since. The rationale I then gave for my coming research was not exactly as I have given it here − much troubled methodological and theoretical water has flowed under the bridge in 22 years − but the essentials were there and have not changed. Aided mightily by George Suci, the first research assistant I ever had, and abetted by interested students and colleagues like Percy Tannenbaum, Al Heyer and Larry O'Kelly, I started exploring semantic space in earnest. We began, of course, by demonstrating in a *Psychological Bulletin* article (Osgood, 1952) the abject wrong-headedness and futility of all previous psychological attempts to measure that elusive thing called "meaning" − including association, generalization and salivation techniques − and set forth both the mediation theory and the fragile beginnings of the SD technique.

ETHNOCENTRICS[2]

The meaning of a sign has been defined as a representational mediation process, a complex reaction divisible into some unknown but finite number of components. This learning theory construct has been tentatively coordinated with our measuring operations by identifying this complex mediation reaction with a point in a multi-dimensional space. The projections of this point onto the various dimensions of the semantic space are assumed to correspond to what component

[2] Excerpts from pp. 31-75 of Osgood, Suci and Tannenbaum, *The Measurement of Meaning,* University of Illinois Press, 1957.

mediating reactions are associated with the sign and with what degrees of intensity. The essential operation of measurement is the successive allocation of a concept to a series of descriptive scales defined by polar adjectives, these scales selected so as to be representative of the major dimensions along which meaningful processes vary. In order to select a set of scales having these properties, it is necessary to determine what the major dimensions of the semantic space are. Some form of factor analysis seems the logical tool for such a multidimensional exploratory task. In this chapter we describe a series of factor analytic studies designed to isolate and identify the major factors operating in meaningful judgments.

Before describing particular factor studies, it will be useful to discuss a few of the general requirements of this approach. One of the most important requirements is, of course, *representative sampling*. Our problem is different from most factor studies in that we are dealing with three sources of variability — subjects, scales, and concepts judged. Since the purpose of our factoring work is to discover the "natural" dimensionality of the semantic space, the system of factors which together account for the variance in meaningful judgments, it is important that our sample be as free from bias as possible. The nature and number of factors obtainable in any analysis is limited by the sources of variability in the original data — in a real sense, you only can get out what you put in — and we wished to avoid both the production of artificial factors by deliberately inserting scales or concepts according to a priori hypotheses and the omission of significant factors through insufficient sampling.

Our sampling has not been entirely satisfactory. Perhaps the greatest inadequacy has been in *subject variance*. Ideally, our subject sample should be a representative crosssection of the general population. For the major factorial studies, however, we have employed college undergraduates. There are some advantages in this choice, of course — having a higher average intelligence they probably yield a clearer picture of the most finely differentiated semantic space. Our greatest care has been taken with the *sampling of descriptive scales*, since it is dimensionality of the scale system in which we are mainly interested. And the chief danger was that some a priori conceptions of what the semantic space should look like would influence our sampling. To avoid such bias, we have sampled scales in terms of an external criterion (with respect to the experimenters). In the first case this criterion was sheer frequency-of-usage in the college population of descriptive terms as qualifiers. Since it became apparent that this criterion resulted in a relative overloading of scales representing the dominant factor, and did not permit identification of many minor factors at all, in a subsequent factorization we used Roget's *Thesaurus* as a source of scales, logically a more exhaustive sampling criterion.

The results of any factor analysis, including the somewhat intuitive identification and labeling of factors, at best merely provides an hypothesis to be tested in further factor analyses. One's confidence in the validity of a particular factor structure grows as this structure persistently reappears in replications of the analysis. However, there is a danger of forcing the same structure to appear again by using the factors obtained in the first study as a criterion for selecting the scales to be used in the subsequent studies. In other words, it is no trick to get the same factors in a second study if one deliberately selects groups of variables to go with, and duplicate, the variables already isolated as factors. But this tests neither the validity nor the generality of the factor structure originally obtained — it merely reaffirms whatever biases were present in the first analysis. Therefore, whenever we have varied the sample of scales, we have made the sampling independent of previous factor results (except for the inclusion of a small number of reference scales).

Analysis I: Centroid Factorization, Graphic Method

Sampling. In obtaining a sample of scales of semantic judgment, a frequency-of-usage or availability criterion was used. Forty nouns were taken from the Kent-Rosanoff list of stimulus words for free association and these were read in fairly rapid succession to a group of approximately 200 undergraduate students. These subjects were instructed to write down after each stimulus noun the first descriptive adjective that occurred to them (e.g., TREE — *green*; HOUSE — *big*; PRIEST — *good*). These subjects were asked not to search for exotic qualifiers, simply to give whatever occurred to them immediately, and the rapid rate of presentation further restricted the likelihood of getting rare associates. These data were then analyzed for frequency of occurrence of all adjectives, regardless of the stimulus words with which they had appeared. These frequently used adjectives were made into sets of polar opposites and served as the sample of descriptive scales used in this study. For theoretical reasons, a few additional sensory continua were inserted in this set of 50; these scales were *pungent-bland*, *fragrant-foul*, and *bright-dark*.

The sampling of concepts presented a less critical problem, since our purpose was a factor analysis of scales of judgment rather than of concepts. It was important, however, that these concepts be others than those on which the adjective sample had been based (the 40 original stimulus words from the Kent-Rosanoff lists), that they be as diversified in meaning as possible so as to augment the total varia-bility in judgments, and that they be familiar to the subjects we intended to use. On these bases the experimenters simply selected the following 20 concepts: LADY, BOULDER, SIN, FATHER, LAKE, SYMPHONY, RUSSIAN, FEATHER, ME, FIRE, BABY, FRAUD, GOD, PATRIOT, TORNADO, SWORD, MOTHER, STATUE, COP, AMERICA. The availability and test-sophistication of the college stu-dent population dictated our sampling of *subjects*. A group of 100 students in introductory psychology served; they were well paid for their work, and internal evidence testifies to the care with which they did a long and not very exciting task.

Procedure. The pairing of 50 descriptive scales with 20 concepts in all possible combinations generates a 1000-item test form. The order-ing of concept-scale pairings was deliberately rotated rather than rand-om; it was felt that this procedure would better guarantee indepen-dence of judgments, since the maximum number of items (19), would intervene between successive judgments of the same concept and the maximum number of items (49) would intervene between successive judgments on the same scale. Each item appeared as follows:

LADY rough   :   :   :   :   :   :   smooth,

with the subject instructed to place a check-mark in that position indicating both the direction and intensity of his judgment.

Treatment of data. The combination of scales, concepts, and subjects used in this study generates a 50 x 20 x 100 cube of data. Each scale position was assigned a number, from 1 to 7 arbitrarily from left to right, and hence each cell in this cube contains a number representing the judgment of a particular concept, on a particular scale, by a particular subject.

Matrix of Intercorrelations. Each subject provides a complete set of 50 judgments on each of 20 concepts — one judgment on each scale. Since both subjects and concepts are replicated, it would be possible to obtain separate matrices of scale intercorrelations for individual subjects (summing over concepts) as well as for individual concepts (summing over subjects). However, since our long-run purpose was to set up a semantic measuring instrument which would be applicable to people and concepts in general, we wished to obtain that matrix of intercorrelations among scales which would be most representative or typical. We therefore summed over both subjects and concepts, generating a single 50 x 50 intercorrelational matrix of every scale with every other scale to which the total data contribute. Another reason for summing over concepts was to avoid spuriously low correlations resulting from low variability of judgments on single concepts. If nearly all subjects call TORNADO extremely *cruel* and also agree in calling it extremely *unpleasant*, the correlation between *kind-cruel* and *pleasant-unpleasant* would approach indeterminacy, despite the fact that over concepts in general there is a high positive correlation between these scales.

Each of the 50 scales was responded to 2000 times, each of the 100 subjects responding once to each of 20 concepts. Thus, every scale can be paired with every other scale 2000 times, each subject contributing 20 pairs to the total and each concept contributing 100 pairs. In computing each correlation — the summations for cross-products — means and variances were taken across both subjects and concepts. If X_{ijv} is the score on the ith scale, for the jth concept, and vth subject, and $\overline{X}_{i..}$ is the mean for the ith scale found by summing over concepts and subjects and dividing by 20 x 100, then the cross-products between scales i and k in deviations from the means were found from:

$$\sum_{j}\sum_{v} (X_{ijv} - \overline{X}_{i..}) (X_{kjv} - \overline{X}_{k..}).$$

The expression for the variance on scale i is then:

$$\frac{\underset{j\ v}{\Sigma\Sigma}\ (X_{ijv} - \overline{X}_{i\ .\ .})^2}{N}$$

These intercorrelations were calculated with IBM equipment.

Thurstone's Centroid Factor Method (1947) was applied to this matrix of correlations. Four factors were extracted and rotated into simple structure, maintaining orthogonality. The rotated factor matrix for this first analysis appears as Table 1. Since orthogonal relations were maintained in rotation, the matrix in this table represents uncorrelated factors.

We stopped extracting factors after the fourth; this factor accounted for less than 2 per cent of the variance and appeared by inspection to be a residual. The pattern of scales having noticeable loadings on it (between .20 and .27) made no sense semantically. It is to be expected that a larger sampling of scales, with less emphasis on the evaluative factor, would allow some number of additional factors to appear.

The problem of labeling factors is somewhat simpler here than in the usual case. In a sense, our polar scales label themselves as to content. The first factor is clearly identifiable as *evaluative* by listing the scales which have high loadings on it: *good-bad, beautiful-ugly, sweet-sour, clean-dirty, tasty-distasteful, valuable-worthless, kind-cruel, pleasant-unpleasant, sweet-bitter, happy-sad, sacred-profane, nice-awful, fragrant-foul, honest-dishonest*, and *fair-unfair*. All of these loadings are .75 or better, and it will also be noted by referring to Table 1 that these scales are "purely" evaluative in the sense that the extracted variance is almost entirely on this first factor. Several other scales, *rich-poor, clear-hazy, fresh-stale*, and *healthy-sick*, while not as highly loaded as the first set on the evaluative factor, nevertheless restrict their loadings chiefly to this factor.

The second factor identifies itself fairly well as a *potency* variable (or, as one of our undergraduate statistical assistants puts it, a "football player" factor): *large-small, strong-weak, heavy-light*, and *thick-thin* serve to identify its general nature, these scales having the highest and most restricted loadings. The tendency for scales representing this factor to be contaminated, as it were, with the evaluative factor is

TABLE 1.   *Rotated Factor Loadings — Analysis 1*

	I	II	III	IV	h²
1. good-bad	.88	.05	.09	.09	.79
2. large-small	.06	.62	.34	.04	.51
3. beautiful-ugly	.86	.09	.01	.26	.82
4. yellow-blue	−.33	−.14	.12	.17	.17
5. hard-soft	−.48	.55	.16	.21	.60
6. sweet-sour	.83	−.14	−.09	.02	.72
7. strong-weak	.19	.62	.20	−.03	.46
8. clean-dirty	.82	−.05	.03	.02	.68
9. high-low	.59	.21	.08	.04	.40
10. calm-agitated	.61	.00	−.36	−.05	.50
11. tasty-distasteful	.77	.05	−.11	.00	.61
12. valuable-worthless	.79	.04	.13	.00	.64
13. red-green	−.33	−.08	.35	.22	.28
14. young-old	.31	−.30	.32	.01	.29
15. kind-cruel	.82	−.10	−.18	.13	.73
16. loud-soft	−.39	.44	.23	.22	.45
17. deep-shallow	.27	.46	.14	−.25	.37
18. pleasant-unpleasant	.82	−.05	.28	−.12	.77
19. black-white	−.64	.31	.01	−.03	.51
20. bitter-sweet	−.80	.11	.20	.03	.69
21. happy-sad	.76	−.11	.00	.03	.59
22. sharp-dull	.23	.07	.52	−.10	.34
23. empty-full	−.57	−.26	−.03	.18	.43
24. ferocious-peaceful	−.69	.17	.41	.02	.67
25. heavy-light	−.36	.62	−.11	.06	.53
26. wet-dry	.08	.07	−.03	−.14	.03
27. sacred-profane	.81	.02	−.10	.01	.67
28. relaxed-tense	.55	.12	−.37	−.11	.47
29. brave-cowardly	.66	.44	.12	.03	.64
30. long-short	.20	.34	.13	−.23	.23
31. rich-poor	.60	.10	.00	−.18	.40
32. clear-hazy	.59	.03	.10	−.16	.38
33. hot-cold	−.04	−.06	.46	.07	.22
34. thick-thin	−.06	.44	−.06	−.11	.21
35. nice-awful	.87	−.08	.19	.15	.82
36. bright-dark	.69	−.13	.26	.00	.56
37. bass-treble	−.33	.47	−.06	.02	.33
38. angular-rounded	−.17	.08	.43	.12	.23
39. fragrant-foul	.84	−.04	−.11	.05	.72
40. honest-dishonest	.85	.07	−.02	.16	.75
41. active-passive	.14	.04	.59	−.02	.37
42. rough-smooth	−.46	.36	.29	.10	.44
43. fresh-stale	.68	.01	.22	−.11	.52
44. fast-slow	.01	.00	.70	−.12	.50
45. fair-unfair	.83	.08	−.07	.11	.71
46. rugged-delicate	−.42	.60	.26	.27	.68
47. near-far	.41	.13	.11	−.05	.20
48. pungent-bland	−.30	.12	.26	.05	.17
49. healthy-sick	.69	.17	.09	.02	.59
50. wide-narrow	.26	.41	−.07	−.11	.25
Per Cent of Total Variance	33.78	7.62	6.24	1.52	.4916
Per Cent of Common Variance	68.55	15.46	12.66	3.08	.9975

apparent in Table 1. The following scales are mainly potency continua, but reflect considerable evaluative meaning as well: *hard-soft,
loud-soft, deep-shallow, brave-cowardly, bass-treble, rough-smooth,
rugged-delicate* and *wide-narrow*. It also should be noted from inspection of this table that in general loadings on the evaluative factor are
higher than those on potency, even where "pure" scales are involved.

The third factor appears to be mainly an *activity* variable in judgments, with some relation to physical sharpness or abruptness as well.
The most distinctively loaded scales are *fast-slow* (.70), *active-passive*
(.59), and *hot-cold* (.46); somewhat different in apparent meaning,
but displaying similar factor loadings, are *sharp-dull* (.52) and *angular-
rounded* (.43). The following scales have considerable loading on this
activity factor, but also as much or more loading on evaluation: *red-
green, young-old* (the subjects were college undergraduates), *feroci-
ous-peaceful,* and *tense-relaxed*. The noticeable tendency for both activity and power to be associated with positive evaluation (e.g., *good,
strong* and *active* tend to go together rather than *good, weak,* and
passive) may represent a cultural semantic bias. We can say that there
appear to be independent *factors* operating, even though it is difficult
to find many specific *scales* which are orthogonal with respect to
evaluation.[3]

The percentages of total variance and common variance accounted
for by the three factors isolated are given at the bottom of Table 1.
These values suggest that the evaluative factor plays a dominant role
in meaningful judgments, here accounting for almost 70 per cent of
the common (extracted) variance, and this impression will be confirmed in subsequent studies to be reported. It is also somewhat startling to
note that, even with college students of considerable sophistication and
intelligence as subjects, almost half of the total variance in meaningful
judgments of 20 varied concepts against 50 varied scales can be accounted for in terms of only these three factors, *evaluation, potency,*
and *activity*. Is it possible that the apparently rich and complex domain of meaning has such a simple structure as this? Although we
shall want to delay any answer to this question until the results of
more factor studies are reported, it nevertheless should be noted that

---

[3] This is also a forewarning of the pervasive tendency of Yang and Yin — see
Volume III, chapter 4 (footnote added in 1974).

50 per cent of the total variance does remain unexplained. Even though some part of this remainder can be attributed to sheer unreliability (error variance), part of it does represent the presence of some unknown number of additional factors, here appearing as specific to particular scales, but potentially extractable in more extensive analyses.

Analysis II: D-Factorization, Forced-Choice Method

The first factor analysis of meaningful judgments raises a number of methodological questions. For one thing, the method used to obtain correlations — summing over both concepts and subjects — necessarily includes the variance attributable to the mean differences between both subjects and concepts. In a small-scale analysis, using only 10 subjects, 10 concepts, and 10 scales drawn from the original data, in which the variance attributable to first subjects and then concepts was held constant statistically, it was found that although there was no change in factor structure attributable to subjects, there was some change due to concepts. To the extent that there are differences in factor structure as between concepts, and to the extent that our sampling of only 20 concepts was nonrepresentative, the factorial results of the first analysis could be biased. For another thing, there was the question of whether our factor results were somehow a function of the graphic method and would not appear when only the polar terms themselves were associated by another technique. The second factor analysis was an attempt to eliminate these possibilities.

Sampling. Since this second analysis was designed as a direct check on the first, it was decided to use exactly the same sample of descriptive continua, e.g., the same 50 sets of polar terms. The subjects were different individuals, but drawn from the same undergraduate college population. There were 40 subjects used in this analysis. A method of collecting data was employed which eliminates concept differences entirely as a variable; since no specific concepts were given for judgment, the factorial structure of the scales obtained cannot be attributed to the particular sample of concepts used.

Procedure. The method used involves a forced choice between pairs of polar terms as to the direction of their relationship. Given the following item for example:

SHARP-dull; relaxed-tense

the subject is asked to simply encircle that one of the second pair which seems closest in meaning to the capitalized member of the first pair. There is no restriction here on the concept (if any) that may be used. Some subjects might think of "people" concepts, others of "object" concepts, and yet others of "aesthetic" concepts. Introspectively (and as judged from the comments of subjects), there is usually no particular concept involved. If 100 per cent of the subjects select *tense*, as might happen in this case, it would indicate that *sharp*-with-*tense* vs. *dull*-with-*relaxed* is an appropriate parallelism or association over concepts in general; if subjects divide randomly (e.g., half one way, half the other) on an item such as

FRESH-stale; long-short

it would appear that either the multitude of conceptual contexts in which these qualities might be related are random with respect to direction or that subjects differ randomly in their judgments of the relation — in either case, no particular concept or set of concepts is forcing the direction of relation.

Treatment of data. The pairing of each of 50 pairs of polar terms with every other pair generates a test comprising 1225 items. Again, a rotational procedure was used to maximize the separation of identical pairs. The measure of relation used in this analysis was simply the percentage of agreement in direction of alignment, e.g., the percentage of subjects circling *noble* as going with STRAIGHT is entered into a 50 x 50 matrix of such percentage for all pairings. Since the number of subjects circling one of the terms entirely determines the number circling the other, calculations are necessary for only one term (the left-hand term was used consistently, since this corresponded to the original direction taken as positive in the first factor study). A perfect relation is inferred from 100 per cent (with left-hand term) or from

0 per cent (with right-hand term); 50 per cent indicates no relation, since equal numbers of subjects choose both terms. The resulting 50 x 50 matrix of percentages was factored by a technique described below and the results compared with those obtained in the original centroid analysis.

Factor Analysis. The method of factoring used in this analysis is based on a slightly different logic than are the conventional factoring techniques. Therefore, a brief description of the method itself will be given before reporting its application to the present problem. We begin with a symmetric matrix of percentages — analogous to a matrix of intercorrelations — of order 50 x 50. The logic is simply this: If two scales are equivalent, i.e., mean the same thing, their percentages of agreement with all the other scales will be equivalent. In other words, we may think of each column of percentages of agreement as sets of scores wherein the higher any single score, the greater the relation between two given scales. If two columns contain perfectly co-varying scores, they are considered equivalent. One can now find the sum of the cross-products between each column of percentages of agreement and every other column and factor the resulting matrix. The factoring may be done by the diagonal method as given by Thurstone (1947), selecting any one of the scales as a pivot to begin with and continuing the factoring until the residuals are zero.

The method has been shown to yield results corresponding closely with those obtained with the centroid method when both are applied to correlation matrices. This technique has been applied to raw score matrices. When this is done the distances (D) between variables can be reproduced. For this reason, the method has been called the D-method of factoring.

The method results in a matrix of coordinates (loadings) for each variable on a set of dimensions (factors) which are orthogonal to each other. Each dimension coincides with a variable chosen as a pivot. The higher the coordinate of a variable on a dimension, the more closely related is that variable with the dimension. The scales which appeared as the successive pivotal dimensions are *good-bad, rugged-delicate, sharp-dull, heavy-light*, and *empty-full*, in this order. After this fifth dimension had been extracted by the present method, it became clear that only dimensions with a single high coordinate (the pivotal variable, a "specific") would continue to emerge, and therefore the analysis was discontinued. Unlike factor loadings, the coordinate of variables against the pivotal dimensions may have absolute values greater than 1.00.

Comparison of Factor Analysis I and II

The five dimensions extracted in the D^2 factor analysis were rotated graphically, maintaining orthogonality among the dimensions. This was not done "blindly", but rather we deliberately tried to maximize the similarity between this structure and that obtained with the centroid method. The question was how close a correspondence between the structures obtained in these two studies could be demonstrated, despite the differences in subjects, methods of collecting data, and methods of factoring. Table 2 gives the coordinates of each variable on the five rotated dimensions.

In comparing these two analyses we refer to "loadings" of variables on "factors" in speaking of results of the centroid method, and to "coordinates" on "dimensions" in speaking of results of the D^2 method. Similarity between the results of the two methods was estimated in three ways: (1) qualitatively, by the extent to which variables heavily loaded on factors also had high coordinates on dimensions; quantitatively, (2) by the magnitude of correlations between factor loadings and dimension coordinates across variables and (3) by the magnitude of indices of factorial similarity, the *coefficient of proportionality*, *e*, between loadings and coordinates across the variables. The latter measure is obtained from the formula

$$e_{ij} = \frac{\sum_k f_{ki} g_{kj}}{\sqrt{\sum_k f_{ki}^2 g_{kj}^2}}$$

where f_{ki} and g_{kj} represent the loading and coordinate respectively of the kth variable on the ith factor and the jth dimension obtained from the two analyses (see Burt, 1948; Tucker, 1951). In the qualitative comparison, "heavily loaded" and "highly coordinate" were defined by arbitrarily selected criterion values: The criteria for "heavily loaded" were that variables have loadings $>.80$, $>.50$, and $>.50$ for fac-

TABLE 2.   *Rotated Dimension Coordinates – Analysis II*

		I	II	III	IV	V
1.	good-bad	2.29	.84	.07	1.54	.00
2.	large-small	.12	1.76	-.02	1.00	-.34
3.	beautiful-ugly	2.40	.41	.38	1.48	-.01
4.	yellow-blue	-.31	-.27	-.15	.73	-.44
5.	hard-soft	-1.39	1.06	.68	.45	.39
6.	sweet-sour	2.29	.71	.14	.98	-.26
7.	strong-weak	.38	1.81	.67	1.36	-.53
8.	clean-dirty	2.38	.46	.60	1.26	-.06
9.	high-low	1.35	1.21	1.00	1.00	-.26
10.	calm-agitated	2.25	.36	-.62	.48	-.14
11.	tasty-distasteful	2.11	1.05	.21	1.21	-.33
12.	valuable-worthless	1.87	1.12	.25	1.53	-.46
13.	red-green	-.59	1.03	.78	.58	-.19
14.	young-old	1.22	.83	1.26	.87	-.33
15.	kind-cruel	2.40	.49	-.18	1.23	-.23
16.	loud-soft	-1.71	1.03	.61	.69	.06
17.	deep-shallow	.30	1.46	-.65	.72	.97
18.	pleasant-unpleasant	2.38	.56	.24	1.38	-.29
19.	black-white	-2.11	.18	-.64	-.53	.13
20.	bitter-sweet	-2.22	-.30	.16	-.82	.43
21.	happy-sad	2.09	.97	.61	1.50	-.22
22.	sharp-dull	.51	1.31	1.88	.53	.00
23.	empty-full	-.62	-1.22	-.05	-.72	1.47
24.	ferocious-peaceful	-2.25	.25	.44	.16	-.09
25.	heavy-light	-1.60	1.68	-.92	.06	.00
26.	wet-dry	-.62	.35	-.46	.00	-.34
27.	sacred-profane	2.29	.58	-.25	1.04	-.24
28.	relaxed-tense	2.17	.24	-.63	.62	-.30
29.	brave-cowardly	1.45	1.56	.40	1.66	-.50
30.	long-short	.59	1.01	.02	.72	-.38
31.	rich-poor	1.31	1.33	.22	1.19	-.36
32.	clear-hazy	1.92	.69	.98	.93	-.09
33.	hot-cold	.42	.83	.65	.57	-.50
34.	thick-thin	-.35	1.48	-.37	.60	-.61
35.	nice-awful	2.39	1.07	-.02	1.15	-.07
36.	bright-dark	1.71	.78	1.32	1.07	-.21
37.	bass-treble	-1.15	.18	-1.42	-.06	.01
38.	angular-rounded	-1.31	.30	.77	-.08	.42
39.	fragrant-foul	2.32	.62	.23	1.12	-.31
40.	honest-dishonest	1.99	.89	.10	1.50	-.37
41.	active-passive	.30	1.64	1.39	.79	-.40
42.	rough-smooth	-2.32	.28	.17	-.07	.31
43.	fresh-stale	2.05	.82	.68	1.27	-.32
44.	fast-slow	.42	1.10	1.50	.63	-.02
45.	fair-unfair	2.22	.89	.37	1.33	-.29
46.	rugged-delicate	-2.41	.60	.05	1.10	.00
47.	near-far	.85	1.09	.67	.74	-.17
48.	pungent-bland	-1.41	.66	.48	.06	-.39
49.	healthy-sick	1.79	1.38	.63	1.81	-.54
50.	wide-narrow	.60	1.24	-.14	.99	-.60

tors I, II, and III respectively; the criteria for "highly coordinate" were that variables have coordinates >2.25, >.30, and >1.30 for dimensions I, II and III respectively.

Table 3 provides a comparison between factor loadings and dimension coordinates for the two analyses. The variables are placed in one of the following categories: Variables having both heavy loadings and high coordinates; variables having heavy loadings but low coordinates; and variables having light loadings but high coordinates. The values for *r* and *e* between factors and dimensions are given at the top of each column.

I. *Evaluation.* The near identity of dimension I with factor I is apparent from both quantitative indices *e* (.967) and *r* (.966), and the qualitative agreement between them is also very high. Even the variables that only meet the criterion on one method are actually close to the criterion on the other — *honest-dishonest* and *fair-unfair* on the factor only, *delicate-rugged* and *smooth-rough* on the dimension only. There is thus no question about identification of the first dimension of the semantic space — an *evaluative factor* is first in magnitude and order of appearance in both analyses.

II. *Potency.* The potency determinant in semantic judgments displays the poorest correspondence between factor and dimension, but even here the evidence is fairly satisfactory. The correlation over all 50 variables is .445 and the index of factorial similarity is .634. The three variables most heavily loaded on factor II are also exactly the same variables having the highest coordinates on dimension II, *strong-weak, large-small,* and *heavy-light.* However, of the two variables meeting the factor criterion only, only *hard-soft* has a sizable coordinate on the dimension. *Rugged-delicate* appears chiefly as an evaluative variable in the forced-choice method. Of the five variables meeting the dimension criterion only, three do have sizable loadings on the corresponding factor — *brave-cowardly, thick-thin,* and *deep-shallow. Healthy-sick,* however, has nearly as high a coordinate on the evaluative dimension, where it belongs according to the first analysis, and *active-passive* has nearly as high a coordinate on the activity dimension (1.39), where it belongs according to the first analysis.

TABLE 3. *Relations Between Factors (Method I) and Dimensions (Method II)*

	Factor I (Criterion,.50)	Dimension I (Criterion,1.30)		Factor II (Criterion,.50)	Dimension II (Criterion,1.30)		Factor III (Criterion,.50)	Dimension III (Criterion,1.30)
	r = .966 e = .967			r = .445 e = .634			r = .682 e = .741	
	Both			*Both*			*Both*	
good-bad	.88	2.29	strong-weak	.62	1.81	fast-slow	.70	1.50
nice-awful	.87	2.39	large-small	.62	1.76	active-passive	.59	1.39
beautiful-ugly	.86	2.40	heavy-light	.62	1.68	sharp-dull	.52	1.88
fragrant-foul	.84	2.32						
sweet-sour	.83	2.29						
clean-dirty	.82	2.38						
pleasant-unpleasant	.82	2.38						
sacred-profane	.81	2.29						
	Factor Only			*Factor Only*			*Factor Only*	
							(none)	
honest-dishonest	.85	1.99	rugged-delicate	.60	.60			
fair-unfair	.83	2.22	hard-soft	.55	1.06			
	Dimension Only			*Dimension Only*			*Dimension Only*	
rugged-delicate	-.42	-2.41	active-passive	.04	1.64	bass-treble	-.06	-1.42
rough-smooth	-.46	-2.32	brave-cowardly	.44	1.56	bright-dark	.26	1.32
			thick-thin	.44	1.48			
			deep-shallow	.46	1.46			
			healthy-sick	.17	1.38			

III. *Activity*. Dimension III and factor III correlate .682 and have an index of factorial similarity of .741. It is also clearly interpretable as an activity determinant on a qualitative basis. The three most high-ly loaded variables, *sharp-dull, active-passive*, and *fast-slow*, are among the five variables having the highest coordinates on dimension III. Of the two variables meeting the coordinate criterion only, *bright-dark* is actually higher on the evaluative dimension, where it belongs accord-ing to the first analysis. *Treble-bass* does not correspond to the results of the first analysis, but its high coordinate on the activity dimension does correspond to the findings of earlier studies on synesthesia in which high notes were typically associated with greater movement.

The two factor analytic studies just described yield highly similar structures among the relations of 50 bipolar descriptive scales. The first determinant operating in meaningful judgments is clearly *evalu-ative* in nature and it accounts for more than half of the extractable variance. The second and third factors to appear in both studies seem to represent what may be called *potency* and *activity* determinants in meaningful judgments, and again there is considerable agreement be-tween the two analyses. Since entirely different subjects and entirely different methods of collecting the data (concepts rated on scales in the first analysis and forced-choice among the scales themselves in the second) were employed, this over-all correspondence increases our confidence that we are dealing with something consistent in the struc-turing of human thinking. The fact that different factoring methods were used would, if anything, be expected to *reduce* the correspon-dence, i.e., the correspondence appears *despite* this difference in me-thodology. The reader may ask if we did not force this correspon-dence by the manner of rotating in the second analysis; in one sense this is true, but on the other hand, had the variables been randomly related, not clustered in similar ways, no placement of the axes could have produced such correspondence.

Analysis III: Thesaurus Sampling

Do the three factors so far isolated, *evaluation, potency*, and *activity*, represent an exhaustive description of the semantic space, the remain-ing 50 per cent or so of the variance being simply attributable to error? Or is there some number of additional factors, probably more restricted in application and appearing as "specifics" in the first two analyses, which a more refined exploration could reveal? In the first place, there are quite a few scales (presumably meaningful) for which very little of the variance is accounted on these general factors: Looking at the h^2 values in Table 1 (proportion of total scale variance extracted), we find that less than one-third of the variance in judgments on *yellow-blue, red-green, young-old, wet-dry, long-short, hot-cold, thick-thin, bass-treble, angular-rounded, near-far, pungent-bland*, and *wide-narrow* is accounted for. It is obvious from inspection that these scales are largely *denotative* in character — they refer to the properties of objects experienced through the senses (with the possible exception of *young-old*) and not dependent upon inference and implication. In the second place, it is apparent also that our original method of sampling scales — depending upon frequency of usage as qualifiers — resulted in an overwhelming proportion of evaluative terms. While this probably reflects a real tendency in human thinking to place high priority on the evaluative significance of things, it also made it difficult for us to obtain a sufficient number of other scales to permit additional factors to appear clearly. For these reasons a third factor analysis was designed, with a sampling procedure that was both more extensive in size and more logically exhaustive with respect to possible dimensions.

Sampling. To obtain a logically exhaustive sampling of *semantic dimensions* which would also be independent of our own theoretical biases and our previous factorial results, we decided to use Roget's *Thesaurus* (1941 edition) as a source. The task set by Roget and his subsequent editors was precisely to provide a logically exhaustive classification of word meanings, and this source had the added advantage that most categories were already arranged in terms of polar opposition. The senior author and a co-worker, independently, went through Roget, extracting from each paired category one pair of polar terms from the adjective listings and trying to select the most familiar yet most representative terms. These two listings were then combined, the judges eliminating in discussion one alternative where their independent selections had disagreed. This procedure resulted in a sample of 289 adjective-pairs.

However, we were also faced with a limitation, imposed by the intended use of the ILLIAC (the Illinois digital computer), that its "memory" could only handle 76 variables in the centroid method of factoring. Therefore, it was decided to employ a preliminary sorting procedure with a small number of subjects to reduce these 289 variables to 76. From an advanced class in advertising copy writing, 18 people who would presumably be sensitive to subtleties in word meanings were individually given a deck of cards containing the 289 polar terms and asked to sort them into 17 piles in terms of similarity of meaning. These subjects were free to define these 17 categories as they pleased, and there was no requirement that the piles be equal in size. Our reasoning was that if a set of variables kept appearing together in the same piles across various sorters, then they would presumably be highly correlated in a subsequent factor analysis, would not contribute to our exploration of the total semantic space, and therefore, all but one of them could be discarded. Since computations on the basis of 18 subjects sorting into 17 categories shows that co-occurrence of variables in the same category in five or more subjects is significant at the 1 per cent level, this criterion of significant clustering or association was used.

Using this clustering criterion, the original sample of 289 variables was reduced to 105. In selecting the alternatives to discard, we tried to eliminate more unfamiliar terms and ones difficult to treat as scales. An additional 29 pairs were finally discarded by the experimenters themselves, using the same criteria, to bring the sample down to 76.

The 100 *subjects* used in the factor analysis of the retained 76 scales were college undergraduates, again for the same reasons given earlier. They were well paid for their less than three hours' work. In sampling the *concepts* to be judged, we tried to draw from a variety of categories so as to increase representativeness; in order to provide a direct tie-in with Factor Analysis I, we included one of the concepts used there in each of the present categories (i.e., five repeat concepts altogether). The 20 concepts used in the present analysis, listed according to the categories they represent and with the repeat concepts italicized, were: *Person Concepts* (FOREIGNER, *MY MOTHER*, ME, ADLAI STEVENSON); *Physical Objects* (KNIFE, *BOULDER*, SNOW, ENGINE); *Abstract Concepts* (MODERN ART, *SIN*, TIME,

LEADERSHIP); *Event Concepts* (DEBATE, BIRTH, DAWN, *SYMPHONY*); and *Institutions* (HOSPITAL, *AMERICA*, UNITED NATIONS, FAMILY LIFE).

Procedure. Rather than rotating the concepts against the scales as had been done in Analysis I, in this case the subject judged the same concept against a series of scales before shifting to another concept. Research had been done between the time of these two factor analyses which indicated that no differences in results were occasioned by these two methods of presentation, and the method used here, in which a single concept is kept in mind while making a series of judgments, is much more satisfying to the subjects. Four-page booklets were made up with 76 scales (seven-step graphic method) appearing in a constant order but random with respect to semantic content; the concept being judged was stamped at the top of each page in these booklets. Each subject thus received 20 booklets, one for each concept. But rather than going through an entire booklet at a time, the subjects were instructed to do all the first pages (through all 20 booklets), then all the second pages, and so on; in this way an increased degree of shifting from concept to concept was obtained, which it was hoped would decrease the boredom inherent to some degree in this task.

The general instructions about the use of the semantic differential — the meanings of the scale positions, the stress on giving immediate impressions and not struggling over individual items etc., as had been used in the first analysis, were repeated here. The subjects gathered in groups of about 20 and were given considerable freedom to take cigarette breaks and the like. The experimenters monitored these sessions and answered in standard fashion occasional questions about the meanings of polar terms (particularly concerning *heterogeneous- homogeneous, tangible-intangible, altruistic-egotistic, inherent-extraneous*, and *heretical-orthodox*).

Treatment of data. The raw data were first transferred to IBM cards, one card for each subject-concept pairing, with the scores (1-7) for the 76 scales arranged in constant order. There were thus 100 x 20 or 2000 cards, and this was the number of pairs entering into each correlation since means, variances and cross-products were taken across both subjects and concepts as had been done in the first analysis (and for the same reasons). These ordered data were transferred directly to punched tape by an automatic machine method, and Pearson product-moment correlations of each scale with every other scale were obtained on the ILLIAC, yielding a 76 x 76 matrix.

This correlation matrix was first factored by *Thurstone's centroid method*, the method used in the first analysis. The analysis was stopped after eight factors had been extracted, since the eighth factor accounted for only about 1 per cent of the variance. The first three factors in this unrotated centroid matrix were clearly interpretable; the remainder were not.

The first factor was again the *evaluative factor* (the scales most heavily loaded on this factor were: *good-bad, kind-cruel, grateful-ungrateful, harmonious-dissonant, beautiful-ugly, successful-unsuccessful, true-false, positive-negative, reputable-disreputable, wise-foolish*). The second was identifiable as the *potency factor* (the scales most heavily loaded being *hard-soft, masculine-feminine, severe-lenient, strong-weak, tenacious-yielding, heavy-light*, and *mature-youthful* in that order). And the third was identifiable as an *activity factor* (the most heavily loaded scales being *fast-slow, active-passive, excitable-calm, rash-cautious*, and *heretical-orthodox* in that order). Factor IV in this unrotated analysis, characterized chiefly by *awkard-graceful, hot-cold, constricted-spacious, private-public* and *excitable-calm*, might possibly be interpreted as some kind of anxiety variable; factor V, characterized by such scales as *masculine-feminine, heavy-light, healthy-sick, unusual-usual, passive-active, blunt-sharp, unimportant-important, public-private*, and *large-small*, defies consistent interpretation; factor VI (*weak-strong, cautious-rash, incomplete-complete, straight-curved, transparent-opaque, rational-intuitive*, and *complex-simple*), factor VII (*light-dark, clean-dirty, small-large*), and factor VIII (*hot-cold, healthy-sick, dry-wet, humorous-serious, straight-curved, stable-changeable*) also yield no obvious interpretation. The relative magnitudes of these factors correspond to what was found in the first analysis — the first factor accounts for about double as much variance in judgments as the next two and these in turn account for about double as much as any of the remaining factors. We conclude (1) that the three dominant factors isolated in the two previous factor analyses are also dominant in the present Thesaurus analysis and (2) that if any clearly identifiable subsidiary factors are to be revealed, some other method of analysis must be employed.

There are some questions as to the value of rotation by the Quartimax method, and in the present case the factors yielded were somewhat dubious as to interpretation. With the correlational matrix and an ILLIAC program available, it was a simple matter to apply *the Square Root method of factoring* (see Wrigley and McQuitty, 1953). In this method, as in Thurstone's Diagonal method (see Thurstone, 1947), scales are selected as pivots through which a given factor is placed, and all variance of other scales in this dimension is exhausted before selecting another scale as a second pivot. Since we already had ample evidence for the presence of three dominant factors, evaluation, potency, and activity, in the unrotated centroid analysis of the present as well as in both previous studies, we decided to select arbitrarily the first three pivotal scales, allowing the ILLIAC to proceed mechanically beyond this point. In other words, in an attempt to clarify the finer factorial composition of our data, we first extracted the three known sources of variance without allowing residual scales to influence the choice of the pivotal scales.

The ILLIAC was instructed to select *good-bad, hard-soft*, and *active-passive* as the first, second, and third pivots respectively. The computer then continued to select *sober-drunk, angular-rounded, new-old, savory-tasteless*, and *aggressive-defensive* in that order; the variance taken out with the last pivot was only half of 1 per cent of the total variance and the factorization was stopped. The increased interpretive clarity of the factors obtained in this manner will be evident in a review of the scales contributing to each.

I. *Evaluative factor*. The scales having the *purest* loading on this factor, regardless of size of loading, are *good-bad* (pivot), *optimistic-pessimistic, positive-negative, complete-incomplete*, and *timely-untimely*. Inspection of the loading patterns of the scales that are chiefly evaluative in nature indicates what may be called "modes" of evaluation — clusters of scales which are dominantly evaluative, but also share sizable loading on some subsidiary factor. We may classify these as follows: "*meek goodness*," having subsidiary negative loading on the potency factor (II), includes *altruistic, sociable, kind, grateful, clean, light* (dark), *graceful, pleasurable*, and *beautiful*; what might be called *"dynamic goodness,"* having subsidiary positive loading on the activity factor (III), includes *successful, high, meaningful, important,* and *progressive*; what might be called *"dependable goodness,"* having subsidiary loading on Factor IV, includes *true, reputable, believing, wise, healthy,* and *clean* — and it should be noted that the scales assigned to factor IV are also positive on factor I; finally, what might be called *"hedonistic goodness,"* having subsidiary loading on factor VII, includes *pleasurable, beautiful, sociable,* and *meaningful* — and again the scales assigned to factor VII generally have positive loadings on factor I. These findings suggest that the general evaluative factor is itself further analyzable into a set of secondary factors — various "modes" of evaluation which are appropriate to different frames of reference or objects of judgment.

II. *Potency.* The scales which have high loadings on factor II are *hard-soft* (pivot), *heavy-light, masculine-feminine, severe-lenient, strong-weak,* and *tenacious-yielding.* Other scales dominantly representative of the potency factor but with less loading, are *constrained-free, constricted-spacious, serious-humorous, opaque-transparent,* and *large-small.* Scales assigned elsewhere in terms of their loading patterns, but including considerable loading on this factor, are *cruel-kind, dirty-clean, dark-light, awkward-graceful, painful-pleasurable, ugly-beautiful, fast-slow, angular-rounded, mature-youthful, insensitive-sensitive,* and *dry-wet.* The common character of potency or "toughness" is apparent in the first terms of these pairs.

III. *Oriented Activity.* The collection of scales loading on the third factor seem to justify the modified label, "oriented activity," rather than plain "activity." Scales having relatively "pure" loading on this factor are *active-passive* (pivot), *excitable-calm,* and *hot-cold.* Scales having positive loading on evaluation as well as activity loading, and justifying the "oriented" characterization, are *intentional-unintentional, complex-simple, successful-unsuccessful, meaningful-meaningless, important-unimportant, progressive-regressive,* and *interesting-boring. Fast-slow* has subsidiary loading on the potency factor and is thus related to *sharp-blunt.* It is also to be noted that in general the scales representing this factor are not as independent of other factors as would be desirable, all tending to be somewhat positive in evaluation and potency.

IV. *Stability.* We turn now to the factors which appeared in the automatic operation of the square root method, after extraction of the evaluation, potency and activity sources of variance. The fourth factor suggests another dimension of the semantic space which we have called "stability," although all of the particular scales characterizing this dimension are also biased toward good evaluation; *sober-drunk* (pivot), *stable-changeable, rational-intuitive, sane-insane, cautious-rash*, and *orthodox-heretical*. Scales assigned elsewhere in terms of loading pattern, but contributing to this stability factor, are *true-false* and *wise-foolish*, also mainly evaluative scales.

V. *Tautness.* This factor is labeled with considerable tentativeness. The scales assigned to this factor in the present analysis are *angular-rounded* (pivot), *straight-curved*, and *sharp-blunt*. Other scales having some loading on this factor are *masculine-feminine* and *fast-slow*.

VI. *Novelty.* Evidence for this type of factor is provided by a small number of scales having quite consistent meaning. Assigned to this factor were *new-old* (pivot), *unusual-usual*, and *youthful-mature*. The only other scales having noticeable loading on this factor were *progressive-regressive* and *complex-simple*.

VII. *Receptivity.* The seventh factor isolated in this analysis, which we have dubbed "receptivity," seems quite clearly identified as to nature by a large number of scales having relatively low loading, i.e., as compared with factor VI above, this is a rather diffuse factor. Scales assigned in this category are *savory-tasteless* (pivot), *colorful-colorless, sensitive-insensitive, interesting-boring, refreshed-weary*, and *pungent-bland*. All of these scales, with the exception of *pungent-bland* are also positive in evaluation, suggesting that even though there may be an independent *factor* of meaning identified here, these particular scales also constitute a "mode" of evaluating. Other scales having some loading here are *sociable, pleasurable, beautiful, meaningful*, and *excitable*, which are consistent with the same interpretation.

VIII. *Aggressiveness.* Only one scale, the pivot item *aggressive-defensive*, has sizable loading on this factor. Slight loadings appear for *progressive, healthy, severe, fast*, and *rash*. It is probably best treated as a "specific" source of variance until further analyses strengthen the evidence for its status.

Variance accounted for by this factor analysis. The proportion of total variance accounted for by the first three factors in the Thesaurus analysis — indeed, by all eight factors — is much less than in the first analysis. This is a direct result of the method of sampling employed in the Thesaurus study, in which tight clusters of scales were deliberately broken up to increase the diversity of the sampling. A moment's consideration of the factorization model will clarify this: Imagine an n-dimensional pin-cushion, with large pins representing the placement of the factors. The more closely aligned a particular scale with a factor, the greater the proportion of its reliable variance extracted, or accounted for, by that factor. Now, if the pins fall in closely related bundles through which the factor-pins are made to run, a relatively large portion of their variance will be accounted for; if, on the other hand, the pins are widely dispersed about the cushion and the same number of factor-pins are run through the space, a smaller amount of their variance will be accounted for. In the Thesaurus study we purposely "pruned" our pincushion before making the quantitative analysis, plucking out and discarding whole clumps of neighboring pins. Of course, this coin has another side too — the fact that this "pruning" procedure did reduce markedly the proportion of the total variance accounted for necessarily means that there are a large number of dimensions (factors) within which meanings can vary.

The Semantic Space

What have we learned about the dimensionality of the semantic space from this series of factor analyses? For one thing, it is clear that it is a multidimensional space. In every analysis more than three factors have been contributing to the meaningful judgments by subjects. It is also clear that these N factors or dimensions are not equally important in mediating judgments, or perhaps better, are not equally used by subjects in differentiating among the things judged. Three factors appear to be dominant, appearing in most of the analyses made and in roughly the same orders of magnitude — *evaluation, potency*, and *activity*.

However, it is also evident the functional semantic space is to some degree modifiable in terms of what kinds of concepts are being judged, i.e., the relative importance and relationship among factors may vary with the frame of reference of judgments. Certainly, specific scales may change their meaning, in the factorial composition sense, as a function of the concept being judged. And finally, it is clear that what we have called the three dominant factors do not exhaust the dimensions along which meaningful judgments are differentiated. Let us look into some of these conclusions more carefully.

1. *Meanings vary multidimensionally.* Many of the phenomena for which psychologists and others have devised measuring instruments seem to be handled satisfactorily on a unidimensional basis — intelligence, manifest anxiety, attitude, and so on are examples. Some attempts to treat meaning in the same manner were noted in the first chapter (e.g., Mosier, 1941; Noble, 1952). Our own research has demonstrated repeatedly that, when subjects differentiate the meanings of concepts, variance along certain scales (e.g., activity scales) may be quite independent of variation along other scales (e.g., evaluation). To put the matter yet another way, some of the things judged "good" may also be judged "strong" (e.g., HERO) but other things judged equally "good" may also be judged "weak" (e.g., PACIFIST). If meanings vary multidimensionally, then any adequate measuring instrument must encompass this fact.

2. *Stability of the evaluative, potency, and activity factors.* In every instance in which a widely varied sample of concepts has been used, or the concept variable eliminated as in forced-choice among the scales, the same three factors have emerged in roughly the same order of magnitude. A pervasive *evaluative factor* in human judgment regularly appears first and accounts for approximately half to three-quarters of the extractable variance. Thus the *attitudinal* variable in human thinking, based as it is on the bedrock of rewards and punishments both achieved and anticipated, appears to be primary — when asked if she'd like to see the *Dinosaur* in the museum, the young lady from Brooklyn first wanted to know, "Is it good or is it bad?" The second dimension of the semantic space to appear is usually the *potency factor*, and this typically accounts for approximately half as much variance as the

first factor – this is concerned with power and the things associated with it, size, weight, toughness, and the like. The third dimension, usually about equal to or a little smaller in magnitude than the second, is the *activity factor* – concerned with quickness, excitement, warmth, agitation and the like. And when other factors can be extracted and identified they typically, again, account for no more than half the amount of variance attributable to the second and third factors.

3. *Modifiability of the semantic space.* When the sample of things being judged is restricted in some fashion, the nature and order of magnitude of the factors may change. For example, when judgments are limited to sociopolitical concepts (people and policies), there seems to be a coalescence of the second and third factors into what might be called a "dynamism factor"; this was apparent in a study of the 1952 presidential election, in a study of ethnic stereotypes, and in a cross-cultural (and cross-language) study of political concepts relating to the Far East. It is as if things in this frame of reference that are "strong" are also necessarily "active" while things that are "weak" are also necessarily "passive." We also noted in factorization of the judgments of a mental patient (case of triple personality) that there was nearly a restriction of the semantic space to a single dimension, combining "good," "strong," and "active." An hypothesis to be explored here is this: the greater the emotional or attitudinal loading of the set of concepts being judged, the greater the tendency of the semantic framework to collapse into a single, combined dimension. Other types of interaction probably operate as well: when, for example, the sample of concepts is limited to aesthetic objects (paintings, in this case), a type of activity factor becomes relatively more prominent.

4. *Dimensionality of the semantic space.* It was made particularly clear in the Thesaurus analysis that the three major factors, evaluation, potency, and activity, do not exhaust the ways in which meanings may vary. Here a broad sample was guaranteed both by discarding highly similar scales and by increasing the total number of scales entering into the analysis. Several additional factors could be tentatively identified: a *stability factor*, a *tautness factor*, a *novelty factor*, and a *receptivity factor*. These subsidiary factors are much less clearly

defined, have not been checked for reliability, and hence should be held as hypotheses for further testing. However, their appearance, along with the large proportion of total variance remaining unaccounted for, indicates that the semantic space for concepts-in-general has a large number of dimensions. We believe that from this point onward the best way to more rigorously identify additonal factors will be to deliberately test for them, i.e., by inserting presumptive clusters in a matrix of reference scales for known factors and seeing if, in the judgment process, they both correlate highly with each other and lowly with other factors. The existence of a large number of dimensions in the total semantic space is not disastrous as far as measurement is concerned; this is because these added dimensions account for relatively little of the total variance.

In What Sense Is The Semantic Differential A Measure Of Meaning?[4]

One of the most serious criticisms of this book probably could have been anticipated at the outset: "Although we understand pretty well what you are measuring and appreciate its value," many readers may say, "why do you call it meaning? Aren't you really measuring the emotive reaction to words rather than 'meaning' as I have understood the term?" Earlier in this chapter (pp. 8-15) I outlined a behavioral theory of meaning that purports to be general. This theory will be elaborated in chapter 5 of volume III. For reasons to be documented (see pp. 88-91), the SD Technique amplifies affective features.

As psychologists we find it necessary to focus on that "state of" or "event in" a sign-using organism that is at once a necessary subsequent condition (r_M) in the decoding of signs and a necessary antecedent condition (s_M) in the encoding of signs. Note carefully that we do not say necessary *and sufficient*. Ultimately it is the job of the psycholinguist to make a science out of the correlations between message events and states of the organism. In our work on what we have been calling "meaning" we have mapped only a small region of this complex set of correlations, and that rather sketchily.

---

[4] Excerpts from pp. 320-325 of *The Measurement of Meaning.* Some up-dating changes in symbolism and wording have been made (footnote added in 1975).

But is it justifiable to use the term *meaning* for the kinds of correlations between signs and organismic states indexed by the semantic
differential? We can best indicate the issue here, perhaps, by setting
up two questions that have frequently been put to us. Both involve
the distinction between what has variously been called denotative,
designative, or referential "meaning" and what has been called connotative, emotive, or metaphorical "meaning."

1. *How can there be interpersonal communication despite connotative disagreement?* Many linguists and philosophers would say (and
have, to us) that two people must first agree on the "meaning" of a
sign before they can disagree on their diverse emotive and other reactions to it. For example, man A may find THUNDER (perceptual
sign) challenging and exciting while man B finds it extremely frighten-
ing, but before they can communicate about this state of affairs they
must agree on the *referent* of the linguistic sign "thunder" in their
common language. As a matter of fact, our data are replete with cases
where individuals differ in their semantic differential profiles for the
same sign-vehicles — one of the major uses of the instrument is to
measure such differences between people. What, then, is the problem
here? If we agree that the *meaning* of "thunder" for A and B must in
some sense be the same because they are obviously referring to the
same object or event, and if we were to claim that the representational
mediation process as we have defined it is a *sufficient* antecedent
condition for language encoding, then the semantic differential profiles we derive from A and B should correspond in some way. A few
moments' consideration shows that we cannot make this claim: Men
A and B will probably experience no more referential confusion on
"thunder" (where their profiles disagree on most factors) than they
do on "blueberry pie" (where their profiles agree closely, let us say).
In other words, we must admit that distances in our semantic space as
between individuals judging the same concepts are not indicative of
degrees of *referential* agreement — if, indeed, one can speak of "degrees" of such agreement.

How can you have referential agreement despite lack of correspondence in the psychological states we index with the differential? A
color-blind person may go through his whole life correctly labeling
and referring to most colored objects and yet in a test case (e.g.,

choosing between particular orange vs. brown ties) show conclusively
that he cannot be "seeing things" the way the rest of us do — what
look obviously different to us look just the same to him! Let us
postulate two hypothetical people: F (father) is normal; S (son) is not
only red-green blind, but he is also allergic to what are commonly
called "apples" — they make him deathly sick. We shall assume that F
has an evaluatively favorable meaning of "apple": part of the gratifying reaction to APPLES-as-eaten has become associated with the perceptual and linguistic signs of this object. Now, on repeated occasions
S is stimulated by APPLE visually (and necessarily has experiences
different from F because he is color-blind); he also sees F point to this
rounded patch of stimulation and say "apple" and point to this and
other similar patches and say "red." Given human learning capacity
and language facility, S rapidly learns to say "apple" to recurrent
appearances of this object and to say "red" to radiant patches similar
to the ones F calls "red" — even though, we must agree, the internal
states of F and S cannot be identical. But even beyond this, F encourages S to bite into the APPLE object, saying it is "tasty" and "good"
— to S it tastes horrible and makes him sick.

On the basis of a number of such experiences, and following the
behavioral principles governing the formation of representational mediation processes discussed earlier, S must develop a "meaning" (in
our sense) of "apple" which is quite different from that of F — and he
would check it quite differently on many of the scales of the semantic
differential as well as displaying different behavior in response to the
object. Here, we have two users of the same language, F and S, who,
despite their manifest differences in mediation processes, will point to
the same things and say to each other "Oh, I know what you mean,"
when they employ the noises "apple" and "red." Similarly, returning
to our original example, it is clear that men A and B may agree on
what "thunder" refers to *even though* the distinctive representational
states in each may differ.

We may summarize our argument on Question 1 as follows: Agreement on the referents of signs implies nothing whatsoever about similarity of the representational states associated with these signs, but
rather that these states have entered into the same sets of relations
between situations and verbal responses. It therefore follows that
agreement on the reference of signs despite lack of profile correspon-

dence on the semantic differential is not evidence for insufficiency of the instrument as a psychological measuring device.

2. *How can there be discriminative encoding despite connotative indiscriminability?* This problem becomes apparent when one considers the lack of perfect reversibility of our measurement operations with the semantic differential. Given only the profile produced by a subject in judging a particular concept, or the point in the space specified by this profile, we are unable to work the system backwards and identify that concept. The force of the argument really is this: Many denotatively distinct concepts may occupy essentially the same region of our semantic space, i.e., may have highly similar profiles — "hero" and "success" as well as "nurse" and "sincere" would be examples. If the state of the speaker which the semantic differential presumably indexes were a *sufficient* condition for selective encoding, how could we account for discriminative selection of "nurse" rather than "sincere," of "hero" rather than "success," when the states in each case are essentially the same?

One possible answer to this problem would be to take the position that the factors or dimensions of the semantic space we have isolated so far are insufficient. Increase the number of factors, this argument goes, and any two concepts would have to be distinguished on at least one dimension. Although we admit the insufficiency of present factors even for our purposes, this solution seems to envisage an almost infinite proliferation of dimensions and becomes practically infeasible. Furthermore, it takes it for granted that variations among representational processes must be a sufficient condition for selective encoding.

A better answer,[5] we think, takes off from the assumption that the representational state indexed by the semantic differential is not the only determinant operating in lexical encoding. It is a necessary but not a sufficient condition. In the simplest cases, this is obvious: given essentially the same semantic process, the speaker will encode "eats" in one linguistic context and "eat" in another depending on whether the subject of the sentence is singular or plural. Here we have selection among two word alternatives on the basis of something other than

[5] I would certainly give more weight to the first "answer" today; see Chapter 4 here (footnote added in 1973).

semantic factors. Going a step further, it has been shown in word association experiments that the form class of the stimulus word markedly influences the form class of the response word from the subject, e.g., given MAN he'll say "woman" but given MEN he'll say "women," given COME he'll say "go" but given CAME he'll say "went." Again, we assume that the "meaning" (in the sense of our measurements) of the stimulus terms stays constant. Coming now to the examples given above, it seems likely that, even with near identical representational states of the sort we hypothesize and try to measure, a speaker will encode "hero" in the context, "The villain was vanquished by the ...," rather than "success"; conversely he will encode "success" in the context, "He is always striving for ...," rather than "hero."

To summarize our argument on Question 2, then: Self-stimulation from the representational system, as indexed by the semantic differential, provides a necessary but not sufficient condition for encoding lexical items; cues from both the linguistic and the situational context combine with those from the representational system to select more discriminatively among alternative responses. By way of analogy, there are some classic experiments in the psychology of the emotions in which the subject is given an injection of adrenalin in a completely neutral, non-arousing situation; the subject typically reports experiencing a vague, stirred-up feeling, a sort of objectless, nameless emotion, as if "something were about to happen." If we could get inside the speaker somehow and produce a particular $r_M \longrightarrow s_M$ without any context, it is possible that he too would experience a kind of "referenceless," "denotation-less" meaning, referable to some region of the semantic space but non-specific as to designation — "something bad, strong, and active, but *what* I do not know."

In what sense, then, are we measuring meaning with the semantic differential? It is certain that we are not providing an index of what signs refer to, and if reference or designation is the *sine qua non* of meaning, as some readers will insist, then they will conclude that this book is badly mistitled. On the other hand, language users do develop representation processes in association with signs and these processes are intimately concerned with their behavior. The psychologist quite naturally focuses his attention on processes that are relevant to the prediction and interpretation of differential behaviors, and, as we have tried to demonstrate, agreement in the reference of signs carries no necessary implication of relatedness of representational states. As we also tried to show, however, the representational states indexed by the semantic differential are not the only determinants operating in language production; linguistic and situational variables also contribute to selective encoding. Perhaps we should admit that the word "meaning" is used in several senses; whether or not it is *meaning* that we are measuring, then, would seem to be merely a matter of choice of terms.

SOME EXCURSIONS

Blind Analysis of a Case of Triple Personality[6]

During the fall of 1953, Osgood and Luria were presented with an unusual opportunity to test the validity and usefulness of the semantic differential as a clinical tool. The then editor of *The Journal of Abnormal and Social Psychology* (Dr. J. McV. Hunt) had received a manuscript entitled "A Case of Multiple Personality," by Drs. Thigpen and Cleckley. Without our knowledge he had suggested to these therapists that it would be interesting to collect semantic data from each of the personalities of their patient and have us interpret them on a blind basis. Thigpen and Cleckley kindly consented to cooperate in this venture and administered a form of the differential twice (at intervals of about two to three months) to each of the three personalities. The form, which had already been used by Luria in some research in psychotherapy, included 15 concepts (LOVE, CHILD, MY DOCTOR, ME, MY JOB, MENTAL SICKNESS, MY MOTHER, PEACE OF MIND, FRAUD, MY SPOUSE, SELF-CONTROL, HATRED, MY FATHER, CONFUSION, and SEX) and ten scales (*valuable-worthless, clean-dirty, tasty-distasteful, large-small, strong-weak, deep-shallow, fast-slow, active-passive, hot-cold*, and *tense-relaxed*).

Before going into the treatment and interpretation of the data, we should state exactly what information we had about this case. We knew that we were dealing with a case of triple personality, and these

[6] Excerpts from pp. 258-271 of *The Measurement of Meaning.*

had been labeled for us as "Eve White," "Eve Black," and "Jane." We also knew, of course, that the patient was a woman, presumably participating in some kind of therapy – but we did not know the stage of therapy or whether or not the woman was hospitalized. To make the interpretation of data on certain concepts meaningful, we also considered it fair to ask (of J. McV. Hunt) if the patient had a child (she did), if she was married (she was), if her parents were alive (the mother was, but he wasn't sure about the father), and if she had a job outside of homekeeping (she did). This was the sum total of our external information about the case. The semantic data consisted of two testings, which we shall identify by the roman numerals I and II, on each of the three personalities. On the basis of these data, we attempted a description of the salient characteristics of each of the three personalities and an interpretation and prognosis about the case as a whole.

Do the factors employed in these three personalities correspond closely in terms of both nature and relative weight? The total data for the initial testing for all three personalities were subjected to factor analysis and rotated by Quartimax on the ILLIAC. Table 4 gives the rotated factor loadings for each of the ten scales for each personality, with the proportion of total variance accounted for by each factor below. The first factor in all three personalities is clearly evaluative (*valuable, clean*, and *tasty*), but what is remarkable is the immense slice of variance taken out by this dimension of judgment, 49 per cent in Eve White I, 59 per cent in Eve Black I, and 48 per cent in Jane I. It is possible to identify the second factor in all three personalities as a kind of potency factor, but the scale *relaxed-tense* (with *relaxed* being potent, perhaps reflecting the therapy context) must be included in this category. Thus the scales loading highest on factor II for Eve White I are *relaxed, strong, deep*, and *large*; for Eve Black I are *large, strong, relaxed,* and *deep*; and for Jane I are *relaxed, tasty, strong*, and *large*. Similarly, the third factor in each personality can be identified as a kind of activity factor by virtue of the relatively high loadings of *fast* and *active* on it – but for Eve White I, at least, *deep-shallow* also has high loading on this factor. We have evidence, then, for essentially the same three major factors operating in the several personalities of this disturbed patient, although there is considerable shifting in the meanings of specific scales between personalities and considerable

TABLE 4. *Rotated factor Loadings and Propositions of Variance for Triple Personality Case*

	Eve White I			Eve Black I			Jane I		
	I	II	III	I	II	III	I	II	III
valuable	.86	-.11	.11	.98	.08	.09	.92	.05	-.11
clean	.98	-.02	-.01	.83	-.03	.05	.93	-.05	-.03
tasty	.89	-.22	-.01	.96	.06	-.07	.73	.59	.05
hot	.86	.16	-.16	.94	-.02	-.18	.93	-.17	.17
large	.66	.23	.14	.26	.88	.13	.83	.21	-.08
strong	.74	.43	-.17	.54	.74	.02	.84	.27	-.09
deep	.77	.25	.41	.67	.53	.12	-.12	-.14	-.05
relaxed	.20	.90	.02	.67	.57	.03	.44	.84	-.06
fast	-.19	-.16	.14	.57	.32	.75	-.05	-.03	.99
active	.07	-.01	.96	.92	.02	.23	.29	-.16	.25
Per Cent Variance	.49	.11	.12	.59	.20	.07	.48	.13	

divergence of this patient in general from most people on whom we have data (e.g., in the use of *hot-cold* and *relaxed-tense*).

The models displayed in Figures 3, 4, and 5 were constructed from the D-matrices computed from factor scores. Within the limits of our type of measurement and our sampling of concepts, the locations and relations among concepts shown here can be thought of as pictures of how this woman perceives herself, the signicant people about her, and certain modes of action — when functioning in her several personalities. For purposes of ready comparison, all of the models are oriented in respect to the concept MY DOCTOR, which stays almost constant in meaning (*good, strong*, and *quite active*) throughout both time and personalities; spatially in these figures, *good* is up and *bad* down, *active* is to the left and *passive* to the right, and *strong* is away from the viewer while *weak* is toward the viewer; the solid ball represents the origin of the space, i.e., a hypothetical "meaningless" concept that would result from checking all 4's on the scales. Since the descriptions and interpretations which follow were made on a blind basis, we shall quote entirely from the article written at that time (Osgood and Luria, 1954). Following submission of our article for publication, the clinical study of the case appeared in print and many of our statements could be checked. Materials taken from this case study (Thigpen and Cleckley, 1954) for purposes of present comparison, but unknown to us at the time are given below.

(From Osgood and Luria): "*Eve White*. Semantic structures for Eve White I and II are shown in Figure 3. The most general characterization would be that Eve White perceives 'the world' in an essentially normal fashion, is well socialized, but has an unsatisfactory attitude toward herself. ME (the self-concept) is considered a little bad, a little passive, and definitely weak. Substantiating evidence is the weakness of her CHILD and the essential meaninglessness to her of MY SPOUSE and SEX. Note also the wide evaluative separation between LOVE and SEX. In the interval between testings I and II, ME and SEX become more bad and passive and simultaneously become almost identical in meaning to her — and note that her conceptions of LOVE (a good, strong thing) and SEX (a bad, weak thing like herself) have moved still further apart."

The above was largely descriptive; in a sense we merely put into words what this woman indicated by her check-marks. The treatment

Fig. 3.   Semantic Space for Eve White

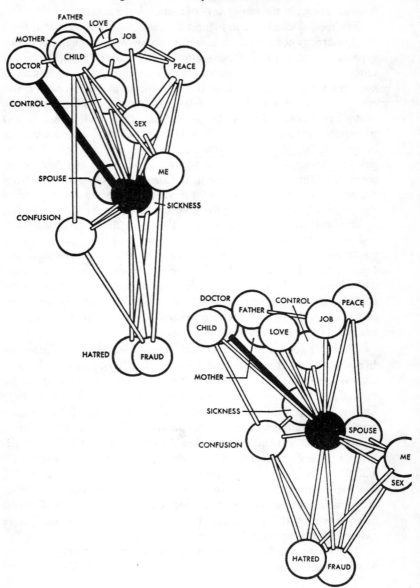

of the data from check-marks to these models is completely objective and any investigator starting from the same checks and following the rules must end up with the same pictures. What follows was, of course, more speculative and interpretive; not only was it on a blind basis, but neither of the authors was a clinician by training.

(From Osgood and Luria): "Eve White is simultaneously the most in contact with social reality and under the greatest emotional stress. She is aware of both the demands of society and her own inadequacies in meeting them. She is concerned and ambivalent about her CHILD, but apparently is not aware of her own ambivalent attitudes towards her MOTHER. Those psychoanalytically inclined may wish to identify EVE WHITE with dominance of the *superego:* certainly, the superego seems to view the world from the eyes of Eve White, accepting the mores or values of others (particularly her mother) but continuously criticizing and punishing herself. If this case came to the psychotherapists with a voluntary, self-initiated plea for help, then it seems likely that Eve White was dominant at the time."

(From Thigpen and Cleckley): "One of us (C.H.T.) had for several months been treating a twenty-five-year-old married woman who was referred because of 'severe and blinding headaches.' ... To the therapist, Eve White — as we shall call her — was an ordinary case with commonplace symptoms and a relatively complex but familiar constellation of marital conflicts and personal frustrations." Now Thigpen and Cleckley describe the sudden appearance of Eve Black on the scene, and contrast her with Eve White: "As if seized by a sudden pain she put both hands to her head. After a tense moment of silence, her hands dropped. There was a quick, reckless smile and, in a bright voice that sparkled, she said, 'Hi there, Doc.' The demure and constrained posture of Eve White had melted into bouyant repose ... . Instead of that retiring and gently conventional figure, there was in the newcomer a childishly daredevil air, an erotically mischievous glance, a face marvelously free from the habitual signs of care, seriousness, and underlying distress, so long familiar in her predecessor." Other incidental evidence about Eve White can be culled from the case history given by Thigpen and Cleckley: "Mrs. White admits difficulty in her relation with her mother, and her performance on the Rorschach and drawings indicate conflict and resulting anxiety in her role as a wife and mother ... . Demure, retiring, in some respects almost saintly ... . Voice always softly modulated, always influenced by a specifically feminine restraint ... . An industrious and able worker; also a competent house-keeper and a skillful cook. Not colorful or glamorous. Limited in spontaneity ... . Consistently uncritical of others."

(From Osgood and Luria): "*Eve Black*. Semantic structures for Eve Black I and II are shown in Figure 4. The most general characterization would be that Eve Black has achieved a violent kind of adjustment in which she perceives herself as literally perfect, but, to accomplish this break, her way of perceiving 'the world' becomes completely disoriented from the norm. The only exceptions are MY DOCTOR and PEACE OF MIND, which maintain their good and strong characteristics, the latter, interestingly enough, becoming also active on II. But if Eve Black perceives herself as good, then she also has to accept HATRED and FRAUD as positive values, since (we assume) she has strong hatred, and is socially fraudulent. What are positive values for most people — CHILD, MY SPOUSE, MY JOB, LOVE, and SEX — are completely rejected as bad and passive, and all of these except CHILD are also weak. Note that it is MOTHER in this personality that becomes relatively meaningless; FATHER, on the other hand, stays good but shifts completely from strong (in Eve White) to weak." Continuing more interpretively: "Eve Black is clearly the most out of contact with social reality and simultaneously the most self-assured. She sees herself as a dominant, active wonder-woman and is in no way self-critical. Those psychoanalytically inclined could say that the *id* looks out at the world through the eyes of Eve Black. Like a completely selfish infant, this personality is entirely oriented around the assumption of its own perfection — personal perfection is apparently the demand acceded to rather than sexuality."

(From Thigpen and Cleckley): "Eve Black's career has been traced back to early childhood. She herself freely tells us of episodes when she emerged, usually to engage in acts of mischief or disobedience. She lies glibly and without compunction, so her account alone can never be taken as reliable evidence." Note the essential masculinity of the following reported by the therapists: " 'When I go out and get drunk,' Eve Black with an easy wink once said to both of us, 'she wakes up with the hangover. She wonders what in the hell's made her so sick.' " And further characterization: "Obviously a party girl. Shrewd, childishly vain, and egocentric ... . Voice a little coarsened,

Fig. 4.   Semantic Space for Eve Black

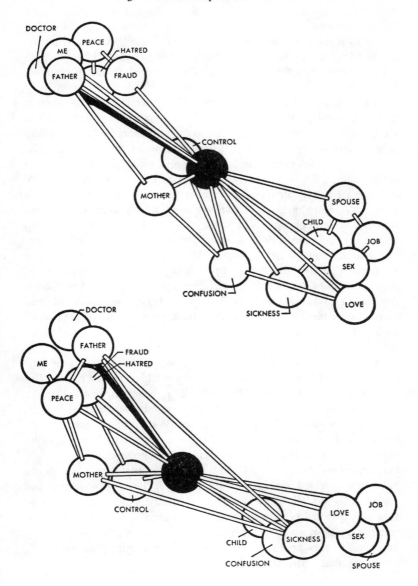

'discultured,' with echoes or implications of mirth and teasing. Speech richly vernacular and liberally seasoned with spontaneous gusts of rowdy wit .... A touch of sexiness seasons every word and gesture." But that this trait of sexiness was superficial in Eve Black is indicated by her relations with a temporary husband, which she finally admitted to the therapists: "Apparently she had no desire for sexual relations but often enjoyed frustrating her supposed husband by denying herself to him."

(From Osgood and Luria): "*Jane.* The general characterization is that Jane displays the most 'healthy' meaning pattern, in which she accepts the usual evaluations of concepts by her society yet still maintains a satisfactory evaluation of herself. Most of the significant persons in her life are seen as good, strong and active. The major modes of behavior, PEACE OF MIND, LOVE, SELF-CONTROL, and MY JOB are seen as equally good and strong, but somewhat passive – as if these ways of behaving and thinking were simply accepted without stress. The self-concept, ME, while still not strong (but not weak, either) is nearer the good and active directions of the semantic space. Her attitude toward her husband, MY SPOUSE, is for the first time meaningful (unlike Eve White) and tending toward the good, strong, active directions, like the other significant persons (unlike Eve Black). And LOVE and SEX (quite unlike Eve White) are both favorable and quite closely identified. The changes from testings I and II are simply such as to strengthen the 'healthy' pattern." The models for Jane are given in Figure 5.

Now, in a more interpretive vein: "Superficially, Jane is a very healthy personality – 'all's well with the world, and day by day I'm getting better and better.' Her SPOUSE is becoming more like the noble DOCTOR all the time, and she is coming to perceive herself, even, as a pleasant and reasonably active (if somewhat weak and submissive) person. But all this is a little too rosy, a little too pat. We note that Jane is becoming more and more 'simple-minded' – all of her judgments tending to fall along a single factor of good-strong vs. bad-weak – which makes the Jane II model the most restricted and undiversified of all. Those psychoanalytically inclined may wish to view this personality as representing dominance of a self-deceptive *ego* which has woven a web of repression as to the state of reality; or, they may wish to view Jane as an essentially strong, healthy, and improving ego-dominated personality."

Fig. 5.   Semantic Space for Jane

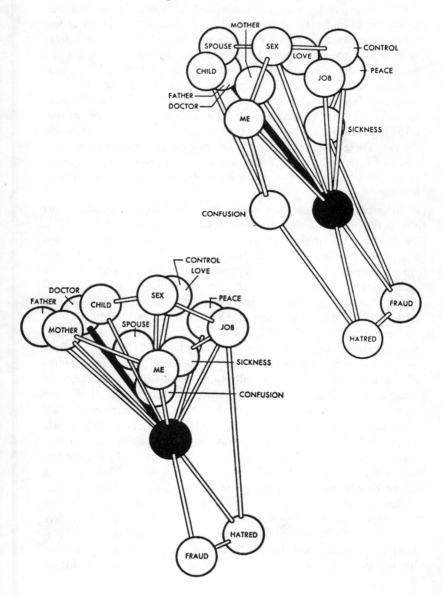

According to Thigpen and Cleckley: "It is easy to sense in her (Jane) a capacity for accomplishment and fulfillment far beyond that of the sweet and retiring Eve White, who, beside this genuinely impressive newcomer, appears colorless and limited. In her are indications of initiative and powerful resources never shown by the other ... . Apparently she is capable of compassion, and, we feel likely of devotion and valid love. She has cooperated with sincerity, and with judgment and originality beyond that of the others." Jane's charitableness toward the other personality (Eve White) whose life and role she was taking appears in a letter she wrote to the therapist: "She must not die yet. There's so much I must know, and so much I must learn from her. She is the substance of 'this above all to thine own self be true.' In her, too, 'the quality of mercy is not strained.' I want her to live — not me!"

Also on the basis of the semantic data, the following guesses about the development of the case were made by Osgood and Luria: "... Jane is both the original personality which broke apart and the terminal personality which is being developed out of therapy ... . The picture of Eve Black is certainly suggestive of an *Electra complex* as the underlying dynamism. In 'real' life, her MOTHER is or was the dominant, threatening figure — moralizing, demanding standards and SELF-CONTROL — and in Eve Black this woman escapes the pressure by rendering both MOTHER and SELF-CONTROL meaningless and simultaneously identifying with and taking her FATHER's place. Suggestive evidence may be found in (that) MOTHER is consistently *colder* than FATHER and usually more *tense* and *fast* ... . We must assume strong and about equal pressures toward solving the *Electra complex*, (a) by identifying with FATHER and asserting the self (id?), and (b) by identifying with MOTHER and devaluating herself (superego?). This produces a two-way split from the Jane pattern, one into Eve Black where selfish needs for superiority and playing the father role are achieved and another into Eve White where societal needs for submission and playing the mother role are achieved ... . The effect of therapy may be to strengthen the self-deceptive organization of Jane without resolving the underlying conflicts dramatized by Eve White and Eve Black. The over-simplified, Pollyanna-like ways of perceiving herself as good along with all the other significant persons in her life yields a superficially happy person who views the world in an acceptable, if rigidly stereotyped, fashion. If (this) interpretation approximates the actual situation, then we feel compelled to predict another breakdown at some later period in this person's life."

Thigpen and Cleckley carefully, and perhaps wisely, avoided any attempt at interpreting the dynamics of their case. Nevertheless, considerable incidental evidence that seems at least consistent with the above interpretation can be culled from their report. (From Thigpen and Cleckley): "Eve Black, so far as we can tell, has enjoyed an independent life since Mrs. White's early childhood. She is not the product of disruptive emotional stresses which the patient has suffered during recent years ... . The parents had had to punish their ordinarily good and conforming six-year-old girl for having disobeyed their specific rule against wandering through the woods ... . On her return Eve received a hearty whipping despite her desperate denials of wrongdoing or disobedience." It had been Eve Black, of course, who wandered off. "The patient is the oldest of three siblings, having twin sisters." In other words, she had a model for a split into Eve White and Eve Black. "Actually the problem started at a much earlier period of life, with a strong feeling of rejection by her parents, especially after the birth of her twin sisters. Mrs. White loves them dearly, Mrs. Black despises them." Of special interest and relevance is the therapists' description of the conditions under which Jane first appeared in therapy. (From Thigpen and Cleckley): "At this point the situation changed for the worse. Eve White's headaches returned. With them also returned the 'blackouts.' ... . Attempts were made with each Eve to work back step by step into early childhood ... . It was hoped that some link or bridge might be found on which additional contact and coalition could grow or be built ... . Sometime after the return of headaches and blackouts, with Eve White's maladjusment still growing worse generally, a very early recollection was being discussed with her. The incident focused about a painful injury she had sustained when scalded by water from a wash pot. As she spoke her eyes shut sleepily ... . After remaining in this sleep or trance for perhaps two minutes her eyes opened. Blankly she stared about the room ... her eyes finally met those of the therapist, and stopped. Slowly, with an unknown husky voice and with immeasurable poise, she spoke. 'Who are you?' " (Jane had appeared at this point.)

It is clear from their report that Thigpen and Cleckley felt that the new Jane was a successful resolution of the personality disturbance, and having developed some identification with this patient ourselves, even though remotely, we certainly hope they are correct. Our reason for doubt on this score was essentially the extreme lack of conceptual differentation in Jane II — her tendency to judge all persons and roles in simple blacks and whites. (It may be added here that since our write-up of the case we have received three more samplings of Jane extending over a period of more than a year; these data show development of even further rigidity in this respect.) Yet, in personal communications we have had from the therapists it appears that Jane is adjusting satisfactorily to her role as mother and wife.[7] In any case this study seems to demonstrate the potential usefulness of the semantic differential as a research instrument in this area.

Pictorial Signs And Symbols[8]

Let us reflect a moment on the probable development of sign processes in the young individual. It is evident that for most of the common objects and situations in the child's environment *perceptual signs* are established prior to *linguistic signs.* The perceptual patterns generated by seeing a BALL or a SPOON, hearing a BARK or a CAR HORN, and feeling a BUTTON or a STRING acquire significance long before the words we use to refer to these objects — we know this because the pre-verbal child displays appropriate meaningful behaviors to these objects, as perceived. Later, the arbitrarily coded noises that constitute vocal signs, and still later, the arbitrarily coded visual patterns that constitute orthographic signs, come to be associated with the same or very similar mediation processes. When a set of physically different stimuli are associated with a process which mediates common overt behavior, we speak of a class of signs having the same significance.

What about *pictorial signs?* Is the outline drawing on a white card

---

[7]   From a personal communication to me by Dr. Thigpen around 1960, it appears now that Jane was actually a *role* being played by Eve Black in an attempt to "win" in therapy; undifferentiated conceptual structures seem to characterized role-playing. cf. Stagner and Osgood, 1941 (footnote added in 1973).

[8]   Pp. 295-299 ol *The Measurement of Meaning.*

of a dog, say, simply a substitute for a perceptual sign? Does the mediation process already associated with DOG as perceived simply generalize to this similar visual presentation? Although generalization may play some role, particularly in highly representational artistic products which skillfully duplicate the conditions of visual perception, this is certainly not true for ordinary pictorial representations. The outline drawing of DOG on a small white card is far removed from the perception of this object; such drawings are actually a very arbitrary class of visual signs (two-dimensional, untrue in color stimulation, etc.) whose significance must be learned, just as the meaning of orthographic signs on the printed page must be learned. Anthropologists are made aware of this arbitrariness when they show drawings or even photographs of common objects to 'primitive' subjects; what is 'obviously' a picture of a cow to the Western white investigators proves to be a complete mystery to the Bantu Negro!

The direct visual perception of an object, the spoken word which labels the object, the printed word for the object, and the conventional picture (outline drawing, painting, photograph, etc.) of the object, then, become a class of alternative *signs* of the object, by virtue of association (through learning) with the same or similar mediation process. But what about a *pictorial symbol*? What is the status, semantically, of the political cartoon of the Democratic DONKEY? Here we have something new – a sign (picture of donkey) which already has its own characteristic meaning being used to represent something other than itself. Our discussion of the basic nature of symbolism in connection with Moss's research on dream symbolism may be recalled.[9] When a person reacts overtly to one sign with the behaviors ordinarily made to another sign, e.g., when he sees his youngster point his forefinger at him and he agreeably simulates fear and raises his hands, he is behaving symbolically. If he maintains the meaningful distinction between the sign and the thing symbolized – recognizing the pointed finger as such and merely behaving as *if* it were a gun – we may speak of *conscious symbolism.* If he does not maintain this distinction, and actually perceives the pointed finger as a gun, as in dream symbolism,

[9] For a presentation of this work on dream symbolism and other clinical matters, see C. Scott Moss, *Dreams, Images, and Fantasy*, University of Illinois Press, 1970 (footnote added in 1973).

we may speak of *unconscious symbolism*. The distinction theoretically lies in whether the sign elicits merely the overt behavior appropriate to the thing symbolized or the mediation process characteristic of the thing symbolized as well.

The experiment described below was designed to study the degree to which the meanings of pictorial signs and pictorial symbols (specifically, political cartoons) replicate the meanings of the things symbolized. Is an outline drawing of an ordinary elephant semantically equivalent to the word ELEPHANT? Is a political cartoon of the Republican elephant, clearly identified as such, semantically equivalent to the words REPUBLICAN PARTY, or is there some degree of compromise in which the meaning of elephant per se interacts with that of REPUBLICAN PARTY? One study [10] employed the semantic differential to investigate these problems. Five groups of 20 undergraduate subjects each, arranged in a Latin-square design, rated each of five classes of animal objects in five different modes of presentation. The animals were BEAR, EAGLE, LION, ELEPHANT, and DONKEY. The modes of sign presentation were as follows: (a) the *orthographic sign* for the animal (e.g., the printed word ELEPHANT); (b) a *pictorial sign* of the animal (e.g., an outline drawing of an ordinary elephant); (c) a *nonpolitical stereotypical pictorial symbol* of the animal (e.g., outline drawing of the elephant cowering before a mouse); (d) as a *political symbol* (e.g., outline drawing of the Republican elephant clearly identified as such); and (e) the *orthographic sign of the thing symbolized* (e.g., the printed words REPUBLICAN PARTY). Ten semantic scales were used — four for the evaluative factor and three each for the potency and activity factors. Each subject rated all 25 stimuli; the order of modes of presentation (types of signs) was held constant, but the order of presentation of the animals was varied from group to group.

Analysis of the data was in terms of profile similarities for the various modes of presentation, as indicated in terms of both D-scores and correlations. Table 5 presents both these indices of similarity for the various types of comparison that will concern us here. Our first question is directed at the *essential equivalance in meaning between*

---

[10]   Conducted by Drs. P.H. Tannenbaum and Jean S. Kerrick at the University of Illinois in 1952.

TABLE 5. *Mean D-scores (Upper Values) and Correlations (Lower Values) Between Various Experimental Conditions*

Animal	1 a vs. b	2 b vs. c	3 b vs. d	4 c vs. d	5 d vs. e
Eagle	1.15	1.29	5.31	7.00	1.81
	.94*	.95*	.41	.12	.98*
Lion	.73	2.97	2.74	5.79	2.48
	.99*	.81*	.76*	.41	.25
Bear	1.09	3.65	4.48	7.67	.92
	.97*	.56*	.59	−.16	.99*
Elephant	1.02	3.11	3.98	7.34	1.03
	.96*	.79*	.43	.11	.93*
Donkey	.96	3.35	4.67	6.71	.97
	.92*	.44	.33	−.08	.91*
Average D	.990	2.874	4.236	6.902	1.442
Average r	.965*	.785*	.525	.085	.930*

* $p < .01$.

the orthographic and pictorial signs for the same object. The main test here lies in comparing conditions *a* vs. *b* (e.g., the word ELEPHANT with the plain drawing of an elephant). Inspection of column (1) in Table 5 shows that the mean D for these comparisons is smaller than those for the other comparisons, and in each case there is a high and significant correlation between the profiles.

A second question is concerned with whether *the meaning of the nonpolitical stereotypical symbol represents some compromise between the meaning of the sign itself and the meaning of the stereotype.* The data in column (2) shows the comparison between the plain drawing of the animal and the drawing of the animal in a nonpolitical stereotyped situation. The D's here are somewhat larger for that in column (1), but there is still some basis for a strong similarity between the profiles, as indicated by the significant correlations. This suggests that the meaning of the nonpolitical stereotyped situation did represent some compromise — e.g., the elephant remains essentially an elephant, although there are shifts on scales appropriate to the stereotypical situation. Indeed, such specific shifts are readily apparent when one examines the scale-by-scale profiles of judgment, not included here for purposes of economy.

What about the *use of the animal cartoon as a political symbol*? Unlike the above findings, here we have practically no evidence of compromise. The D's between conditions *d* and *e*, as shown in column (5), are all lower than those between conditions *d* and the other drawings, i.e., in columns (3) and (4). Also, the correlations between the political drawing and the political word are, with one exception, high and significant. Only in the case of the lion as a symbol of Great Britain did this relation fall down — one possible explanation of this is that midwestern undergraduates failed to perceive a drawing of a lion with a Union Jack flag on its chest as a symbol of Britain.

These results support the conclusion that for certain pictorial symbols, at least, the meaning of the symbol may be shifted completely to that of the thing symbolized. The standard political cartoon symbols carry very little of the sign being used as a symbol — the elephant as a symbol of the Republican party bears little resemblance to the judgment of an elephant per se. That this is not a universal characteristic of symbols is at least suggested by the results with the nonpolitical pictorial symbols; here there is evidence for compromise between sign-meaning per se and meaning-as-symbol, although the case would have been stronger had Tannenbaum and Kerrick also presented words referring to the stereotyped characteristics for rating (e.g., the word COWARDLY in the case of the elephant set). Finally, it is clear that, at least for the sign classes used here, ordinary pictorial signs are semantically equivalent to linguistic signs.

The Semantic Effects Of Word Combination [11]

The meaning of a word in ordinary speech is influenced by the context of other words with which it occurs. Speakers select adjectives to modify nouns and adverbs to modify verbs, and they arrange word sequences to change meanings in desired directions and to desired degrees, thereby greatly expanding the discriminatory power of the communication system. An AGGRESSIVE LEADER is somewhat different in meaning from a POWERFUL LEADER, and both in turn are quite different from a SYMPATHETIC LEADER. An experiment by

---

[11]   Excerpts from pp. 275-284 of *The Measurement of Meaning.*

Howes and Osgood (1954) demonstrated that the probabilities of various associative responses to a given stimulus word can be changed by varying the antecedent verbal context; while this is evidence that meaning is influenced by linguistic context, it provides no insight into the laws that might be operating. In the present study, a set of adjectives is combined with a set of nouns in all possible pairs, and we are interested in the degree to which the meanings of these combinations are predictable from knowing the meanings of their components. [12]

Materials and Procedure. It was necessary to select verbal materials whose meanings would be as widely distributed throughout the semantic space as possible and whose combinations, therefore, would yield as wide a variety of amounts and directions of change as possible. It was also necessary to have components whose combinations would be as "natural" and credible as possible. The combination of adjective and noun into the nominal phrase seemed to be the linguistic form most suited to our purpose. To satisfy the credibility criterion, we tried to avoid nouns having a rigid connotative significance, e.g., a HAPPY BOULDER would be rather hard to swallow cognitively! Nouns referring denotively to classes of persons were finally selected: NURSE, SCIENTIST, THUG, PROSTITUTE, HUSBAND, COMEDIAN, IMP, and SECRETARY. The following adjectives were selected on a priori grounds as giving a fairly wide coverage of the semantic space: ARTISTIC, HAIRY, LISTLESS, AVERAGE, SINCERE, SHY, TREACHEROUS, and BREEZY. To make the prediction situation as rigorous as possible, and to avoid any bias in choosing particular combinations, the eight adjectives were combined in all possible ways with the eight nouns, i.e., 64 word mixtures.

Since it was desirable not to have a subject judge more than one combination using the same component, it was necessary to employ eight groups of subjects. These groups ranged from an N of 21 to an N of 29, averaging an N of 25. Each group differentiated the meanings of all 16 component words (the eight adjectives and eight nouns) and then subsequently differentiated the meanings of eight of the 64 pos-

[12] Mr. Donald C. Ferguson collaborated with the senior author on this research, supported by an Undergraduate Research Fellowship with the Social Science Research Council. We gratefully acknowledge this support.

sible combinations. Group I had ARTISTIC NURSE, Group II had
BREEZY NURSE, Group III had TREACHEROUS NURSE, and so
on.

The scales used in this study were nine in number, three to represent each of the major factors isolated in our factor analytic work:
evaluation (*valuable-worthless, admirable-deplorable, good-bad*); potency (*robust-delicate, intense-mild, powerful-powerless*); and activity
(*quick-slow, active-passive*, and *restless-quiet*). These scales appeared
on mimeographed sheets with the component term or combination to
be judged printed at the top; the order of the components and combinations was randomized in the booklets handed out to the subjects.
Beyond the standard instructions, the following special instructions
for judging the combinations were given:

On the following pages you will find descriptive pairs of words such as
PIOUS THIEF, which you might find easier to judge if you try to
recall some character who seems to fit the description — for example,
one from a movie, play, or book. Here, too, do NOT look back and
forth through the booklet or try to remember how you marked similar items earlier, but make each item a separate and independent
judgment.

The basis for prediction. The problem of predicting the meaning of
word mixtures is somewhat analogous to that of predicting the color
of wave-length mixtures. In both cases we are dealing with the locations of component stimuli in an *n*-dimensional space and are seeking
general principles governing their interaction. The direction of a point
from the origin of our semantic space is analogous to the wave-length
of a visual stimulus; the distance from the origin out to the point is
analogous to the colorimetric purity of a visual stimulus. Thus we
might speak of AGGRESSIVE as being *strong, active*, and *slightly
good* in "hue" and quite intense or "saturated." One of the laws of
color mixture is that if two component stimuli lie on the same straight
line through the origin and on opposite sides of it (complementary
colors), their mixture will merely cancel toward neutral gray. Will the
combination of words of opposed meaning also tend toward a meaningless "neutral gray," e.g., the meaning of a SUBTLE OAF? Another
law is that the hues of mixtures must always lie between those of the

components. Will the point in semantic space corresponding to a CAT-LIKE WRESTLER necessarily fall somewhere on a line between the points representing CATLIKE and WRESTLER? In color mixture the saturation of a mixture cannot be greater than that of the most saturated component. Must the meaning of STURDY TREE be equally or less polarized than STURDY?

In predicting the semantic effects of word mixture, use was made of *the congruity principle*, which is similar to, but not identical with the laws governing color mixture. [13] The essence of the principle is that when two cognitive events are simultaneously elicited, each exerts a modifying pressure on the other, in proportion to its own degree of polarization and in the direction of the other's position of perfect congruence. If such a principle can be shown to operate along one of the dimensions of meaning (the attitudinal or evaluative dimension), it seems reasonable to expect that it will operate simultaneously along all semantic dimensions. The present study, in part, may be considered a test of this expectation.

If two words of known meaning (i.e., measured meaning), such as the adjective SINCERE and the noun PROSTITUTE are combined in a linguistic phrase, SINCERE PROSTITUTE, the meaning of the compound should be predictable by applying the congruity formula simultaneously along all three dimensions *evaluation, potency*, and *activity*. There are several ways in which this situation differs from that described for attitude change: (1) Here we assume that we are always dealing with a positive, associative assertion, i.e., that the modification of a noun by an adjective is equivalent to the assertion that the noun *is associated with* the adjectival characteristic. (2) We also assume that the subject is always credulous of the combination, that he accepts any adjectival characterization of any noun. (3) And rather than dealing with *change* in the meaning of a concept due to interaction, we deal with the resolution of component meanings into the "new meaning" of the compound. The formula we use is

$$d_m = \frac{|d_a|}{|d_a| + |d_n|} (d_a) + \frac{|d_n|}{|d_a| + |d_n|} (d_n)$$

[13] See Chapter 5 of *The Measurement of Meaning* for more detail; also Ch. 3 ("Cognitive Dynamics in Human Affairs") in Volume II and Ch. 4 ("From Yang and Yin to *And* or *But*") in Volume III of this series (footnote added in 1974).

where $|d|$ is deviation or polarization from neutrality on the scales regardless of sign, d is deviation from neutrality with respect to sign (i.e., location along a continuum from -3 to $+3$), and the subscripts m, a, and n refer to *mixture, adjective,* and *noun* respectively. This formula is applied separately to each of the three semantic dimensions.

Results. The raw data were first transformed to factor scores by averaging over the three scales representing each factor; for each subject's judgment of each component word we then had three scores. Using the congruity formula above, a table was generated giving the predicted scale values for all combinations of these factor scores; entering this table with a particular subject's scores for the adjective and noun components contributing to a given combination, the predicted factor scores for the combination were read off and listed. The obtained factor scores were computed directly from the same subject's actual judgments of the word combinations. The main concern of the experiment is with the accuracy of prediction, i.e., how close the obtained meanings of the word combinations are to those predicted from the component terms. We may look first at analyses based on the *means for groups.* Figure 6 illustrates the prediction problem: the upper solid line gives the mean factor scores for the noun, SECRETARY, and the lower solid line the means for the adjective, SHY; the dashed line gives the means of the predicted factor scores for the combination, SHY SECRETARY, and the remaining solid line gives the means of the obtained factor scores for this combination. It will be noted that the measured meaning of SHY SECRETARY consistently deviates from the prediction in the direction of the adjective; this dominance of the adjectival component is typical of our data.

Perhaps the best estimate of prediction accuracy here is the correlation between predicted and obtained mean factor scores across the 64 word combinations. For the evaluative factor $r = .86$; for the potency factor, $r = .86$; and for the activity factor, $r = .90$ — all highly significant. Summarizing these results on the "cultural meanings" of word mixtures, we find that the obtained factor scores, as predicted with the congruity formula, are consistently within the limits set by the meanings of the components, deviate from predictions on the average by amounts attributable to unreliability (except for the evalu-

Fig. 6. Cultural Meanings for SHY SECRETARY

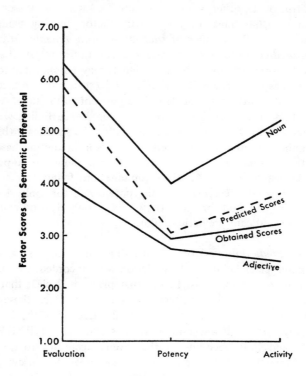

ative factor), and correlate very highly with predicted factor scores.

More sensitive tests of the accuracy of predictions can be obtained from the data on individual subjects. Two such tests were made: (1) *Constant errors as determined by sign test.* For each word combination on each of the three factors we have approximately 25 pairs of obtained and predicted scores. If there were no constant errors in prediction (the null hypothesis here), then the obtained factor score for each subject should have a 50/50 chance of being larger or smaller than his predicted factor score. The Dixon-Mood Sign Test was run separately for each word combination on each factor to determine if predictions were significantly displaced from obtained meanings. Constant errors were plainly occurring for the evaluative factor, 40/64 items having errors significant at the 5 per cent level or better; this was not true of the other two factors, only 7/64 items for the potency factor and 14/64 items for the activity factor showing significant constant errors. (2) *Number of subjects showing reliable difference between predicted and obtained factor scores*. In test-retest reliability data the factor scores of individual subjects may be expected to vary by as much as 1.00 scale unit on factor I, 1.50 scale units on factor II, and 1.33 scale units on factor III only 5 per cent of the time. Assuming that these values establish 5 per cent confidence limits, we may ask of each factor for each word combination if a significant (by sign test) number of subjects show reliable errors in prediction based on congruity. By this criterion, also, prediction is shown to be poorest for the evaluative factor, 42 of 64 combinations failing to meet this criterion of good prediction; for the potency factor, only 4 of 64 combinations fail, and for the activity factor, only 8 of 64 combinations show significant prediction failure.

Nature of Prediction Failures. Restricting our attention to the 38 cases where "clear failures" of prediction were recorded, we may try to discover some lawfulness. In the first place, it is clear that most errors occur on the evaluative factor. In the second place, these errors are almost always in the direction of the adjective (31 of the 38 cases) — and only three nouns, seemingly the most "loaded," THUG, PROSTITUTE, and IMP, account for the seven exceptions to this rule. Finally, inspection of the direction of error shows that in every case deviation is in the unfavorable direction of the semantic space, i.e., toward the *bad, weak*, and *passive* directions. These results are consistent with what might be dubbed the "evaluative stickiness" of some concepts — resistance of concepts having strong evaluative loading to meaning change. Thus every combination made with LISTLESS deviates from the predicted meaning toward the location of this adjective; all combinations made with THUG (except with the adjectives LISTLESS and SHY) deviate toward the location of this noun. However, it is really "*pessimistic* evaluative stickiness" that seems to be operating. It is as if the more unfavorable, unpleasant, or socially derogatory components were always dominant in word mixtures. Whereas the meaning of NURSE can easily be devalued by attaching TREACHEROUS to it, attaching SINCERE to PROSTITUTE fails to budge the immoral connotation of the fallen woman. A TREACHEROUS NUR-SE is definitely not to be trusted, but a SINCERE PROSTITUTE is still a prostitute!

But isn't there some simpler, or at least less esoteric, way of accounting for these errors? What about the *angle* in the semantic space between the components contributing to a combination? In an earlier chapter Suci has argued that concepts are comparable to the extent that they share the same characteristic attributes. If this is a general condition for cognitive interactions, then congruity effects should also operate to the degree that the interacting concepts share characteristic attributes. Since concepts will share the same atributes in proportion to how close they lie to a common dimension through the sematic space, accuracy of prediction should vary inversely with the cosine of the angle between adjective and noun components. Accordingly, cosines of the angles between all adjective and noun pairs were computed from the mean factor scores of these components when judged separately, and these values were then correlated with the accuracy of predicting the meanings of their combinations via congruity (as estimated from the numbers of subjects showing reliable errors). A significant correlation, 69, was obtained, indicating that errors in prediction do, in fact, increase with the angular displacement of the components in the semantic space.

Summary. Quite apart from the validity of the congruity principle as a basis for predicting the meanings of word mixtures, this experiment demonstrates the usefulness of the semantic differential as a tool for testing certain psycholinguistic notions. In this case it was possible to measure in comparable units at least certain aspects of the meanings of both individual words and of phrases in which they were combined, and thereby to test for the lawfulness of semantic change under conditions of combination. The results of this study show that the semantic effects of word combination are neither haphazard nor unique. In terms of the average meanings of the word combinations, semantic effects follow the expectations from a congruity principle quite closely. Analysis of the data from individual subjects, however, reveals consistent errors in prediction with the congruity formula: particularly on the evaluative factor, the measured meanings of combinations regularly deviate by being more unfavorable (*bad*, *weak*, and *passive*) than predicted. It was also shown that the congruity formula predicts less and less well as the angular displacement of word components in the semantic space increases. In other words, the less comparable two signs that are put in combination, in terms of the sharing of characteristic attributes, the less congruity interaction they display, and the failure of congruity under these conditions typically appears as dominance of the unfavorably evaluative component. It is entirely possible, of course, that some formula other than that derived from the congruity principle would incorporate these word mixture results more adequately.

Chapter 2

SEMANTIC DIFFERENTIAL TECHNIQUE: ANTHROPOCENTRICS

STRATEGY OF CROSS-CULTURAL RESEARCH[1]

In the near-decade of work from 1950 to 1957, the generality of the Evaluation-Potency-Activity (E-P-A) structure of what I now call "affective meaning" had been amply demonstrated for the American English language/culture community. Since this generality has been shown to hold across various methods of obtaining judgments and factoring, across various types of subjects (males vs. females, age and I.Q. levels, Republicans vs. Democrats, and even schizophrenics vs. normals), across various independent procedures for sampling bipolar adjectival scales, and across various samples of concepts (whether they be ordinary nouns in English, pictorial signs or even whole paragraphs, e.g., describing Charles Morris's "Ways to Live," Osgood, Ware, and Morris, 1961) we seemed to have the answer to one of the major questions with which we had begun our exploration: *given diversified samples of concepts, scales and native informants, the E-P-A structure of the semantic space obtained in replications of the SD technique is non-arbitrary*. Just as there is non-arbitrariness of the geophysical space, determined by gravity, the rotation of our planet and the location of the magnetic pole, so there seemed to be non-arbitrariness in the affective meaning space.

There was one serious limitation upon this conclusion, however; nearly all of our research up to this point had been highly *ethnocentric* — focussed on humans sharing a common (American) culture and speaking a common (English) language — and the few exceptions (e.g., by Kumata and Schramm, 1956, and by Suci, 1960) had been subject to the bias of translation. It was at least *conceivable* that the dominance of Goodness-Badness, Strength-Weakness and Activity-Passivity

---

[1] Excerpted from a version of "Explorations in Semantic Space: a Personal Diary" appearing in the *Journal of Social Issues*, 1971, *27*, 5-64. Kurt Lewin Memorial Award Address.

in our data was attributable to something peculiar, either about American culture or about the English language — or both. In 1958-59 — while I was a Fellow at the Center for Advanced Study in the Behavioral Sciences at Palo Alto and had a chance to sit back and look at the larger pattern of things — it became clear that the next step in our exploration of semantic space should be a shift from ethnocentrics to what might be called *anthropocentrics*, with a focus upon mankind in general and a hope of discovering something universal about human semantic systems.

Recent developments in technology — in transportation, in communication and in industrialization generally, to say nothing of pollution and weaponry — are driving us willy-nilly toward mutual interdependence, either One World or No World. The same technological developments have made it possible to do cross-cultural research on a scale that would have been inconceivable only a decade or two ago. Certainly our own cross-cultural research on human semantic systems would have been inconceivable without the developments — even within the 11-year span of the project so far — of speed in communication, in transportation and, particularly in computation. I am also convinced that, had our project been initiated circa 1980 rather than circa 1960 — only 20 years later — much of the cultural uniqueness still evident in our data would have been obliterated in the sweeping tide of cultural homogeneity, also evident in our data, for the younger generations who constitute our samples.

There are many hypotheses about human nature that demand cross-cultural and cross-linguistic designs, if we are to successfully disentangle what is common to the human species from what is peculiar to specific segments of it. However, comparisons across cultures are particularly difficult when what anthropologists term *non-material* traits are under study. It is one thing to compare skull shapes, scraping tools, potsherds and other artifacts; it is quite another to compare values, feelings, stereotypes and, most generally, meanings — what I have come to call "subjective culture." Whereas elements of objective culture may leave their physical traces on and in the earth, elements of subjective culture certainly cannot. But more important, subjective culture is most naturally and directly assessed through the medium of language, and therefore what is called "the language barrier" must somehow be pierced.

Many years ago Edward Sapir and then Benjamin Lee Whorf phrased what would now be called "the hypothesis of psycholinguistic relativity," according to which how we perceive, how we think, and even how we formulate our implicit philosophies depend upon the structure of the language we speak. If this were literally true, then cross-linguistic comparisons of subjective culture would be impossible in principle. However, recent comparative studies in psycholinguistics are making it clear that, although languages do display uniqueness in phonology, grammar and semantics that render them mutually unintelligible, they also display certain universals in phonology, grammar and semantics that render them mutually translatable. The critical thing is this: in order to note differences within any domain and order them in a rigorous fashion, one must have certain similarities in the dimensions of variation. Only to the extent that physical objects share such attributes as size, weight and volume — and to the extent that these attributes can be abstracted and quantified — can comparisons among them be made on anything other than an intuitive basis. The same holds true for subjective culture.

So, in 1960, with initial support on a small scale from the Human Ecology Fund, Geppetto and his Pinocchio set out across the world looking — not for fame and fortune — but for friends in foreign lands who might catch some of their excitement and join in the exploration of semantic space. Put a bit less romantically, my purposes were twofold; first, on the theoretical side, to test the generality — or lack thereof — of the E-P-A structure of affective meaning across a matrix of human communities differing in both language and culture; second, on a more practical bent — if the generality of the E-P-A system could be demonstrated as common dimensions of variations in meaning — to devise comparable semantic differential tools in various languages for measuring similarities and differences in subjective cultures.

HYPOTHESIS-TESTING AND TOOL-MAKING

We wished to test the hypothesis that the major dimensions of affective meaning are independent of variations in both language and culture. Ideally, the whole world should be our oyster, but the funds available in 1960 were very limited and our estimates of expenses for travel, for field work. for data-processing, for salaries and all those other mundane matters strongly suggested an initial sample of only six language/culture communities. [2] After much discussion at a planning conference in late 1959, including anthropologists, linguists, psychologists and some social scientists from foreign countries — which is a good, if obvious, strategy in this type of research — we settled upon six locations which we felt would would maximize linguistic and cultural differences and yet provide literate speakers of "national" languages, i.e., "high cultures." These were Finnish in Finland (Finno-Ugric language family), Arabic in Lebanon (Semitic), Farsi in Iran (Indo-European, but remote from English), Kannada in Mysore, India (Dravidian), Chinese in Hong Kong (Sino-Tibetan), and Japanese in Japan (its own language family) — with American English in Central Illinois as a kind of "control," since it was necessarily the source language for translation.

If you could imagine a map of the world, with all of the 25 locations in which we are now working indicated by pins with city names on them, three things would immediately become apparent to you: (1) we have something of an over-representation in Europe, 10 of our 25 if you include our two Scandinavian groups and three Mediterranean ones (this is the result of the availability of interested and trained people, in large part); (2) the southern hemisphere is very poorly represented, with no site as yet in South America and only the Nigerian samples (Hausa and Yoruba in Ibadan, and this work was disrupted by the Biafran conflict) in Africa; (3) the two largest countries in the world, the Soviet Union and the Peoples Republic of China, are not included (in the former case we have made unsuccessful overtures and in the latter it seemed completely infeasible until very recently). Otherwise, the sample seems reasonably representative and extensive. We also proved to be surprisingly efficient, in terms of standardization of the basic procedures and computarization of all but the most raw of the data. By the time we were into the sixth year of work — now with support jointly from the National Institute of Mental Health and

---

[2]   I use this term since in some cases we have several languages in one country (e.g., Bengali, Hindi and Kannada in India), in others the same language in several countries (e.g., Mexican, Yucatansan, and Costa Rican Spanish), and yet other closely related languages in two countries (e.g., Netherlands Dutch and Belgian Flemish, Iranian Farsi and Afghan Dari).

the National Science Foundation, which we gratefully acknowledge[3] — we were handling twice the number of sites that we had originally bargained for and without any request for increased funds. This, I have been told, is well-nigh unheard of in granting-agency circles!

As far as sampling *within* communities was concerned, we were faced with a dilemma common in cross-cultural work: *did we want representativeness within each country or equivalence across countries*? Maximizing representativeness within usually means minimizing equivalence between, and vice versa. Since our primary purpose was to compare semantic systems *as a function of gross differences in language and culture,* we decided to maximize equivalence, using teen-age male students in average high schools in urban settings.

At the same planning conference we had to face another dilemma common to cross-cultural researchers: *how we were to walk the fine line between standardization and naturalness*? Scientists regard standardization of procedures, quite correctly, as one of the safeguards of scientific rigor. Its purpose is to render data from diverse samples comparable. In public opinion polling as well as in anthropological ethoscience, it is well-known that what questions one asks and how one asks them can markedly influence the data. In within-culture research this usually means identical instructions and procedures; in cross-cultural research — paradoxically — it may mean deliberately varied instructions and even procedures. On the other side of this coin, what passes for "standardization" in cross-cultural work may in fact impose a foreign mold upon the experimental tasks and press out quite unnatural and therefore valueless data. In our case, we wished to expose native speakers to the same task, functionally, and yet leave their responses completely free of Western influence. We desired procedures which would maximize the opportunity for cultural uniqueness to appear and yet be sufficiently standardized so that comparisons could legitimately be made.

And this led us into yet another dilemma faced by cross-cultural strategists: *how were we to assure sufficient standardization and yet avoid the pitfall of translation bias*? The most common strategy for circumventing the language barrier is that of using "translation-equiva-

[3] Grants #07705 I through 5 from the National Institute of Mental Health and # GS 360 from the National Science Foundation.

lent" instruments; not only does this involve many tactical problems, but a test in language X that is literally translated into language Y is, in a sense, a direct imposition of the culture of X upon the culture of Y. To use a crude example, one cannot reasonably ask Bantu subjects in Africa "would you accept Black families in your neighborhood?" as part of an attitude scale. However, we did use a version of "translation equivalence" as the starting point of our research — as will be seen. Another strategy is the use of "language-free" instruments; the late Hadley Cantril's self-anchoring "ladder device," in which subjects in different communities establish their own best-possible and worst-possible worlds in their own terms as anchors of a scale, is a case in point (*The Patterns of Human Concerns*, 1965). Various perceptual devices, including a Graphic Differential which we have worked on, are also usually considered to be "language-free," but this obviously assumes some absolute distinction between linguistic and non-linguistic (perceptual) signs. A third strategy — and by all odds the best, in my opinion — is the development (or perhaps better, discovery) of "language invariant" instruments. Its success depends upon the demonstration of language universals.

Keeping all of these hazards of cross-cultural research in mind, I would like now to trace briefly the actual procedures we followed in the first "tool making" (and hypothesis-testing) phase of our own work. The reader can judge for himself how successful we were in resolving the dilemmas and dodging the pitfalls.

(1) Selecting a basic list of substantives

You will recall that in the original explorations in American English (AE for short) we had sampled qualifiers (adjectives) from existing frequency lists (Thorndike-Lorge) and semantic catogorizations (Roget's *Thesaurus*). How was one to get a representative set of qualifiers for languages which have neither Thorndike-Lorge nor Roget types of listings? The solution that would occur immediately to any experimental psychologist would be some kind of word-association test — modified to elicit adjectival forms, of course. But what elicitors should be used? In AE, nominal forms typically elicit adjectival forms — that is, people seem to have a natural tendency to qualify substantives, and one might hope that this is a human universal. Fair enough. But should one devise a standardized list of substantives (nouns) or let our colleagues in each locus devise their own stimulus lists? It seemed obvious that different types of nouns (e.g., names of physical objects vs. names of emotions) would produce quite different types of qualifiers, even in the same language, so we decided to establish a standardized list of translation-equivalent nouns which would be culture-common even if not necessarily culture-fair (I don't really know what the latter means). But what list? The Kent-Rosanoff stimuli for word-association are obviously a product of Western Culture. Participants in our planning conference pointed out that items used in glottochronological studies of rates of linguistic changes (cf., Swadesh, 1950; Lees, 1953) were deliberately designed to be culture-common. Relying mainly on these lists, we assembled a pool of 200 substantives.

The next step was to determine the translation fidelity of these verbal items. All 200 substantives, nouns in AE, were given to panels of about 10 fluent English/Mother-tongue bilinguals in each of the six original languages we planned to work with (Arabic, Cantonese, Finnish, Japanese, Kannada and Persian). These bilinguals were instructed to give both a preferred and a second translation, *not* using a dictionary, and rate each on a four-point scale for translation difficulty. If any item failed to show a clear majority agreement on either first or second translations in any language, *it was dropped from the list for all languages*. This pruned our list to 108 surviving nouns. Both for reasons of elegance and to more equally balance abstract and concrete concepts, we threw away an additional 8 concretes, ending up with the set of 100 substantives shown in Table 1. Even a brief inspection of this list will convince you of the familiarity of these concepts — HORSE, GIRL, DOG and CLOUD but also abstractions like TRUST, SYMPATHY, PAIN and RESPECT. Testimony to the culture-commonness of these concepts is the fact that, based upon successful translation in only 6 languages, this list has subsequently been translated into over 20 additional languages with at the most three and usually none of the items failing to pass the fidelity test.

I would like to say one more thing about the role of translation in our research. This initial point — translation of the 100 substantives to be used in qualifier elicitation — is the *only* point in the entire research at which translation bias could in any way *affect the data*, the actual results. Everything else is done entirely in the native language,

TABLE 1. *The 100 Culture-Common Concepts Used in Qualifier Elicitations*

1. House	21. Bird	41. Cat	61. Success	81. Man
2. Girl	22. Hope	42. Poison	62. Snake	82. Wednesday
3. Picture	23. Heat	43. Tree	63. Hand	83. Chair
4. Meat	24. Map	44. Hunger	64. Mother	84. Guilt
5. Trust	25. Husband	45. Choice	65. Knot	85. River
6. Tooth	26. Rain	46. Noice	66. Life	86. Peace
7. Defeat	27. Truth	47. Need	67. Head	87. Hair
8. Book	28. Stone	48. Doctor	68. Thunder	88. Food
9. Lake	29. Pain	49. Anger	69. Luck	89. Danger
10. Star	30. Ear	50. Tongue	70. Author	90. Policeman
11. Battle	31. Respect	51. Horse	71. Music	91. Father
12. Seed	32. Laughter	52. Marriage	72. Sleep	92. Fear
13. Sympathy	33. Moon	53. Game	73. Future	93. Root
14. Progress	34. Courage	54. Color	74. Egg	94. Purpose
15. Cup	35. Work	55. Heart	75. Crime	95. Fire
16. Wind	36. Story	56. Friend	76. Sun	96. Rope
17. Thief	37. Punishment	57. Death	77. Belief	97. Power
18. Bread	38. Wealth	58. Smoke	78. Money	98. Window
19. Love	39. Woman	59. Freedom	79. Knowledge	99. Pleasure
20. Fruit	40. Cloud	60. Dog	80. Fish	100. Water

blindly, by computers — although non-Roman scripts must be transliterated, of course, according to a set of rules (our computers only speak Roman!). In other words, beyond this point the data are untouched by (American) human minds. This applies only to quantitative facts, of course; we do obtain translation at each stage to keep an eye on what's happening, and when at last we come to *interpretation* of the data, translation problems — both linguistic and cultural — return with a vengeance.

(2) Qualifier elicitation and selection

With instructions adapted to each language and culture (not simply translated), 100 teen-age boys in ordinary classroom situations were asked to write for each substantive the first qualifier that occurred to them. The 10,000 qualifier tokens (100 subjects x 100 stimuli) generated in this manner in each location were tabulated (and transliterated if necessary) in the field and airmailed to our Center at Illinois, where the data were punched onto IBM cards. Our computer is programmed to apply three criteria in deriving an ordered list of qualifiers from such data: (a) *frequency of usage* (total incidence of each type of qualifier across all noun stimuli); (b) *diversity of usage* (number of different nouns producing each qualifier type); and (c), having ordered all qualifier types according to the Information Theoretic statistic, *H*, which combines frequency and diversity, *independence of usage* (having correlations in distribution of usage across the 100 nouns *less* than a criterion value with all higher-ordered qualifiers). What this procedure does — blindly — is to select and order *the most productive modes of qualifying* in each language and then prune from the ordered list those less productive modes which are redundant with modes already selected. In the absence of usage-frequency lists and Thesauri, this procedure seems reasonable: it combines properties of both, and it is standardized across all languages.

A productivity-ranked and pruned list of 60-70 qualifiers was sent back to each community, where a small group of native speakers was asked to produce *opposites* for each term — again, with appropriately adapted instructions. Any qualifiers which did not have familiar and agreed-upon opposites were eliminated, and a final list of 50 adjective-pairs was thus obtained. What is interesting here is that in *none* of the 28 language/culture communities where this stage has been reached — and this now includes several non-urban and/or non-literate groups — has any difficulty been experienced in eliciting qualifier-opposites. It would appear that the tendency to organize modes of qualification in terms of polar opposition is yet another universal of human languages.

(3) Concept-on-scale factorization

Another group of teen-age male subjects in each community was given the task of differentiating the same 100 translation-equivalent concepts against the bipolar scales derived uniquely for their own language and culture. The usual instructions for this task — again, adapted for each place — were given, including careful definitions of the seven scale positions. These data were then tabularized and shipped to Illinois. Two types of factorization were applied.

(a) *Indigenous analyses.* Imagine, if you will, some 25 data cubes (like the one previously described for our ethnocentric AE work), one for each of our language/culture communities. The only difference is that now — consistent with the implications of Jack Carroll's review (1959) of our earlier work — we have expanded the concept dimension from 20 to 100. For the indigenous factorizations, each of these data cubes was analysed independently of the others, just as in our earlier work. I will summarize the results for 20 communities (only 8 are shown in Table 2): For all language/culture groups the 1st factor, accounting for the largest proportion of variance, is clearly Evaluation. For 13 of the 20 communities, factors clearly identifiable as Potency and Activity are 2nd and 3rd in order of magnitude; for four groups (Belgian Flemish, Netherlands Dutch, Greek and Calcutta Bengali), Activity accounts for more variance than Potency. For Afghan Dari, a factor characterized by the qualifiers *humane, religious, learned, moslem, courageous*, and *immaculate* takes 2nd position in front of A and then P; for Chinese a factor characterized by *extreme, difficult, strange, deep* and *red* displaces A to fourth position; and for Lebanese Arabic a kind of Scarcity factor (*rare, little, particular, hidden, thin* and *light*) displaces A. Although this is a most gratifying conclusion, I am sure that you will have noted with some glee that in order to interpret these results — indeed, to even communicate them — I have had to rely upon translation and your intuitive feelings about the semantics *of English*. Is there any way out of this translation dilemma? I think there is — and this is by putting the data from all communities into one simultaneous factor analysis.

(b) *Pan-cultural analysis.* To put the data derived from separate collections into a single mathematical space for factor analysis, it is necessary that *at least one of the sources of variance* be common or shared. In our three-mode situation this would mean that across the indigenous data cubes either the subjects be the same (which they obviously are not), or the scales be the same (which they obviously are not, with *nectar-like/poisonous* showing up only in Hindi, with *moslem/heathen* only in Afghan Dari, and so forth), *or* the concepts be the same. What about this last possibility? On the one hand, as you have seen, the 100 concepts used in the tool-making phase were carefully translation-equivalent, and on the basis of this equivalence we can organize the data for correlational purposes — in the same sense that, in identical vs. fraternal twin studies, we pair the data for Jones A with Jones B, Smith A with Smith B, and so on, rather than at random. But, on the other hand, we can by no means claim that, just because 23 communities' terms for PAIN are translation-equiva-

TABLE 2. *Factor Analysis of Full-Scale Instrument As Used in Concept-Scale Task*

American English*

I (45.5%)		II (12.0%)		III (5.6%)	
nice-awful	.96	big-little	.81	fast-slow	.64
sweet-sour	.94	powerful-powerless	.75	noisy-quiet	.56
heavenly-hellish	.93	deep-shallow	.69	young-old	.55
good-bad	.93	strong-weak	.68	alive-dead	.55

Calcutta, Bengali

I (30.6%)		II (10.2%)		III (9.8%)	
beautiful-ugly	.94	warm-cold	.75	huge-minute	.74
lovely-homely	.93	intense-mild	.64	deep-shallow	.66
finest-poorest	.93	powerful-powerless	.60	long-short	.66
good-bad	.93	restless-quiet	.59	big-small	.65

Finland, Finnish*

I (30.8%)		II (9.2%)		III (7.8%)	
nice-not nice	.88	agile-clumsy	.68	long-short	.56
light-gloomy	.88	delicate-sturdy	.63	sharp-dull	.52
pleasant-unpleasant	.85	capricious-steady	.60	energetic-unenergetic	.50
sweet-sour	.82	flexible-rigid	.58	large-small	.49

Greece, Greek

I (35.2%)		II (7.3%)		III (6.2%)	
worthy-unworthy	.90	strong-weak	.65	big-small	.81
honest-dishonest	.88	quick-slow	.64	long-short	.61
polite-impolite	.88	active-passive	.52	many-few	.57
filotimos-afilotimos	.88	difficult-easy	.52	rich-poor	.46

TABLE 2.(continued)

Iranian Farsi

I (35.1%)		II (14.4%)		III (9.4%)	
good-bad	.91	big, large-small	.77	exciting-spiritless	.76
safe-dangerous	.91	thick-thin	.74	active-inactive	.74
harmless-harmful	.90	heavy-light	.70	fast, sharp-slow, dull	.70
lifegiving-killing	.90	stalky-slim	.68	burning-frozen	.68

Sweden, Swedish

I (28.7%)		II (9.7%)		III (7.5%)	
good-bad	.94	strong-weak	.77	lively-apathetic	.81
nice-nasty	.94	firm-frail	.69	swift-slow	.77
kind-evil	.90	big-small	.66	active-passive	.76
friendly-angry	.90	high-low	.60	bloody-not bloody	.53

Thailand, Thai*

I (47.3%)		II (8.5%)		III (4.6%)	
right-wrong	.95	heavy-light	.67	quick-inert	.86
comfortable-uncomfortable	.95	old-young	.67	fast-slow	.76
happy-suffering	.94	big-small	.61	loud-soft	.48
good-bad	.94	hard-soft	.60	little-much	.28

Japan, Japanese*

I (41.0%)		II (13.0%)		III (8.5%)	
pleasant-unpleasant	.96	heavy-light	.76	cheerful-lonely	.76
comfortable-uncomfortable	.95	difficult-easy	.71	colorful-plain	.68
good-bad	.94	strong-weak	.65	noisy-quiet	.68
happy-sad	.93	brave-cowardly	.63	active-inactive	.61

* Factor Analysis represents unrotated Principal Component Solution.

lent, PAIN therefore "means the same thing" to the teenage speakers in these communities. However, it can be legitimately argued that this makes no difference mathematically and, in fact, that lack of sameness in meaning can only work *against* our E-P-A hypothesis by introducing "noise" and reducing the correlations toward zero.

When we began this cross-cultural project in 1960 I wouldn't have believed that our computers could ever handle the factor analysis of a monstrous cube involving (for 23 communities) 1150 scale variables × 100 concept variables — but by the time we were ready to do it, they were ready to do it. Figure 1 is an earlier representation of this sort — then for 19 cultures. As the upper diagram shows, the scale means are organized horizontally by community blocks and vertically by a constant order of the 100 concepts; as the lower diagram shows, in the correlational matrix the triangles along the diagonal are nothing other than our indigenous inter-scale correlation matrices ($L_1 L_1$, $L_2 L_2$, etc.) while the body of the matrix is the inter-community matrix ($L_1 L_2$, $L_1 L_{19}$, etc.). Each indigenous scale is thus correlated with every other scale — all other indigenous scales as well as all scales for all other communities and the entire matrix is factored. Now suppose that scale #21 for AE (language 1) is *good-bad* and that scale #37 for JP (Japanese, language 19 in the diagram) is *iwa-matsu* — meaning what, we have no idea; further suppose that JP *iwa-matsu* has a high correlation with AE *good-bad*, those concepts having high scores on the former (like MOTHER and PEACE) also having high scores on the latter and, conversely, low scores for both on other concepts (like PAIN and DANGER). We would have to conclude — *without depending on translation* — that *iwa-matsu*, however it translates, *functions* for the Japanese in very much the way that *good-bad* functions for Americans in the differentiation of these 100 concepts. We are thus applying the psycholinguistic definition of similarity of meaning — similarity in distribution of usage — *across* languages.

The proof of this particular pudding, however, lies in the *results* of the factoring. If nothing easily interpretable in the way of factors comes out, then we can make no strong claim for universality of our affective meaning structure, despite the results of indigenous analyses — because of their dependence on translation into English. If, on the other hand, E, P and A come out loud and clear, then we have a strong case for universality, indeed, since identification of the factors

Fig. 1. Schema of Pan-cultural Factorization Input and Correlations

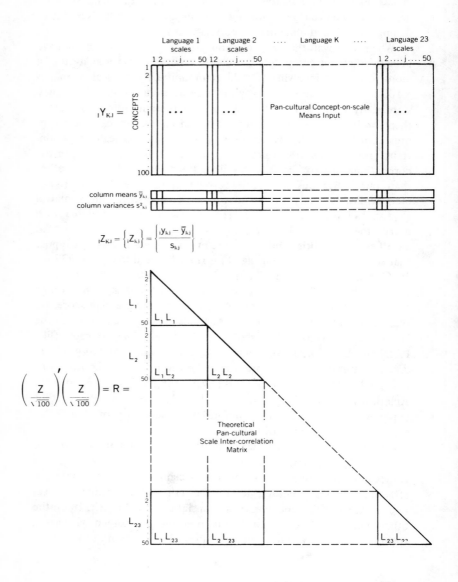

is entirely independent of translations from particular languages and all errors of measurement (differences in the actual meanings of translation-equivalent concepts) are working against us. But, of course, we must still rely upon translation for communication to an American English audience, and also leave it to the audience to judge the strength of the case.

Table 3 gives for 20 language/culture communities,[4] their four highest-loading scales (identified only by their positive terms, to save space) on each of the first three factors of a pan-cultural factor analysis. Table 3(A) shows the first factor, and it is clearly identifiable as Evaluation. The numbers shown are the factor-loadings of the scales, where the maximum (omitting the decimal point) would be 100. Note that with a single exception − MK, Mysore Kannada − the four scales for each community all have loadings on the 1st pan-cultural factor in the 80's and 90's. This, as anyone familiar with the results of ordinary factor analyses will acknowledge, is most remarkable. And, as casual inspection will show, all scales are clearly evaluative in nature.

Table 3(B) gives analogous data for the 2nd pan-cultural factor. The loadings here are lower, ranging in the 40's through 60's − indicating that this factor is less concentrated in the space − but they are very respectable nevertheless. The semantic flavor is quite consistent, the terms as translated representing variations on the themes of physical magnitude and strength (*great, big, strong, deep, heavy*, and the like); qualifiers like *brave, important, high, difficult* and *severe* also appear. I think you will accept my identification of this second pan-cultural factor as Potency. Factor III in magnitude, shown in Table 3 (C), has more varied loadings across these 20 communities. Quite high loadings, in the 60's and even 70's, appear for Belgian Flemish (BF), Finnish (FF), Hong Kong Chinese (HC), Dutch (ND) and Swedish (SW); relatively low loadings, all in the 30's, appear for Lebanese Arabic (LA) and Mysore Kannada (MK). As to semantic flavor, the most frequent and generally highest-loading scales, as translated, are

---

[4] Communities are represented by two-letter symbols, usually with the location indicated by the first letter and the language by the second (thus AE for American English, AF for Afghan Farsi, BF for Belgian Flemish, and so forth); where locus and language coincide, and there is no ambiguity, the two letters simply stand for the language (thus FR for French, GK for Greek, IT for Italian, JP for Japanese, and so forth). See Osgood, May and Miron (1975) for details.

TABLE 3. *Pan/Cultural Principal Component Factor Analysis*

(A) Factor 1, Evaluation

AE	AD	BF	CB	DH
94 Nice	88 Good	91 Good	93 Beautiful	83 Glad
92 Good	85 Well	89 Magnificent	93 Lovely	83 Good
90 Sweet	84 Safe	88 Agreeable	91 Kind	81 Ambrosial
89 Helpful	82 Lovely	88 Beautiful	91 Finest	80 Superior

FF	FR	GK	HC	IF
88 Nice	90 Pleasant	93 Superb	92 Lovable	92 Good
87 Pleasant	89 Good	91 Good	92 Good (not bad)	89 Worthwhile
86 Good	88 Nice	88 Friendly	91 Good (not poor)	88 Best
81 Light	86 Magnificent	85 Useful	90 Respectable	88 Auspicious

IT	JP	LA	MK	MS
93 Valuable	93 Good	90 Sound	78 Merciful	93 Admirable
92 Beautiful	92 Pleasant	90 Good	76 Good	93 Agreeable
92 Desirable	91 Comfortable	90 Beautiful	75 Delicate	92 Good
92 Good	91 Happy	89 Enlivening	74 Calm	92 Friendly

ND	SW	TH	TK	YS
91 Pleasant	86 Good	88 Useful	91 Beautiful	93 Pleasant
91 Happy	84 Nice	87 Comfortable	90 Good	92 Good
90 Good	82 Right	87 Right	90 Tasteful (art)	91 Loveable
87 Nice	82 Kind	87 Loving	90 Pleasant	89 Beautiful

TABLE 3. *(continued)*

(B) Factor 2, Potency

AE	AD	BF	CB	DH
68 Big	55 Great	57 Strong	62 Huge	47 Strong-of-its-kind
68 Powerful	45 Military	57 Big	60 Powerful	47 Brave
57 Strong	40 Absolute	54 Heavy	55 Big	46 Heavy
57 Deep	37 High, Loud	50 Deep	54 Strong	44 Difficult

FF	FR	GK	HC	IF
60 Large	68 Large	60 Big	76 Tall, Big	62 Heavy
59 Sturdy	59 Strong	59 Strong	75 Big	50 Severe
51 Heavy	57 Huge	46 Brave	72 Strong	47 Thick
40 Rough	52 Heavy	39 Difficult	68 Significant	42 Stout

IT	JP	LA	MK	MS
68 Big	66 Heavy	51 Large	44 Wonderful	60 Giant
55 Strong	63 Big	42 Strong	41 Huge	58 Big
54 Wide	59 Difficult	41 Long	41 Big	55 Major
49 High, Tall	56 Brave	38 Heavy	34 Great	54 Strong

ND	SW	TH	TK	YS
57 Big	50 Difficult	50 Heavy	67 Big	72 Big
55 Heavy	50 High	49 Deep	58 Heavy	67 Bulky
54 Strong	46 Strong	43 Old	53 Large	67 Strong
48 Special	45 Long	42 Big	51 High	55 High, Tall

TABLE 3. *(continued)*

(C) Factor 3, Activity

AE	AD	BF	CB	DH
61 Fast	51 Fast, Rapid	69 Quick	47 Alive	47 Gay
55 Alive	41 Sharp	65 Active	43 Fast	36 Thin (slim)
44 Young	40 Tender, Soft	42 Bloody	43 Active	34 Soft
42 Noisy	36 Narrow	40 Impetuous	38 Light	30 Loquacious

FF	FR	GK	HC	IF
67 Fast	61 Lively	55 Quick	68 Agile	53 Active
66 Flexible	57 Fast	52 Young	54 Fast	52 Exciting
64 Agile	56 Living	39 Active	49 Alive	41 Fast, Sharp
52 Lively	42 Young	39 Thin	46 Red	31 Warm

IT	JP	LA	MK	MS
66 Fast	48 Noisy	35 Fast	35 Loose	56 Active
47 Mortal	45 Active	31 Infirm	34 Unstable	46 Young
47 Young	44 Soft	30 Thin	33 Fast	44 Fast
40 Sensitive	42 Fast	29 Alive	27 Few	37 Soft

ND	SW	TH	TK	YS
72 Active	66 Bloody	56 Agile	50 Fast	63 Lively
71 Fast	63 Swift	44 Fast	47 Living	54 Fast
51 Fascinating	62 Lively	39 Thin	43 Soft (flexible)	45 Young
48 Warm	54 Sensitive	28 Naughty	42 Young	41 Soft

fast or *quick, active, alive* or *lively*, and *young*, and these seem to justify labeling this pan-cultural factor as Activity. Whether the highest-loading scales for DH (Delhi Hindi — *gay, thin, soft, loquacious*) and MK (Mysore — *loose, unstable, fast, few*) warrant this label is certainly questionable, but I must remind you that we are dealing with single-term translations.

The large number of scales and concepts entering into this pan-cultural factor analysis made it possible to identify five additional factors that appear to be human universals. I shall attempt to label them and characterize them only briefly: IV. a Concreteness/Stability factor (the highest loadings being for terms like *concrete, stable, solid, firm, steady, tame, reliable, deep*, and *untransparent*); a Human/Non-human factor (*human* or *person* (vs. *animal*), *humane, learned, serious* and *colorless*); VI. What I have called a Thermal-Dermal factor (characterized by *freezing, cold, wet*, and *blue* and *green*); VII. an Ordinariness factor (*ordinary, limited, slow, empty, common, easy, near* and *cheerful*); VIII. an Age factor (*old, old-fashioned, aged, quiet, round, eternal, few, lonely, solitary, plain* and *natural*). Some of these factors are more like the semantic features familiar to linguists and philosophers, but it should be kept in mind that, compared with E, P and A, they are very small in magnitude and account for very little of the variance in subject judgments.

ON THE POWERS AND LIMITATIONS OF SEMANTIC DIFFERENTIAL TECHNIQUE

The SD was my first vehicle for exploring semantic space. It has proved to be a hardy, space-worthy ship, and I am still travelling in her, but she does have her limitations. Let me now say something about her virtues and vices — which I can do without embarassment, since she responds only to feeling, not reason! The strength of the SD technique lies, first, in its natural adaptability to the very powerful procedures of *multivariate statistics*, in which factor analysis is a means of discovering semantic features and distance analysis is a rigorous means of specifying semantic similarites and differences among concepts. It lies, second, in the fact that it is a *componential* model and has all of the efficiency of such models — describing the meanings of a large number of concepts in terms of a relatively small number of distinguishing features — but, unlike most componential systems, its features are continuous rather than discrete in coding and paradigmatic rather than hierarchical in organization (i.e., there is no *logical* priority of certain features over others). Its power lies, third, in the fact that it provides a *systematic sampling* of the distributions of usage of terms rather than the haphazard "compelling examples" characteristic of most linguistic and philosophical semantics.

When the SD technique is applied cross-linguistically and cross-culturally, we have seen that it yields strong evidence for the universality of Evaluation, Potency and Activity as affective features of meaning. And — reflecting back on my discussion of the pitfalls in cross-cultural research — let me emphasize that, although the procedures at all critical points were standardized, the subjects in each language/culture community were free to create *any* kind of semantic space their minds might hold. Even though they had to produce qualifiers to substantives as stimuli, *what* qualifiers they produced and with *what* frequencies and diversities was entirely in their minds; even though they had to create all possible "sentences" involving 100 concepts and 50 scale-pair adjectives, what "sentences" they created, e.g., *TRUST is quite strong* rather than *TRUST is slightly weak*, was entirely in their minds. Therefore the overwhelming dominance of Evaluation, Potency and Activity as semantic features of language stands as a universal fact about Humanness.

But why E, P and A?[5]

It has nothing to do with connotations of the term "connotation" (which I used to call what the SD measures), but rather, I think, with the importance of emotion or feeling in human affairs. I believe it was M. Brewster Smith who first pointed out to me the essential identity of our E-P-A factors to *the dimensions of feeling*, as described in introspective studies of feeling by Wundt in the last century and in studies of communication via facial expressions by Schlosberg (1954) and many others in the present century. In the next chapter I will report some explorations into the semantics of communication via

---

[5]   The remainder of this chapter written specifically for this volume (footnote added in 1973).

facial expressions and their relation to affective meaning generally.

Consistent with my behavioristic theory of meaning, it is these pervasive affective features which dominate much of our behavior, including language behavior; we really are — Chomsky and the rationalists to the contrary — still animals at base. I simply refer you to the latest News for confirmation. What is important to us now, as it was back in the age of Neanderthal Man, about the sign of a thing is: First, does it refer to something *good* or *bad* for me (is it an antelope or a saber-toothed tiger)? Second, does it refer to something which is *strong* or *weak* with respect to me (is it a saber-toothed tiger or a mosquito)? And third, for behavioral purposes, does it refer to something which is *active* or *passive* (is it a saber-toothed tiger or merely a pool of quicksand, which I can simply walk around)?

But this leads us to another question: *why does the SD technique,* as ordinarily applied, *yield these massive affective features* (which lexicographers pay little attention to) rather than equally ubiquitous denotative features, like Concrete/Abstract, Animate/Inanimate and Human/Non-Human (which lexicographers regularly exorcise)? The answer, in a nutshell, is that the SD technique literally *forces* the metaphorical usage of adjectival scale terms, *and shared affect appears to be the common coin of metaphor*. Since, in SD technique, every concept must be rated against every scale, this means that TORNADO must be judged *fair* or *unfair*, MOTHER must be judged *hot* or *cold* and SPONGE must be judged as *honest* or *dishonest*. While the philosophers among you writhe, let me add the fuminous fact that, among the 100 concepts used in our cross-cultural studies, only a few will be denotatively relevant for making "sentences" with, for example, *hot-cold* and *hard-soft*; yet our subjects must somehow deal with *hot defeat* vs. *cold defeat* and *hard power* vs. *soft power*. The fact that they *do* deal with such items — and deal with them in a very consistent way — is a fact to conjur with.

The "why" of E-P-A is simultaneously the reason that the SD technique is insufficient as a general vehicle for discovering features in semantic space. The pressure toward metaphorical usage of adjectival terms means that most scales used with most concepts will *rotate* in the semantic space toward that affective feature on which they have their dominant loading — *sweet-sour* toward E, *hard-soft* toward P, *hot-cold* toward A. Since, in factor analysis, the major dimensions are mathematically inserted through the largest clusters of variables, this means that the shared affective features, E, P and A, will be amplified and the many subtler denotative features of meaning damped. This is why the SD technique does not provide a sufficient characterization of the meanings of concepts. For example, NURSE and SINCERITY˙ have near identical E-P-A factor scores, but they obviously do not have the same meanings; I can say *she's a cute nurse*, but I cannot say *she's a cute sincerity*. But in fairness let it be pointed out that *any* sub-set of semantic features must be equally insufficient: if I use only the familiar hierarchical features Concrete/Abstract, Animate/Inanimate, and Human/Non-human, then all of the ways in which speakers differentiate among humans — male vs. female kin-cepts, skilled vs. unskilled occupation-cepts, old vs. young organism-cepts — disappear, and WIFE means the same as HUSBAND, LAWYER the same as BEGGAR, and BOY the same as MAN.

Damping out E, P and A

Is there any way in which the influence of the dominant affective features of meaning can be themselves "damped" in the SD technique, so as to allow other features characterizing a domain to appear? One cannot minimize the influence of E-P-A merely by eliminating from the SD task those scales which normally load high on these factors, since these features are "in the heads" of our subjects and contribute to judgments on all scales. However, one càn determine the *partial correlations* of all scales with E, P and A factors, eliminate the portions of inter-scale correlations these account for, and then re-factor the residual correlation matrix. What this does, in effect, is to minimize the influence E, P and A features of meaning presumably had in determining subjects' judgments of *all* concept-scale items — accomplishing statistically what some mysterious surgery might accomplish by making subjects affectively aphasic!

Working with personality concepts, one of our colleagues in Finland, Jorma Kuusinen, made this significant methodological contribution, as well as providing further evidence for variation in qualifier factor structure as a function of concept domain (Kuusinen, 1969). He found that when a total of some 60 scales — most elicited by personality concepts and relevant to them, but some representing E-P-A in the Finnish Pan-cultural SD results with heterogenous concepts —

were factored in the usual way, the familiar E-P-A system appeared loud and clear, but little else. Table 4 gives the highest loading scales for the first four factors in this analysis. Note that the first factor, clearly E, accounts for 52% of the total variance. Factor two is a version of Activity and factor four a version of Potency, while factor three does look like a new feature of personality concepts. When the partialing and re-factoring process was applied to the data for this *homogeneous* domain of personality concepts, a very different picture emerged, as shown in Table 5. Six readily interpretable "personality" factors appear, and the total variance is spread more evenly across them. We have (I) a Trustworthiness factor (19%), (II) what might be called a Self-righteousness factor (19%), (III) a Rationality factor (16%), (IV) a Predictability factor (12%), (V) a Tolerance factor (12%)[6] and (VI) a Sociability factor (8%). Although these factor

TABLE 4.   *Finnish Personality Differential: Varimax-Rotation of Six Factors, Whole Data*

Factor I (52%)

moral-immoral	.98
reputable-disreputable	.97
obedient-disobedient	.96
trustworthy-untrustworthy	.95
predictable-unpredictable	.94
good-bad	.93
diligent-lazy	.93
tangible-intangible	.93
honest-dishonest	.93
necessary-unnecessary	.92
clean-dirty	.92
rational-irrational	.92
faithful-unfaithful	.90

Factor III (10.9%)

broadminded-narrowminded	.90
relaxed-tense	.71
sense of humor-no sense of humor	.67
individualistic-regular	.65
tolerant-intolerant	.63

Factor II (11.5%)

fast-slow	.91
agile-clumsy	.89
courageous-timid	.67
inventive-uninventive	.67
attentive-inattentive	.65
individualistic-regular	.63

Factor IV (8.5%)

sturdy-delicate	.95
large-small	.92
heavy-light	.86
strong-weak	.67

[6]   Kuusinen assures us that the Finnish scale translated as *sad-glad* does have this orientation with respect to the Tolerance factor, and appropriately so.

TABLE 5. *Finnish Personality Differential: Varimax-Rotation of Six Factors, Partialed Data*

Factor I (19.3%)

trustworthy-untrustworthy	.96
honest-dishonest	.93
faithful-unfaithful	.83
straight-crooked	.78
reputable-disreputable	.76
clean-dirty	.70

Factor II (18.7%)

selfish-unselfish	.90
wholesome-unwholesome	.87
impatient-patient	.78
proud-humble	.77
tough-tender	.76
excitable-calm	.74
self-confident-insecure	.67

Factor III (15.6%)

logical-intuitive	.89
rational-irrational	.83
knowing-unknowing	.82
attentive-inattentive	.75
wise-stupid	.69
inventive-uninventive	.66
careful-careless	.66

Factor IV (11.9%)

usual-unusual	.88
predictable-unpredictable	.79
poor-rich	.69
regular-individualistic	.67
obedient-disobedient	.67

Factor V (11.7%)

sense of humor-no sense of humor	.85
sad-glad	.73
broadminded-narrowminded	.72
tolerant-intolerant	.66
relaxed-tense	.60

Factor VI (8.3%)

sociable-solitary	.84
beautiful-ugly	.81
gregarious-self-contained	.63
polite-impolite	.58

names are imposed, I think the reader will agree that the factors label themselves reasonably well in terms of the scales having the highest loadings on them.

What happens when the same partialing procedure is applied to SD data drawn from a *heterogeneous* concept domain? The Kuusinen procedures were applied to the American English cross-cultural Concept-on-Scale data (100 diverse concepts against 50 scales). The unpartialed data yielded the usual E-P-A system. Table 6 gives the results of the partialing analysis. Again we note the more even distribution of variance across factors and, for the most part, the factors seem interpretable: an Aesthetic factor of sorts (I), an Honesty factor (II), some kind of Visual Brightness factor (III), a sharp Thermal-Dermal factor (IV), a Utility factor (V) and what might be called a Have vs. Have-not factor (with faithfulness being attributed to the Have-nots!). But for this heterogeneous concept domain, as compared with Kuusinen's homogeneous personality domain, the number of scales having appreciable correlations with others after partialing was much smaller — 26% *r*'s .50 or higher for Kuusinen's data, but only 1% *r*'s of this magnitude in our cross-cultural data.

The general point seems to be that only when most scales are denotatively relevant to most concepts in the domain will significant and interpretable variance remain after the metaphorically based E, P and A are partialed out. However, *within* such homogeneous domains of concepts as personality (here), occupations, physical artifacts, and so on, the partialing technique appears to be a means of going beyond

TABLE 6. *Varimax Rotation of American English Data (100 Heterogeneous Concepts X 50 Scales) With E, P and A Influences Partialed Out*

Factor I (16.3%)		Factor IV (10.8%)	
soft-hard	.67	hot-cold	.90
soft-loud	.64	burning-freezing	.90
tender-tough	.58	dry-wet	.60
smooth-rough	.56		
beautiful-ugly	.56		
Factor II (16.3%)		Factor V (9.0%)	
smart-dumb	.79	useful-useless	.82
straight-crooked	.75	helpful-unhelpful	.75
honest-dishonest	.71	needed-unneeded	.72
sane-mad	.68		
true-false	.62		
Factor III (12.9%)		Factor VI (7.8%)	
shiny-dull	.66	rich-poor	.79
light-dark	.63	full-empty	.48
sharp-dull	.63	unfaithful-faithful	.46
white-black	.62		
tough-tender	.60		

E-P-A.[7] Nevertheless, this is a somewhat cumbersome procedure —
and the additional features which fall out (Trustworthiness, Rationality, and the like) still do not have the denotative "feel" of features
like Count/Non-count, Concrete/Abstract, and Animate/Inanimate. It
was because of these limitations upon the SD technique that, in recent
years, I began investing in a new vehicle for exploring semantic space
— a Semantic Interaction Technique — which takes more fully into
account the contextual determinants of acceptable usage of word-
forms in syntactically defined frames. Some of the results of explorations with this technique will be reported in Chapter 4 here.

AN ATLAS OF AFFECTIVE MEANINGS[8]

Comparable SD measuring instruments (efficient 12-scale forms, based
on the pan-cultural factor analysis described above) are now available
for 30 language-culture communities. The primary "tool-using" research to date has been the compilation of an *Atlas* of affective meanings of over 600 diversified, translation-equivalent concepts for these
30 communities. Organized into some 50 conceptual domains, these
data provide a means for "Probing Subjective Culture" — (Osgood,
1974) — thus, an *objective* subjective social indicator. Although this
phase of our cross-cultural work will not be covered here, a detailed
account is available in chapters 5 and 6 of *Cross-cultural Universals
of Affective Meaning* (Osgood, May and Miron, 1975).

---

[7]   More recently Dr. Oliver Tzeng (1972) has improved upon Kuusinen's partialing procedure by applying a varient of three-mode factor analysis, and his
results for British English, Finnish and Japanese personality-differential data
strongly suggest that, once affective E, P and A are controlled, there are culturally unique "theories of personality."

[8]   This brief section added in 1975.

Chapter 3

DIMENSIONALITY OF THE SEMANTIC SPACE
FOR COMMUNICATION VIA FACIAL EXPRESSIONS

ORIENTATION[1]

Research on facial expressions as a means of interpersonal communication has recently enjoyed a revival of interest. This has been due in
part to increasing concern with non-verbal or paralinguistic communication of affect in psychotherapy, but it has also been due in considerable part to a series of papers by the late Harold Schlosberg (1952,
1954). Schlosberg succeeded in transforming study of the semantics
of emotions from discrete labeling to continuous, multidimensional
scaling.

There are several, quite different, questions that can be asked
about communication via facial expressions.

(1) *Validity questions.* Are facial expressions faithful indicators of
the actual emotional states of the source? This question necessarily
refers to spontaneous expressions in natural situations, e.g., of pa-
tients during psychotherapy. But since much of the research in this
field, to say nothing of much of facial communication in ordinary
interpersonal discourse, involves posed expressions, the validity question often becomes: are facial expressions dependable indicators of
the *intentions* of the source, regardless of what his actual emotional
state may be?

(2) *Situational questions.* Are natural, spontaneous expressions as
easily read as artificial, posed expressions? Are live, moving faces more
communicative than still, photographed faces? Or, in general, to what
extent does *context* contribute to ability to decode the meanings of
facial expressions?

(3) *Structural questions.* What are the physiological correlates of
emotion or feeling? What features of the face (eyes, nose, mouth) are

[1] This chapter originally appeared under the same title in the *Scandinavian
Journal of Psychology*, 1966a, 7, 1-30.

related to what states of feeling and by what manner of movement?
Are the correlations between emotional state and facial movement
products of inheritance or learning or both?

(4) *Communication questions.* Are the components of facial expressions analogous to the phonemes of a language, and do they combine
into meaningful wholes analogous to morphemes? That the correspondence to spoken language is more than an analogy is a primary assumption of *kinesics* (Birdwhistell, 1960). In information theory
terms, what is the stability and fidelity of the facial-visual channel as a
communication system? What is the dimensionality of the semantic
system within which facial expressions are interpreted?

The classic literature on the expression of emotion at one point or
another has involved all of these questions. Darwin (1872) was concerned with structural questions, particularly the inheritance of correlations between states and expressions, as was Piderit (1859), but
more with motor patterning *per se.* Sherman (1927) and Munn (1940)
illustrate early concern with the role of situational context, the former with facial expressions of infants and the latter with unposed
photographs of adults in *Life* and *Look* magazines; both concluded
that the face is quite ambiguous in the absence of situational cues.
The major concern of early investigators was with validity questions:
After inducing and photographing facial expressions in intense labora-
tory situations, Landis (1924) concluded that no expression other
than the smile could be considered typical of any situation. Many
investigators working with posed photographs reported very low
accuracy in labeling. This classic literature is summarized excellently
by Schlosberg (in Woodworth & Schlosberg, 1954) and need not be
further detailed here.

There is an obvious conflict between the ambiguity of judgment
typical of the experimental literature and the confidence with which
most people feel they can judge emotional states from the face. Resolution involves more than simply stating that in everyday life people
are really judging the total situation, not just the face. The basic issue
appears to be *what question is put to the observer?* If he is asked to
name the emotional state presented, as is typical in the early literature, he usually does very poorly — the language of emotions appears
to be much richer than the territory it is designed to cover, and it is
therefore full of quasi-synonyms. If, on the other hand, the observer is

asked to judge the *feeling* being expressed in terms of dimensions rather than labels, he does much better. Even the classic literature is consistent in showing that giving credit for near misses (i.e., clustering labels into groups of quasi-synonyms) markedly improves accuracy scores. In other words, if facial expressions primarily communicate *affective* meaning rather than *referential* (or denotative) meaning, as is usually assumed, then the question asked of observers should be designed to tap affect.

The development of attempts to map facial expressions — first into nominal types, then onto unidimensional scales, and finally into multidimensional spaces — is described by Abelson & Sermat (1962) and by Nummenmaa (1964). The attempt can be traced back at least to F. Allport (1924), who suggested a list of six nominal types of expression — I. Pain-Grief, II. Surprise-Fear, III. Anger, IV. Disgust, V. Pleasure, and VI. "The Attitudinal Group". Somewhat later, striving to rationalize the clearly non-random confusions among judgments in various labeling experiments, Woodworth (1938) proposed a unidimensional scale, running from I. Love-Happiness-Mirth, through II. Surprise, III. Fear-Suffering, IV. Anger-Determination, V. Disgust, to VI. Contempt. Schlosberg (1941) discovered that sortings of the Frois-Wittman Series of poses (cf. Hulin & Katz, 1935) into the Woodworth bins yielded a circular rather than a linear scale, i.e., Contempt judgments tended to spill over into Love-Happiness-Mirth and vice versa. He proposed a *post facto* two-dimensional surface, the dimensions being Pleasant-Unpleasant and Attention-Rejection. Subsequently, Schlosberg (1952) demonstrated that, after having these dimensions defined for them and being provided with anchoring stimuli, subjects could reliably distribute samples of the Frois-Wittman poses in this two-space. In 1954, Schlosberg — presumably influenced by increasing evidence for neurophysiological activation mechanisms — introduced a third hypothetical dimension of facial expression, Sleep-Tension, and subsequently he and his associates (Engen, Levy & Schlosberg, 1957, 1958), using a new series of photographs (posed by Marjorie Lightfoot), demonstrated that all three dimensions could be used reliably.

The recent history of this problem has not been concerned so much with reliability of judgments as with the nature, number and independence of the dimensions involved. Using the Lightfoot Series

and Greek subjects, Triandis & Lambert (1958) found that the Schlosberg dimensions could be used reliably cross-culturally, but that the
shape of the hypothetical emotion solid (i.e., the orientation of the
dimensions) was different for Greeks than for students at Brown University. Using a new series of 27 poses (which may be called the
Ristola Series after the actor) and a somewhat different method of
multidimensional analysis, Nummenmaa & Kauranne (1958) concluded that two bipolar dimensions, Pleasure—Anger and Surprise-
Rejection, were sufficient. Frijda & Philipszoon (1963) used poses by
a professional actress and a 27-scale semantic differential; factor analysis of the judgments yielded four orthogonal dimensions accounting
for 80 per cent of the total variance, these factors being identified as
Pleasantness-Unpleasantness, Submission-Condescension, Intensity-
Control, and Attention-Disinterest.

Abelson & Sermat (1962), after having 13 poses in the Lightfoot
Series judged for global similarity of all possible pairs, subjected these
judgments to multidimensional scaling (Torgerson, 1958); of the five
dimensions required, 73 per cent of the variance was accounted for by
only two — which were identified with Pleasant-Unpleasant and either
Attention-Rejection or Sleep-Tension (the latter two being highly redundant). In a very similar (in time, method and materials) but independent study, Gladstones (1962) applied the complete triads
method of multidimensional scaling to 10 poses in the Lightfoot
Series; the first two dimensions were readily identifiable as Schlosberg's Pleasant-Unpleasant and Sleep-Tension, but the third only correlated moderately with Attention-Rejection, and the investigator preferred to label it Expressionless-Mobile. In the most recent study of
this type of which we are aware, P. Ekman (1965) had photographs
drawn from psychotherapeutic interviews judged against Schlosberg's
three dimensions; he found Pleasant-Unpleasant and Sleep-Tension to
be independent of each other, but Attention-Rejection was moderately correlated with *either* Pleasantness or with Activation (depending upon whether the face or the body was being judged). And finally
we have a recent paper by Tomkins & McCarter (1964) in which
evidence is given for nine "primary affects" — I. Enjoyment, II. Interest, III. Surprise, IV. Fear, V. Anger, VI. Disgust, VII. Shame, VIII.
Distress, and IX. Neutrality — which brings us round-about, full-circle
to where the categorizing problem began.

The purpose and design of the experiment to be reported in this paper can be described in terms of the distinctions made above. The primary purpose is (1) to determine the dimensional structure of the semantic space within which facial expressions are judged. Secondary questions to which the study contributes some information include: (2) the stability and fidelity of the facial-visual channel as an information transmitting system; (3) the typology of the "primary" emotions; (4) the validity of the James-Lange feedback theory of the emotions; (5) the correlation between effectiveness in expressing and in interpreting emotions via the face; and (6) the comparative reliability of judging referential *vs.* affective meanings of the face. This experiment was a "naming" study, with live (but still) expressions being posed by student actors and interpreted by student judges. Judgmental data are analyzed so as to yield information about dimensional structure of the semantic space as well as about clustering of types of intentions and significances.

METHOD

The data of this experiment were collected at Yale University in 1944, where the author was then teaching the introductory courses in psychology. It was designed as a combined demonstration and experiment with students serving both as actors and judges. The data were simply tabulated[2] at that time, but have since then been analyzed in various ways and at various times. The original purposes were to test an implication of the James-Lange theory of the emotions (namely, that mimicking posed expressions should improve accuracy of judgment) and to test the hypothesis that accuracy in interpreting the facial expressions of others is correlated with accuracy in expressing one's own intentions. The design developed for these purposes proved, upon much later consideration, to make possible an analysis of the semantics of facial-visual communication.

---

[2]   The author wishes to express his sincere thanks to Mr. Raymond Jewett, then a student in the course, who undertook the labor of summarizing these data into usable form.

Materials

Labels for 40 emotional states were drawn from various earlier studies (particularly as described in Woodworth, 1938) and complemented by selections by the author. The criteria were primarily two: coverage of all of the categories evident in the literature and inclusion of subtle and complex states as well as pure or simple ones. The 40 labels are given in Table 1; the ordering here is in terms of a subsequent cluster analysis, not as they were actually posed. Instances of all of the categories and dimensional poles discussed in the Introduction – with the possible exceptions of Love (Woodworth), Submission (Frijda) and Shame (Tomkins) – will be found within the list. For the student actors, these labels (on slips of paper) specified the emotional *intentions* they were to express; for the student judges, the labels (all written on the blackboard) specified the set of possible emotional *significances* of the expressions they would see.

Subjects

The introductory psychology course from which the subjects came met once a week in five small sections (the actual N's were: I. 26; II. 32; III. 24; IV. 19; V. 24). Ten members of each section were selected at random to serve successively as *actors*, each receiving in turn a slip with four of the 40 labels typed on it. The order in which the slips were given out was randomized, and therefore the order in which intentions were posed was also random across sets of four; care was taken in the original assignment of labels to slips to diversify the types of emotional states among the four in each set. There were thus 5 different actors posing each intention, one in each section. The number of *judges* of each expression was constant, but the number of judgments varied somewhat about an average of 110; this was because of variation in number of blanks recorded. Each actor was also a judge for all expressions but those he posed.

Procedure

The 40 labels were already on the blackboard when the subjects entered the classroom. On the desk at the front had been placed a specially
designed window-frame equipped with a screen that could be quickly
raised and lowered. A strong light was placed just behind and to the
side of the window-frame, oriented so as to maximally etch with light
and shadow the face of an actor. After a brief introduction to the
problem of judging facial expressions, the subjects were told that ten of
their number had already been selected at random to serve as actors and
to each of them in their turn would be given a slip containing four of the
labels listed on the blackboard. Each actor was to "prepare" his expression of the first labeled emotion with the screen down, then raise the
curtain for 10 seconds (timed by the experimenter) while holding that
expression, and then lower the screen and prepare for his next expression
while the others looked at the blackboard and recorded their judgments.

The special experimental variable — mimicking vs. merely observing — was handled by dividing each section physically in half (spatial
separation) and approximately in half numerically. In preparing their
data sheets (ten numbered sets in order with four lines in each set,
numbered 1 to 4), the subjects on one side put an M beside the
odd-numbered sets and those on the other side placed an M beside the
even-numbered sets. Thus, in effect, each subject served as his own
control for the mimicking vs. observing test. While each actor was
taking his place, the experimenter reminded the groups of which role
they were to play as judges.

It was stressed that each of the 40 emotional states listed on the
board would only be expressed once, by some one of the actors, but
that the judges were free to use the same label more than once; that is,
they could re-use a given label if they later saw an expression that
seemed to fit it (but they were not to change any earlier judgments).
Aside from occasional groans from students when they suddenly discovered that they were to become an actor, and occasional muffled
laughter from the judges when a particularly startling expression appeared before them in the window, the experimental hour proceeded
smoothly in each section. In the experimenter's estimation, the attempts at mimicking varied markedly in success, but the attempts
were earnestly made.

RESULTS

Preliminary Treatment of Data

Under each of the 40 intentions, the frequencies of the 40 possible significances (judgments) were tabulated as bar diagrams. These basic data sheets for each intention distinguished in each row (judged significance) among the actors doing the posing by colors (five, one in each section) and between mimicking and merely observing by inscribing an M: in the appropriate cells. Thus each cell on a given intention sheet represented a single judge, indicating simultaneously the significance he gave to the expression being posed, which section he was in (and hence which actor he was judging) and whether he was mimicking or merely observing. These data provide the basis for all of the following analyses.

However, for most of the questions being put to these data, the distinction between mimicking and simply observing and the distinction between the five actors on each intention (one for each group) were not considered relevant and were not maintained. As a matter of fact, using five different posers and five different sets of judges for each intention increases the generality of the results, the effects of interaction between particular emotional intentions and the peculiarities of particular individuals as actors or judges being reduced. The design of this experiment does not permit an over-all analysis of variance, but it is evident from inspection of the basic data that there is considerable interaction between actor and intention. For example, for the four emotional states on one slip (CYNICAL BITTERNESS, SILENT LAUGHTER, FEAR, and SULKINESS), the within-cluster accuracy scores (based on within-cluster scoring; see below) for the five actor-group combinations were as follows: I. 2, 12, 1, 1; II. 5, 8, 4, 13; III. 1, 8, 10, 7; IV. 3, 14, 0, 4; V. 2, 7, 4, 4. Note that while there is a general tendency for SILENT LAUGHTER to be most accurately judged, this is most evident in Groups I and IV; the actor in Group II was most accurately judged when posing SULKINESS and the actor in Group III when posing FEAR.

Therefore, the first treatment of the basic data was a summation of judgments over the five actor-group combinations into an *intention-significance matrix*. A small portion of this matrix is reproduced here as Figure 1. The columns are defined by the emotional states *intended*

FIGURE 1.   Portion of Summary Intention-significance Matrix (Frequency of Attributing Each Significance to Each Intention)

Significances:	Intentions									etc. to 40
	1	2	3	4	5	6	7	8	9	
1. Physical pain	16	2	3	1	1	0	0	1	1	
2. Acute sorrow	4	3	0	0	4	2	0	0	0	
3. Dismay	4	1	6	5	3	3	2	4	3	semantic similar- ity
4. Despair	2	6	2	3	4	7	2	0	1	
5. Pity	1	3	6	7	3	5	6	0	4	
6. Dreamy sadness	1	11	1	14	4	9	0	1	2	
7. Fear	1	0	4	4	0	0	7	7	3	
8. Horror	6	1	7	2	2	1	11	30	7	
9. Dread	4	2	4	3	1	0	7	17	8	
etc. to 40			expression similarity							

by the actors (as determined by the labels on their slips) and the rows
are defined by the emotional states *signified* to judges (as determined
by the labels they selected from the 40 on the blackboard). Frequencies in the diagonal (italicized) indicate exactly correct judgments.
Thus when PHYSICAL PAIN was the state being portrayed by the
actor in each group, 16 judges in the total experiment correctly judged it to be *physical pain*, 4 saw it as *acute sorrow*, 4 as *dismay*, 6 as
horror, and so forth down column 1. Note that it is not infrequent for
an intention to be more often perceived as something else than as
what was intended, e.g., DESPAIR, as posed, was more often seen as
dreamy sadness than judged correctly.

Relations between the columns of this matrix, including correlations and factor analyses based upon them, are assumed to reflect
expression similarity. (Note that we cannot say *intention similarity* in
this case, since the rules for encoding intentions into facial movements
may vary from actor to actor.) Relations between the rows of this
matrix are assumed to reflect *semantic similarity*. Regardless of what
may have been intended by the actors, if two labels display a high
correlation in usage by the judges, this indicates that they are similar
in meaning. In other words, we may treat intentions simply as the
occasions for producing a sample of facial stimuli, the labelings of
which provide evidence for the structure of the *language* of emotions.

Results and Specific Discussion

(1) *Label usage, expression codability, and accuracy of naming*. Table 1 presents some summary measures derived from the intention-
significance matrix. Column 1 gives the frequencies with which intentions were judged, i.e., the sums of columns in the matrix. As would
be expected, variation is small, simply reflecting occasional failures to
attribute any significance to certain poses. The large difference here
between JOY (125) and GLEE (103), otherwise very similar, as will
be seen, presumably merely indicates that chance assignment of actors
to intention-sets happened to give GLEE to more opaque, less communicative actors.

Column 2 gives the frequencies with which the various labels were
used in making judgments, i.e., the sums of rows in the matrix. Here

much larger differences are found, but the reasons are not immediately obvious. Collecting together those labels selected 140 times or more and comparing them with labels selected 70 times or less in the total experiment, we have as "salient" or "popular" labels *surprise, amazement, boredom, determination, annoyance, contempt, quiet pleasure, complacency, expectancy, intrigued interest, incredulous doubt, suspicion* and *distrust*, while we have as "obscure" or "unpopular" labels *physical pain, acute sorrow, pity, dismay, excitement, despair, fear, rage,* and *worried laughter*. Keeping in mind that the judges knew each label would serve as the intention only once in their group, we may informally test several hypotheses: it cannot be frequency of usage in English (*contempt* and *surprise* are "popular" but *pity* and *fear* are not); it cannot be intensity of meaning (*surprise* and *incredulous doubt* are "popular" but *fear* and *rage* are not); however, it *is* apparent that, with the possible exception of *excitement*, all of the "unpopular" labels are unpleasant states for ego. Are the names of ego-threatening states somehow avoided, either in perceiving the emotions of others or in scanning labels themselves? Tomkins & McCarter (1964) suggest that such is the case; after noting that Fear, Anger and Shame fail to be correctly identified when present and also fail to be attributed incorrectly to other states, they say, "we interpret this as evidence for the probable operation of a denial mechanism" (p. 148).

Column 3 of Table 1 gives the percentage of judgments (in all tables expressed in proportions) for each intention that were precisely correct, i.e. fall in the diagonal of the intention-significance matrix. The over-all average accuracy of naming is only 13 per cent. However, as noted earlier, the language of emotion contains many quasi-synonyms; in the intention-significance matrix FEAR, for example, is more often named horror than correctly, SURPRISE is more often named amazement, DISGUST named contempt, JOY named glee (and vice versa), and so on.

A cluster analysis, to be described subsequently, was used to assign the 40 labels to 12 groups in terms of similarities in label usage. The labels in Table 1 are actually grouped according to these clusters (A, B, C, ... L). Column 4 gives the percentage of correct within-cluster naming, counting as correct all judgments of an intention which employ labels within its cluster (e.g., labeling intended PHYSICAL PAIN as *physical pain, dread* or *anxiety* would all be scored correct). Com-

TABLE 1.   Some Summary Data on the 40 Emotional States Sampled in the Experiment

States	(1) Judgment frequency	(2) Label usage frequency	(3) % correct naming	(4) % correct cluster naming	(5) Mean D	(6) H-rank	(7) % correct mimicking Cluster	Exact
A								
Physical pain	115	40	.14	.21		4.31	.81	.88
Dread	109	105	.07	.15		4.62	.44	.63
Anxiety	108	108	.04	.05		4.40	.33	.50
			.08	*.14*	*51*	*4.44*		
B								
Acute sorrow	114	40	.03	.19		4.10	.48	.00
Pity	112	62	.03	.18		4.60	.38	.67
Dreamy sadness	114	120	.08	.21		4.31	.44	.22
Sulkiness	106	86	.14	.24		4.25	.48	.53
Cynical bitterness	112	106	.02	.10		4.57	.39	.50
			.06	*.18*	*46*	*4.37*		
C								
Dismay	111	70	.06	.41		4.08	.51	.67
Bewilderment	108	128	.06	.24		4.33	.48	.27
Surprise	115	140	.10	.38		3.75	.51	.36
Amazement	113	153	.23	.51		3.47	.54	.62
Excitement	110	43	.05	.34		3.87	.44	.80
Awe	109	104	.18	.46		3.97	.49	.50
			.11	*.39*	*49*	*3.91*		
D								
Despair	110	61	.03	.20		4.39	.46	.6
Boredom	105	143	.38	.38		3.64	.42	.48
Adoration	110	100	.24	.27		4.06	.67	.69
			.22	*.28*	*51*	*4.03*		
E								
Fear	111	48	.06	.16		4.56	.47	.57
Horror	114	114	.26	.33		3.20	.53	.57
			.16	*.25*	*41*	*3.88*		

TABLE 1. (continued).

F	Sullen anger	110	90	.09		.39			3.86		.46	.70
	Rage	116	65	.17	.10	.39	.35	39	4.12	4.17	.50	.55
	Stubbornness	110	76	.05		.31			4.31		.49	.67
	Determination	111	147	.10		.31			4.37		.49	.36
G	Annoyance	109	147	.05		.38			3.96		.48	.20
	Disgust	111	75	.13		.60			4.03		.57	.57
	Contempt	110	190	.12	.10	.38	.45	36	4.25	4.05	.53	.69
	Scorn	112	138	.16		.54			4.00		.46	.44
	Loathing	111	98	.03		.43			4.01		.48	.3
H	Silent laughter	104	80	.15		.40			3.67		.43	.4
	Quiet pleasure	111	154	.34	.22	.55	.41	33	3.36	3.66	.46	.58
	Complacency	106	142	.18		.27			3.95		.52	.42
I	Joy	125	83	.19		.58			3.15		.49	.29
	Glee	103	112	.21	.15	.55	.41	13	2.88	3.38	.52	.45
	Worried laughter	112	32	.06		.30			4.11		.61	.71
J	Expectancy	106	161	.14	.16	.22	.27	27	4.13	4.22	.44	.47
	Intrigued interest	109	177	.17		.31			4.31		.47	.53
K	Puzzlement	109	110	.10	.13	.16	.21	37	4.60	4.40	.42	.55
	Incredulous doubt	113	212	.15		.25			4.19		.63	.65
L	Suspicion	109	165	.12	.18	.25	.26	34	4.35	4.15	.60	.84
	Distrust	107	183	.24		.27			3.95		.45	.42

paring columns 3 and 4, and noting particularly the within-cluster means, it can be seen that increases in accuracy attributable to more relaxed scoring vary markedly across clusters; clusters A and D show very little improvement, whereas clusters C, F, G, H, and I about triple in per cent correct. It may be noted that clusters A and D have the largest mean within-cluster distances (column 5), i.e., are the "loosest" or least clearly defined, however, cluster C is also a relatively poorly defined cluster. The overall average proportion correct with cluster-scoring is .30, which is still not very impressive.

Tomkins & McCarter (1964) specify eight categories of "primary affects" (and one "neutral" category) and report high accuracies of judgment of poses when judges are allowed to choose among clusters of terms (e.g., afraid, frightened, panicky, terrified) defining these affects. Identifying that single intention, or cluster if appropriate, in our experiment which seems to correspond best with each of the Tomkins and McCarter categories, we may ask if our data also support the notion that certain 'primary' affects are particularly well communicated. Table 2 presents the Tomkins-McCarter primaries, their correspondents (assumed) in our experiment, along with the percentages of within-cluster correct judgments for both. The higher over-all accuracy for the Tomkins-McCarter study as compared with the pre-

TABLE 2. *Proportions of Correct Within-cluster Judgments for 'Primary Affects' (Tomkins & McCarter) Compared with Data from the Present Experiment*

Primary affects	Prop. correct (Tomkins & McCarter)	Correspondents here	Prop. correct here
Enjoyment	.92	Joy, Glee,	.56
		Quiet pleasure	.55
Interest	.58	Cluster J (Intrigued interest, Expectancy)	.27
Surprise	.86	Surprise	.38
Fear	.63	Fear	.16
Anger	.65	Sullen anger, Rage	.39
Disgust	.78	Disgust	.50
Shame	.67		
Distress	.73	Acute sorrow	.19
Neutrality	.67	Complacency (?)	.27

sent experiment is probably due to two facts: they selected their three best poses of each affect category for this analysis; their judges were given the nine clusters to select among rather than an array of single labels. Nevertheless, a general correspondence is evident in Table 2: their three most accurately judged affects (Enjoyment, Surprise, and Disgust) are also the most accurately judged here; their two least accurately judged affects (Interest and Fear) are among the least accurately judged here. However, although Enjoyment and Disgust are clearly above average in being communicated in the present experiment, Interest, Fear, and Distress are below average, and one would have to question their 'primacy' if this is the criterion.

Column 6 in Table 1 gives the entropy (H) values for the expressions as an index of their *codability*. If all judges selected exactly the same label (correct or not) for the expressions of a given intention, H would be zero and codability maximum; if all 40 labels were selected equally, H would be maximum and codability zero. It can be seen that the H-values tend toward their maximum (H_{max} = 5.32 for 40 alternatives) rather than their minimum, which supports the conclusion that facial expressions are not discretely namable (codable) to a very satisfactory degree. It is important to keep in mind that the H-index indicates the extent to which poses for each intention succeed in narrowing down the range of possible significances, without any regard for correctness of judgments. Thus judges could agree perfectly with each other that a given expression meant *incredulous doubt* when the actor was striving to communicate *pity* (and, as a matter of fact, attempts to pose PITY did receive 13 votes for *incredulous doubt* as against only 3 for *pity!*). Are the 'primary affects' particularly codable according to this index? JOY, GLEE and QUIET PLEASURE are highly codable (relatively); none of the others listed in Table 2 are particularly codable.

(2) *Mimicking vs. simply observing.* According to Woodworth & Schlosberg (1954, pp. 107-8), "the James-Lange theory, which created quite a stir because of its reversal of the common-sense view of emotion, states that the sight of a bear in the woods causes running, rapid breathing and heartbeat, etc., and that the sensations resulting from such bodily changes fuse with the perception of the object (or situation) to produce the experience of fear." It would seem to follow

from such a feedback theory that mimicking with one's own face the contortions seen on another's should facilitate accuracy of judgment, by producing in part the same kind of sensory feedback present when one is experiencing that emotional state himself. To test this hypothesis we compare accuracy of labeling under mimicking and control conditions. Since the judges in each section were divided into two groups, half mimicking for odd-numbered sets of expressions and half for even-numbered, experimental and control conditions are distributed evenly over the total experimental design.

Column 7 of Table 1 gives the percentages of all *correct* within-cluster and exact judgments which occurred under the mimicking condition. With the more liberal method of scoring, successes under the two conditions of observing hover about the chance, 50/50, level; however, 13 intentions are more often identified under the mimicking condition, 26 under the passive observing condition, and there is one tie — which by sign test is significantly *contrary* to the hypothesis at nearly the 5 per cent level of confidence. This would imply that trying to mimic in some way interferes with interpreting facial expressions. But when we use the more stringent method of scoring — exactly correct naming — a quite different picture emerges. Twenty two intentions are more often identified correctly under the mimicking condition, 15 under the passive condition, and there are three ties — this is not significant, but it clearly represents a reversal in trend. If we look at the *direction* of shift between loose and tight scoring, 26 intentions improve under mimicking and precise scoring, 13 improve under passive observing and precise scoring, and there is one tie — which, again, is significant at nearly 5 per cent level by sign test. That correct identification of PHYSICAL PAIN is facilitated by mimicking is evident from the frequencies under both methods of scoring (cluster method, 21 correct with mimicking to 5 without; exact method, 14 correct with mimicking to 2 without).

How are we to interpret these results? In the first place, only a positive result would have had significance. Negative or ambiguous results could be explained away, and the feedback theory retained, by arguing (a) that exaggerated mimicking is strange to adult subjects and interferes with the judgment process, or (b) that the actors in this experiment were so poor in facial communication, as indicated by low accuracy scores, that mimicking their expressions would be misleading, or (c) that people normally mimic each other spontaneously, not deliberately, and thus not having precise control over their own facial muscles, our student judges often gave themselves false feedback cues. Since we certainly do not get clear positive results, any or all of these explanations could be maintained. But then we are faced with the fact that certain expressions (e.g., of PHYSICAL PAIN) are clearly facilitated by mimicking on their own right, and with the fact that in shifting from loose to precise scoring there is a tendency, significant at approximately the 5 per cent level, for mimicking judges to do better than passive observers.

(3) *Are the best actors the best judges?* It is obvious from everyday observation that people vary widely in their expressiveness, from the man who wears the same poker-face for all occasions to the man whose face fluently mirrors every fleeting change in feeling. It is also obvious that people vary in their sensitivity to the facial communications of others; in this experiment, a few subjects correctly identified 20 of the 40 poses (cluster scores) and a few got none correct (even with cluster scoring). The design of this experiment, with each actor serving as a judge except when he himself was posing, allows us to determine whether there is any relation between expressing and interpreting. The James-Lange feedback theory would seem to imply that there should be some correlation, the person with the more expressive face being better able to mimic and hence empathize with the feeling of others.

Since the different actors in each section were given different sets of emotional states to pose, and since these states have been shown to vary considerably in the accuracy with which they are judged, we cannot correlate expressing and interpreting over the entire experiment nor over the 10 actors in each section. We can only compare across the five actors who attempted the same poses, each in a different section; there were 10 sets of labels used and hence 10 comparisons are possible. Table 3 gives per cent accuracy scores, both by clusters and by exact labeling, for judging actors ranked in terms of their own accuracy in judging others. Thus, for intention-set I, the best actor in terms of *his* accuracy of judgment (rank 1) earned 19 per cent correct cluster judgments and 6 per cent correct exact judgments, whereas the worst actor in terms of judging others (rank 5)

TABLE 3. Percent Accuracy in Judging Expressions of Actors Ranked According to Their Accuracy in Judging Others

	Rank 1		Rank 2		Rank 3		Rank 4		Rank 5	
	(Cluster)	(Exact)	(Cluster)	(Exact)	(Cluster)	(Exact)	(Cluster)	(Exact)	(Cluster)	(Exact)
I	.19	.06	.16	.10	.29	.10	.24	.10	.29	.10
II	.50	.15	.44	.06	.19	.06	.49	.06	.18	.10
III	.24	.10	.24	.07	.24	.05	.32	.05	.38	.05
IV	.42	.12	.31	.17	.30	.22	.30	.06	.32	.14
V	.44	.14	.44	.28	.42	.06	.42	.09	.27	.00
VI	.28	.10	.55	.33	.42	.17	.37	.17	.35	.17
VII	.17	.10	.31	.23	.46	.18	.33	.18	.36	.24
VIII	.38	.08	.38	.12	.38	.14	.32	.10	.25	.10
IX	.21	.14	.28	.10	.28	.18	.37	.18	.17	.18
X	.31	.15	.31	.08	.57	.11	.33	.15	.29	.14
	31.4	11.4	34.2	15.4	35.5	12.7	34.9	11.4	28.6	12.2

earned 29 per cent correct cluster and 10 per cent correct exact judgments. There are no significant differences among the means whatsoever; indeed, as can be seen, the worst actor-judges are as correctly
interpreted as the best actor-judges.

(4) *Stability and fidelity of the facial-visual channel as an information transmitting system.* Osgood and Wilson (1961) have described
applications of information theoretic and other measures to various
communication situations, and the data in the intention-significance
matrix (Fig. 1) were used to illustrate one type of communication
situation, that in which information is transferred between non-
coupled but corresponding systems via a channel. The corresponding
systems here are the semantic-intentional systems of the actors (as
indexed by the labels on the slips given them) and the semantic-significance systems of the judges (as indexed by the labels they select from
the blackboard). These systems are 'corresponding' in the sense that
they are capable of existing in the same states, of displaying the same
alternatives. The channel connecting these corresponding semantic
systems is the facial-expression system — such expressions being simultaneously the output of the source and the input to the receiver — and
its characteristics can be described in information theoretic terms.

Since this type of analysis of facial communication has been described in some detail elsewhere (Osgood, in Quastler, 1955), only a
brief summary will be given here.[3] Let X be the set of emotional
states (labels) the actors intend to portray and Y be the set of emotional states (labels) the judges select as their judgments. Since we have
the same number of alternatives in each system (40), the maximum
uncertainty for both is

$$H_{\max} = \log_2 40 = 5.32$$

or about 5 potential bits of information that could be transmitted.
The actual uncertainty of the dependent, semantic-significance system
is somewhat less than its maximum,

$$H(Y) = \Sigma - \Sigma \, p(y) \log_2 p(y) = 5.20$$

[3] Dr. Kellogg Wilson made the extensive computations required for this information theory analysis and his help is gratefully acknowledged.

due to unequal usage of the available labels by the judges. This measure is obtained from the row totals of the matrix illustrated in Fig. 1. The measure in which we are particularly interested is the conditional predictability (the converse of conditional uncertainty) of the dependent judgments given occurrence of the expressions, i.e., the degree to which significances are predictable from intentions. In this communication situation, Osgood & Wilson (1961) refer to this measure as the degree of *contact* (C) between the corresponding systems via the channel. The value for this intention-significance matrix is

$$H_x(Y) = - \Sigma p\,(x, y)\,\log_2\,p_x(y) \;\; = 4.24, \;\; C = H(Y) - H_x(Y) = 0.96$$

or in relative terms approximately 1/5 of the maximum possible information that might be transmitted (1 bit rather than 5). It should be noted that this information theory measure takes no account of either the correspondence between states of X and Y (the correctness of judgments) or the similarities between states (a near miss is as bad as a wild miss). The measure of *communication* between corresponding systems, as Osgood & Wilson (1961) define it, is simply the percentage of events falling in the main diagonal of a matrix like Fig. 1, i.e., the percentage of exactly correct judgments, and as we have seen this value is only 13 per cent. This information theoretic analysis confirms our impression that the facial communication system is a noisy and unreliable one — when the task for the subject is selecting names in a context-free situation. On the other hand, as we have also seen, judgments are by no means completely random.

(5) *Dimensional structure of the significance space.* When multidimensional analysis is applied to relations among the *rows* of the intention-significance matrix (Fig. 1), it is the semantic system of the judges which is being investigated. Thus, if the frequencies of selecting *contempt* and *scorn* rise and fall together across the array of 40 intentions, we assume that these words in the language have similar meaning, regardless of any correspondence to what the actors intended. Two different types of multidimensional analysis have been made of these Yale data.

(a) Generalized distance method. In 1950, Osgood & Heyer[4] applied a method of dimensional analysis that was being developed by Osgood & Suci (1952), employing both mean difference and profile information to these facial expression data. With the frequencies in the intention-significance matrix (Fig. 1) transformed to percentages, 'distances' between labels in terms of their usage were computed as

$$D_{1.2} = \sqrt{\ \Sigma[p(x, y_1) - p(x, y_2)]^2} \ ,$$

where $p(x,y_1)$ and $p(x,y_2)$ are the probabilities of an actor's intention of x being judged as y_1 or y_2 respectively. The 40 X 40 matrix of distances obtained in this manner proved to plot into a solid, three-dimension model with reasonable accuracy — although by no means perfectly, indicating that more than three dimensions are actually involved.

The solid model was generally pyramidal in shape: One dimension (identified as Pleasantness) was defined at its top by *joy* and *glee* and at its bottom by a host of unpleasant states, running from *contempt* at one end through *rage* to *horror* at the other; a second dimension (identified as Intensity) ran from a point to the rear defined by *complacency* forward to the front surface of the model defined by the entire array of intense emotions, the *joy-glee* group, the *rage* group and the *horror* group; the third dimension (identified as Control) ran across the densely populated front surface of the model, from *contempt* and *cynical bitterness* through *rage* and then *dismay* to *fear* and *horror* at the other side. It should be noted that the dimensions inferred from this distance model, *prior* to Schlosberg's work and hence uninfluenced by it, correspond reasonably well to those proposed by him independently in 1954; our Pleasantness dimension is the same as his Pleasant-Unpleasant, our Intensity dimension looks very much like his Sleep-Tension, and our Control dimension, going as it does from expressions like *contempt* to expressions like *horror*, seems to be at least similar to his Rejection-Attention.

It will be recalled that information theory measures take no ac-

---

[4] Dr. Albert Heyer assisted the author in computing this distance matrix and in constructing its three-dimensional model, the former being unbearably dull work but the latter rather fun.

count of either the correspondence between intention-states and significance-states (i.e., correctness) or the similarities among states (i.e., ordering of rows and columns). Using projections of the 40 labels onto each of the three dimensions in the model successively, it was possible to simultaneously re-order the rows and columns of the intention-significance matrix (Fig. 1), first according to Pleasantness, then according to Intensity, and finally according to Control. Product-moment correlations were computed between intentions and significance under each re-ordering. These correlations were 0.38 for Pleasantness, 0.32 for Intensity, and 0.50 for Control. The multiple correlation for all three dimensions combined was 0.71. This looks much more impressive than the 1 bit (out of a potential 5 bits) of reduction in uncertainty given by the information theory analysis, but this is simply a matter of our habits of interpreting correlation *vs.* uncertainty measures. A correlation of 0.71 accounts for precisely one half the total variance in judgments, and 1 bit of information likewise reduces total uncertainty by one half.

(b) Factor analytic method. In 1958 the usual factor analytic and rotational computer programs were applied to the same basic data in the intention-significance matrix illustrated in Fig. 1, the correlations again being between rows (significances). A centroid factor analysis was carried through 12 factors, which together accounted for 84 per cent of the total variance; however, only 6 factors accounted for 66 per cent and only 3 for 46 per cent. Unrotated loadings for the first 6 factors are given in Table 4: Factor I is clearly identifiable as Pleasantness (*joy* and *glee* best defining one pole and *dread* and *anxiety* the other); Factor II is clearly identifiable with the Control dimension of the earlier analysis (one pole defined best by *annoyance, disgust, contempt, scorn* and *loathing* and the opposite pole by *dismay, bewilderment, surprise, amazement*, and *excitement*); and Factor III can be identified as Intensity, or what we might now call Activation, following Schlosberg (one pole defined by *sullen anger, rage, disgust, scorn* and *loathing* and the other pole better defined by *despair, pity, dreamy sadness, boredom, quiet pleasure, complacency* and *adoration* — thus, the 'passive' states). Of the next three factors, only Factor IV appears interpretable, as some kind of Interest dimension (defined only in one direction by *expectancy, pity, determina-*

TABLE 4. *Unrotated Centroid Factor Loadings for Labels as Selected by Judges (First Six Factors)*

	I	II	III	IV	V	VI
Physical pain	.38	.06	.17	− .18	− .29	.16
Acute sorrow	.55	.32	− .31	− .11	− .21	.29
Dismay	.36	− .70	− .06	.26	− .12	.09
Despair	.33	.07	− .65	.24	− .17	.05
Pity	.53	.09	− .46	− .46	− .10	.26
Dreamy sadness	.48	.46	− .42	.09	.09	.13
Fear	.32	− .49	.23	.15	− .22	− .47
Horror	.21	−.57	.26	.33	− .12	− .14
Dread	.63	− .15	.30	.06	− .17	− .07
Anxiety	.77	− .08	.12	− .32	− .11	.19
Bewilderment	.41	− .68	− .38	.10	.20	− .10
Surprise	.15	− .73	− .06	− .17	.43	− .06
Amazement	.26	− .67	.15	09	.26	− .15
Sullen anger	.28	.44	.37	− .21	− .18	− .37
Rage	.23	.23	.46	− .19	− .27	− .49
Sulkiness	.38	.47	− .32	− .07	− .16	.10
Stubbornness	.39	.44	.28	− .24	− .15	− .38
Boredom	.15	.24	− .42	.34	.17	− .10
Annoyance	.31	.58	.31	.18	.42	.17
Determination	.39	.40	.13	− .43	.18	− .37
Disgust	.40	.55	.37	.23	.38	.19
Contempt	.52	.57	.23	− .08	.28	.27
Scorn	.24	.61	.35	.24	.35	.15
Loathing	.38	.22	.46	.33	.51	.19
Cynical bitterness	.55	.50	− .22	− .16	.17	.12
Silent laughter	− .36	.28	− .25	− .26	.37	− .29
Joy	− .59	− .13	.18	− .39	.33	.23
Glee	− .58	− .16	.14	− .37	.26	.28
Excitement	.17	− .75	.14	.06	.22	− .21
Expectancy	.10	− .25	− .39	− .56	.38	− .13
Quiet pleasure	− .29	.21	− .46	− .23	.31	− .39
Complacency	− .08	.32	− .55	− .19	.38	− .32
Awe	.38	− .59	− .29	.07	.12	.11
Adoration	.14	− .24	− .48	.20	.13	− .12
Intrigued interest	.24	− .26	− .32	− .42	.43	− .29
Puzzlement	.62	− .15	− .28	− .24	− .28	.15
Suspicion	.44	.48	.08	− .29	− .14	.13
Distrust	.55	.34	.07	− .38	.12	.21
Incredulous doubt	.62	− .45	− .21	− .28	− .08	.21
Worried laughter	− .54	− .21	.18	− .41	.40	.20

TABLE 5. *Clustering Determined by (1) Generalized Distance Measures over Six Unrotated Significance Factors, (2) Varimax Rotation of Significance Factors, and (3) Varimax Rotation of Intention Factors*

(1) D-Method	(2) Varimax significances	(3) Varimax intentions

CLUSTER A
  physical pain
  dread
  anxiety		

CLUSTER B
  acute sorrow
  pity
  dreamy sadness
  sulkiness
  cynical bitterness
		FACTOR V
		  despair, .69
		  pity, .62
		  dismay, .56
		  sulkiness, .51
		  dreamy sadness, .49

CLUSTER C
  dismay
  bewilderment
  surprise
  amazement
  excitement
  awe
	FACTOR II
	  amazement, .85
	  suprise, .81
	  bewilderment, .76
	  excitement, .72
	  awe, .66
	  dismay, .59
		FACTOR X
		  awe, .83
		  bewilderment, .61
		  surprise, .52
		  amazement, .42

CLUSTER D
  despair
  boredom
  adoration
	FACTOR III
	  boredom, .82
	  despair, .82
	  dreamy sadness, .57	

CLUSTER E
  fear
  horror
	FACTOR IX
	  dread, .79
	  fear, .71
	  horror, .60
		FACTOR III (+)
		  horror, .86
		  dread, .85
		  fear, .79
		  amazement, .65
		  surprise, .62

CLUSTER F
  sullen anger
  rage
  stubbornness
  determination
	FACTOR I
	  stubbornness, .85
	  rage, .82
	  sullen anger, .71
	  determination, .63
		FACTOR IV
		  determination, .84
		  sullen anger, .83
		  stubbornness, .82
		  rage, .58

CLUSTER G
  annoyance
  disgust
  contempt
  scorn
  loathing
	FACTOR V
	  loathing, .88
	  disgust, .88
	  annoyance, .87
	  scorn, .84
	  contempt, .76
		FACTOR I
		  contempt, .92
		  disgust, .86
		  scorn, .84
		  loathing, .74
		  annoyance, .60
		  cynical bitterness, .57

TABLE 5 *(continued)*

(1) D-Method	(2) Varimax significances	(3) Varimax intentions

CLUSTER H
  silent laughter
  quiet pleasure
  complacency
	FACTOR IV
	  quiet pleasure, .94
	  silent laughter, .86
	  complacency, .74
		FACTOR III (−)
		  complacency, − .46
		  quiet pleasure, − .39

CLUSTER I
  joy
  glee
  worried laughter
	FACTOR VIII
	  joy, .88
	  glee, .86
	  worried laughter, .78
		FACTOR II
		  glee, .88
		  joy, .87
		  excitement, .61
		  worried laughter, .57
		  silent laughter, .44

CLUSTER J
  expectancy
  intrigued interest
	FACTOR VII
	  intrigued interest, .79
	  expectancy, .76
		FACTOR XII
		  expectancy, .46
		  intrigued interest, .39

CLUSTER K
  puzzlement
  incredulous doubt		

CLUSTER L
  suspicion
  distrust		

	FACTOR VI
	  pity, .84
	  anxiety, .76
	  acute sorrow, .74
	  distrust, .72
	  puzzlement, .63
	  incredulous doubt, .59
	  suspicion, .56
	  physical pain, .44
	  cynical bitterness, .43
		FACTOR VI
		  distrust, .77
		  puzzlement, .63
		  incredulous doubt, .59
		  suspicion, .54

		FACTOR VII adoration, .73
		FACTOR VIII physical pain, .86

		FACTOR IX
		  boredom, .73
		  dreamy sadness, .46
		  anxiety, − .54
		  worried laughter, − .38

tion, intrigued interest, and *worried laughter*). No other factors seemed interpretable.

(6) *Cluster analysis.* Using differences between labels in factor loadings across the first 6 factors of this unrotated matrix, and applying the generalized distance formula given above, a 40 X 40 distance matrix was generated. Distances varied from a minimum of 10 (*joy* and *glee*) to a maximum of 153 (*bewilderment* and *scorn*). Working simultaneously with two criteria — to keep the number of clusters as few as possible and their mean within-cluster D as small as possible — the 12 clusters (A through L) listed in the first column of Table 5 were isolated. Table 6 gives the mean within-cluster and between-cluster distances. The within-cluster distances (along the diagonal of Table 6) are always smaller than any between-cluster distances, although some clusters are close enough to suggest possible amalgamation (e.g., A with K, B with L). With the exception of Cluster D (*despair, boredom, adoration*), these groupings make reasonable intuitive sense.

A Varimax rotation over all 12 unrotated factors accomplished what also appears to be a kind of 'cluster analysis'; all rotated factors are essentially unipolar (significant loadings in only one direction), and the clusters defined by high loadings on each factor correspond very closely with those defined above by the generalized distance measure. These clusters, along with loadings on the factors they represent, are given as the second column in Table 5. Subsequent Varimax rotations, based on the first 6 unrotated factors, yielded a progressive coalescence of these clusters into bipolar sets of contrastive clusters increasingly resembling the original three factors of the unrotated solution.

(7) *Dimensional structure of the intention space.* When correlations and subsequent factor analyses are based on relations among the *columns* of the intention-significance matrix (Fig. 1), the semantic system of the actors is being studied — but as necessarily confounded by their modes and skills in expression, as well as by the fact that five different actors contributed to each intention. One might therefore anticipate a less easily interpretable factor structure, and for the unrotated Centroid analysis, shown as Table 7, this proves to be the case. The first three factors account for 44 per cent of the total variance,

TABLE 6. *Mean Within (diagonal) and Between Cluster Distances* $(\overline{D})$

	A	B	C	D	E	F	G	H	I	J	K	L
A	*51*											
B	82	*46*										
C	97	120	*49*									
D	102	79	95	*51*								
E	86	132	74	106	*41*							
F	83	97	132	118	109	*39*						
G	98	95	137	117	132	96	*36*					
H	134	105	131	89	140	109	124	*33*				
I	134	142	122	133	135	135	133	102	*13*			
J	109	103	88	95	118	113	134	79	103	*27*		
K	62	85	84	109	101	114	129	126	139	90	*37*	
L	65	57	129	132	127	71	77	111	128	106	84	*34*

TABLE 7.   *Unrotated Centroid Factor Loadings for Intentions as Expressed by Actors (First Six Factors)*

	I	II	III	IV	V	VI
Physical pain	.15	− .21	.18	− .40	.27	.20
Acute sorrow	.41	− .34	− .25	− .14	.19	.26
Dismay	.13	− .64	.17	− .26	.33	− .14
Despair	.43	− .43	− .30	.09	.12	.13
Pity	.15	− .51	− .15	− .17	.27	− .22
Dreamy sadness	.21	− .35	− .55	.38	.17	− .24
Fear	− .31	− .53	.48	− .12	.26	− .21
Horror	− .35	− .40	.58	− .08	.26	− .26
Dread	− .43	− .42	.52	− .20	.16	− .19
Anxiety	− .26	− .42	.18	− .27	.15	.24
Bewilderment	− .29	− .73	.19	− .08	− .06	.19
Surprise	− .58	− .36	.46	.14	− .27	− .03
Amazement	− .52	− .38	.08	.12	− .24	− .08
Sullen anger	.60	.39	.32	− .16	− .34	− .24
Rage	.25	.15	.33	− .31	− .18	− .13
Sulkiness	.60	− .05	− .25	.15	− .15	− .15
Stubbornness	.52	.26	.16	− .33	− .39	− .27
Boredom	.22	− .13	− .26	.36	.17	− .30
Annoyance	.68	.11	.21	.12	.08	.23
Determination	.46	.23	.29	− .29	− .24	− .24
Disgust	.52	.33	.30	.37	.08	.22
Contempt	.55	.43	.33	.33	.15	.33
Scorn	.69	.30	.26	.17	.13	.24
Loathing	.54	.38	.29	.19	.10	.20
Cynical bitterness	.50	.54	.05	.20	.23	− .05
Silent laughter	− .39	.60	− .33	− .19	.28	− .07
Joy	− .44	.47	− .27	− .27	.15	.18
Glee	− .47	.53	− .25	− .31	.16	.15
Excitement	− .56	.24	− .09	− .23	− .21	.24
Expectancy	− .68	.12	− .16	− .07	− .29	.14
Quiet pleasure	− .30	.46	− .37	.19	.13	− .34
Complacency	− .07	.22	− .52	.34	.09	− .45
Awe	− .46	− .45	.19	.30	− .31	.24
Adoration	− .30	− .25	− .22	.33	.12	.16
Intrigued interest	− .28	− .23	− .31	.14	− .44	.23
Puzzlement	.19	− .55	− .30	− .24	− .20	.18
Suspicion	.68	− .20	− .23	− .16	− .07	− .12
Distrust	.49	− .18	− .18	− .24	− .29	.11
Incredulous doubt	.21	− .60	− .16	− .22	− .25	.26
Worried laughter	− .44	.47	− .29	− .30	.25	.20

proportions of variance beyond this dropping to 5 per cent or less with no prominent loadings. Factor I is characterized by *annoyance, contempt* and *suspicion* toward one pole and by *expectancy, surprise* and *excitement* toward the other (thus resembling the Control Factor of the significance analysis); Factor II is characterized by *silent laughter, cynical bitterness, joy* and *glee* toward one pole and by *bewilderment, dismay*, and *incredulous doubt* toward the other (not resembling any of the previous factors); Factor III is characterized by *horror, dread, fear* and *surprise* toward one pole and by *complacency, dreamy sadness* and *quiet pleasure* toward the other (thus resembling the Activation Factor). No clear Pleasantness Factor is evident, unless one conveniently forgets the presence of *cynical bitterness* above.

The Varimax rotation of these factors, on the other hand, yields clusters similar to those found in the use of labels by judges. Returning to Table 5, it can be seen that certain clusters hold up across all three methods:[5] Cluster C (*surprise, amazement, bewilderment,* and *awe*), Cluster E (*fear* and *horror*), Cluster F (*sullen anger, rage, stubbornness,* and *determination*), Cluster G (*annoyance, disgust, contempt, scorn* and *loathing*), Cluster H (*complacency* and *quiet pleasure*), Cluster I (*joy, glee* and *worried laughter*) and Cluster J (*expectancy* and *intrigued interest*). With the exceptions of their Neutrality, Distress and Shame categories, these clusters replicate the Tomkins & McCarter 'primary affects', and they also correspond well with the Woodworth (1938) categories.

Comparing the D-method with the two Varimax solutions, we note the following: First, Cluster A (*physical pain, dread* and *anxiety*) is evident in neither Varimax solution and therefore, given the relatively large within-cluster $\bar{D}$ for this cluster, its members probably should be redistributed — at least, *dread* to Cluster E (*fear* and *horror*). Second, Clusters K and L (*puzzlement* and *incredulous doubt* vs. *suspicion* and *distrust*) are merged in both Varimax solutions and so perhaps should be considered a single category, despite the relatively large $\bar{D}$ and the apparent denotative distinction. In general, it is evident that the labels in each cluster, even those that are consistent across all methods, are

---

[5] In interpreting the information in Table 5 it should be realized that the factor loadings given in each cluster in columns (2) and (3) are the *highest* on each factor involved — no labels with higher loadings are omitted.

synonymous affectively but not denotatively — *bewilderment* is not *awe*, nor is *sullen anger* the same as *rage*, but perhaps it requires situational context to differentiate them. This is why we refer to 'quasi-synonyms'.

Comparing the two Varimax solutions — one for clusters among significances (column 2) and the other for clusters among intentions (column 3) — observe first the considerable correspondence between them. All but one of the nine factors for significance find corresponding clusters among the eleven factors for intentions (note, however, that Factor III for intentions is bipolar and contributes to two clusters). This seems to indicate that the same semantic system is operating in both expressing and interpreting emotion. However, the mapping is not exact. When a group of labels falling into one cluster for *intentions* is spread about several clusters for significance, the expressions of them must have been ambiguous, but in consistent ways. Thus actors' expressions of *amazement* and *surprise* are clustered with those for *horror, dread* and *fear*, despite the fact that judges use these two sets of terms discriminatively — perhaps the actors tended to 'over-do' *amazement* and *surprise*. The same seems to hold true for attempts to portray *excitement* and *silent laughter* (intention Factor II). Conversely, when a group of labels falling into one cluster for *significances* is spread about several clusters for intentions, the ambiguity would seem to lie within the language itself. Thus the expressions produced when intending *pity* (V), *anxiety* (IX), *physical pain* (VIII) and *cynical bitterness* (I) were differentiated from each other and from the *distrust, puzzlement, doubt, suspicion* cluster (VI) by the actors, yet in their general usage of labels judges confuse these terms, some calling a given expression *pity* while others are calling it *puzzlement* and yet others are calling it *physical pain*, as evident from the single Factor VI for significances. Again, the rather loose coupling between intentions and significances, via facial expressions, is evident.

Finally, we may record the confusions among Clusters A through L (in Table 5, column 1) and relate them both to mean distances between the clusters, given in Table 6, and to similar confusion data reported by Tomkins & McCarter (1964). Table 8 gives the frequencies over all actors with which intentions in one cluster were confused with those in another, as indicated by 20 per cent or more of the judgments of a given expression falling in some *particular other*

TABLE 8.   *Confusions Among Clusters*

Intention	Significance											
	A	B	C	D	E	F	G	H	I	J	K	L
A	—	3	2	0	2	2	6	0	0	1	2	4
B	0	—	0	5	0	2	0	2	0	1	5	8
C	4	0	—	1	2	0	0	0	1	11	3	1
D	1	5	3	—	0	0	2	2	0	0	1	0
E	5	1	6	0	—	1	1	0	0	1	0	0
F	1	1	2	0	0	—	10	0	0	3	3	3
G	0	5	0	0	1	4	—	0	0	0	0	0
H	0	2	3	0	0	1	2	—	1	1	0	1
I	1	0	1	0	0	1	2	4	—	3	0	0
J	0	0	1	0	1	0	0	1	1	—	3	0
K	2	1	5	0	1	0	3	0	0	1	—	2
L	0	0	0	0	0	2	6	1	0	0	3	—

cluster than the correct one. We would expect confusion among clusters to be an inverse function of the distance between them in the semantic space, and this proves to be the case. The following are the major confusions, along with the distances ($\overline{D}$) involved: A/G (98); B/D (79) and B/L (57); C/J (88); E/C (74); F/G (96); L/G (77). In contrast, of the 57 cases where there is *never* confusion by this criterion (indicated by zeros in Table 8), only seven have distance values as small as the largest (98) reported above.

Now we may relate our findings to the confusion data of Tomkins & McCarter (1964): They find that Enjoyment generates no common confusions; we find that Clusters H (*quiet pleasure*) and I (*glee*) are only confused to any degree with each other. They find Interest confused with Surprise and vice versa; in our data Cluster C (*surprise*) is confused with J (*interest*), but not vice versa. They find Surprise confused with Fear and vice versa; we find Cluster E (*fear*) confused with C (*surprise*), but not vice versa. In other words, for us the confusions in this series seem to be regularly from intense to mild, but not the other way. Anger is confused with Disgust for Tomkins & McCarter, and to lesser extent the reverse; we find exactly the same relation for Clusters F (*anger*) and G (*disgust*) — which again fits the notion of more intense feelings being perceived as less intense. In general, then, our confusion data confirm those of Tomkins & McCarter.

GENERAL DISCUSSION

Dimensionality of the Semantic Space for Emotional Meanings

The primary concern of the recent literature in this field, and of this paper, has been with number and nature of dimensions required to account for variance in judgments. Estimates of number have varied from two to as many as seven or eight, and suggestions as to nature have ranged from high agreement on Pleasantness to unique candidates like Submission-Condescension (Frijda & Philipszoon, 1963).

(1) *Number of dimensions.* The issue here has been whether at least three dimensions are necessary or only two sufficient. (Actually, of course, there must be many dimensions, so the real question is how many are needed to account for the lion's share of the variance.) Schlosberg felt obliged to move from two (1952) to three (1954). Triandis & Lambert (1958) find three appropriate to their Greek data, Frijda & Philipszoon (1963) and Harrison & MacLean (1965) include analogues of Schlosberg's three among their four, and Gladstones (1962) also reports three, with the third weak and ambiguous. On the other hand, Nummenmaa & Kauranne (1958) find only two sufficient, as do Abelson & Sermat (1962), and P. Ekman (1965). We have found three dimensions (at least) clearly required in all analyses (in a model based on distance measures, in factor analysis of label-usage by judges, and in factor analysis of expressions by actors); however, the agreement among these analyses is not surprising since they were based upon the same raw data. Before attempting to resolve this issue, some methodological points must be made.

First, number of dimensions discovered in a particular experiment is easily influenced by limitations on the number and diversity of scales of measurement. For the second experiment in this series (Hastorf, Osgood & Ono, 1966), for example, twelve semantic differential scales were deliberately selected to represent what we thought were the major factors in the present experiment — to be used as a measuring instrument in studying the semantic effects of fusing different facial expressions in a stereoscope. The fact that only three factors, accounting for 95 per cent of the variance, were obtained in this second experiment, whereas many more factors were found in the present study (with the first three accounting for only about 50 per cent of the variance) is not surprising: it follows from restriction in scale selection.

Second, when a small sample of poses is used, as in the Abelson-Sermat study (13 Lightfoots) and the Gladstones study (10 Lightfoots), the chances of certain dimensions happening to be correlated, or simply not represented, is increased. Other things equal, evidence for more independent dimensions when larger numbers of stimuli are used should outweigh evidence for fewer dimensions when small numbers of stimuli are used.

Thirdly, experiments reporting on dimensionality have varied markedly in the how and the what of measurement: in kind of response required, *global similarity* (Nummenmaa & Kauranne; Abelson & Sermat; Gladstones), *labeling* (this experiment), or *scaling* (Schlosberg; Triandis & Lambert; P. Ekman; Frijda & Philipszoon; Hastorf, Osgood & Ono — the latter using semantic differentials); in kind of stimulus applied, *live-posed-still* (this experiment), *photographed-unposed* (P. Ekman), *artificial caricatures* of faces (Harrison & Mac-Lean), or *photographed-posed* (all others).

Following our own data, and the rule that three independent and interpretable factors can never be explained in two, we conclude that at least three dimensions are involved in communication via facial expressions. This conclusion also seems justified by the following common-sense: Suppose there were only two dimensions, Pleasantness and Activation (the two usually agreed upon): any pair of expressions in the same quadrant, e.g., Unpleasant and Active, should be differentiable only by intensity or by degrees of these two qualities; what, then about the rather obvious differences among *loathing*, *rage*, and *horror*? They all seem equally intense, as well as equally Unpleasant and Active, yet they represent three "primary affects" (Tomkins & McCarter, 1964).

(2) *Nature of dimensions.* In the available literature there is complete agreement on Pleasantness as one dimension of feeling and nearly as complete agreement (in the recent literature, at least) on Activation as another dimension. It is the third, which Schlosberg (1941) had early labelled Attention-Rejection, about which most of the debate has arisen. Triandis & Lambert accept it (with certain reserva-

tions concerning the shape of the emotional solid); Nummenmaa & Kauranne accept it, but relegate Activation to an intensifier within the other two dimensions; Frijda & Philipszoon's Attention-Disinterest seems to say the same thing. But Abelson & Sermat choose Tension-Sleep at the expense of Attention-Rejection as the second of only two necessary dimensions; Gladstones prefers to call this third, rather wobbly, dimension Expressionless-Mobile; and P. Ekman rejects Attention-Rejection as being redundant. Schlosberg himself says "*Anyway*, I am not happy about A-R, and want a better term." (Letter from Harold Schlosberg to the author, dated Oct. 13, 1959.)

And this seems to be the problem — *naming* the third dimension. The third factor in the present experiment was defined by the *disgust*, *contempt*, *loathing* groups at one pole and the *surprise*, *amazement* group at the other, and this held for both significances and intentions; we termed this the Control dimension. Thinking about, and in fact mimicking, the kinds of facial expressions characterizing each pole, we selected for the second, fusion experiment (Hastorf, Osgood & Ono, 1966) the scales *tight-loose*, *hard-soft*, and *closed-open*. But this experiment showed that these scales were used primarily to represent Pleasantness, *tight-hard-closed* being Unpleasant. In retrospect, it appears that we had described the physical characteristics of the faces rather than the emotional states behind them. One scale, *intentional-unintentional*, did a better job of defining the third dimension. It now appears that scales like *intentional-unintentional*, *deliberate-impulsive*, *controlled-uncontrolled*, and perhaps even *strong-weak* would better describe the third dimension — but this remains to be demonstrated.

Shape of the Emotional Expression Solid

It appears possible to resolve the issues of the nature and number of dimensions of emotional expression in a way that will explain both the difficulty in naming the third dimension and the fact that it is often correlated to some degree with either or both Pleasantness and Activation. Figure 2 represents the hypothetical space of emotional expression (intentions as well as interpretations) as a pyramid, truncated at its rear end — on the assumption that *sleep* is really not a facial expression at all, involving no communicative intention. The

Fig. 2.

The Space of Emotional Expression as a Truncated Pyramid.

Dimensions: P, Pleasantness; A, Activation; C, Control.

Clusters: C, surprise; E, horror; F, anger; G, loathing; H, complacency; I, joy;
                   J, interest.

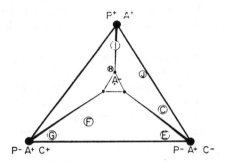

shape is like a *triangular megaphone* with its large end toward the
viewer. As indicated by the symbols at the corners of the solid, Activation increases through the third dimension, from rear to front, being
maximal over the front surface which is assumed to be perpendicular
to the viewer (that is, *Joy*, *Horror* and *Loathing* are assumed to be
equally activated). Pleasantness is maximal at the forward peak of the
pyramid and decreases downward toward the base (*Loathing* and *Horror* thus being equally unpleasant, albeit quite different states). The
Control dimension extends across the face of the pyramid, from left
(controlled *Loathing*) to right (uncontrolled *Horror*).

    The pyramidal shape has some interesting implications. For one
thing, Control as a source of variation in emotional meaning, must be
maximal for Active-Unpleasant states and decrease in significance as
emotional states become either more Pleasant or more Passive. Hence
the difficulty in naming this third factor — the labels should include
the Unpleasantness connotation at both ends. For another thing,
Active states must be more differentiated than Passive states, and
Unpleasant states more differentiated than Pleasant states; and furthermore, Pleasant states should vary primarily in how Activated they
are. These "predictions" seem to hold up: Among our 40 emotion
labels, we count 28 that would be considered Unpleasant, 7 that are

clearly Pleasant, and 5 (*surprise, amazement, excitement, expectancy*, and *intrigued interest*) that might be either; we count only 9 (*despair, pity, dreamy sadness, sulkiness, boredom, quiet pleasure, complacency, awe*, and *adoration*) states that could really be called Passive; and our two clusters for Enjoyment are the *Joy* group and the *Complacency* group, which clearly vary in degree of Activation. Needless to say, the 40 labels were not chosen with this hypothetical solid in mind.

It is this pyramidal structure which seems to explain the frequent (but rather low) correlations between Attention-Rejection (Control here) and either Activation or Pleasantness (Abelson & Sermat, 1962; P. Ekman, 1965). Unless sampling of states is perfectly balanced on the Control dimension or very large, decreases in Activation or increases in Pleasantness will be accompanied by decreases in the extremeness of expressions along the Control dimension, and hence usually yield some correlation.

By virtue of its truncated nature, this pyramidal solid has *six* corners rather than the three it would have if perfectly pyramidal, or the eight it would have if cubic (all three dimensions full-blown throughout). We do not seem to be able to differentiate, nor do we seem to have labels for, states which are highly Active and Pleasant, but *either* Controlled *or* Uncontrolled − in controlling Great Joy we seem to have to pacify it! The same seems to hold true for states which are simultaneously Pleasant and Passive − even the terms "Controlled Complacency" and "Uncontrolled Complacency" have a strange feel about them (not at all like "Controlled Anger" and "Uncontrolled Anger"). Do these six corners suggest six "primary affects"? They would be as follows: P+, A+ (Joy); P−, A+, C+ (Loathing); P−, A+, C− (Horror); P+, A− (Complacency); P−, A−, C+ (Boredom); P−, A−, C− (despair). It should be noted that for the last three "primaries", the rear corners, the degrees of Pleasantness and Control differentiation are necessarily small − hence we would expect *complacency, boredom* and *despair* to be easily confused.

How might such a system for expressing emotion develop? Figure 3 traces a purely hypothetical sequence of stages in the development of the individual human being, the transitions being conceived as a series of progressive differentiations. In *stage 1*, which may be observed in neonates, there appears to be a single dimension combining Pleasantness and Activation, with passive, relaxed states being pleasant

Fig. 3.

Hypothetical Stages in the Development of Emotional Expression.

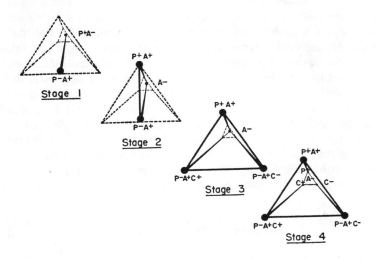

(post-feeding, being cuddled) and active, tense states being unpleasant (hunger, wetness, pain, shock, and so forth). Sherman's (1927) finding that expressions of infants produced under conditions designed to excite Rage, Fear, Pain, and Hunger could not be distinguished, while these as a group could be distinguished from non-agitated states, is consistent with this view. *Stage 2* would be defined by differentiation of the Active expressions into Pleasant *vs*. Unpleasant — the cooing, smiling, crowing kind of Activation being distinguishable from the still undifferentiated rage, fear, hunger, pain kind (about three to four months?). *Stage 3* involves differentiation of the Unpleasant states into a gross Control dimension — probably Rage, Determination, Rejection and the like *vs*. Surprise, Shock, Anxiety, Interest, and the like (about one year?). The final *stage 4* shown here represents a working backward of the differentiations already achieved for Active states to the Passive states, which (if our solid is valid) never is fully developed. The fact that Active states are differentiated earlier than Passive states seems consistent with the notion that uninhibited, all-or-nothing reactions are easier than finely graded, partially inhibited reactions. Beyond this stage, there is presumably continuous refinement — filling in of the solid — and clustering of affects in terms of cultural norms.

The developmental picture drawn here — as a series of progressive differentiations in terms of affective "features" — has much in common with Jakobson's description (Jakobson & Halle, 1956) of phonemic development in terms of progressive differentiation of phonetic distinctive features. This again emphasizes that facial expressions share characteristics of other human communications systems. Is there any other evidence for such a pattern of development? Phylogenetic studies of facial expressions in lower animals do not appear to have been reported with the question of dimensionality in mind. Studies on facial expressions of congenitally blind children seem consistent with the idea that the basic dimensional system is innately determined (cf. Woodworth & Schlosberg, 1954), but again development does not appear to have been a focus of concern.

Dimensions vs. Types of Expression

The history of this problem began with typologies (Allport, 1924), moved through dimensional analyses (Schlosberg, 1941; 1952, 1954), and, in recent work of Tomkins & McCarter (1964), has come around to typology again. The distinction is not a matter of *either-or* but of *both*. Given a space defined by several dimensions (three major ones in this case), the labels by which we refer to either particular intentions or particular significances may be represented by points within the space, each point having some projection onto (degree of) each dimension. Thus *surprise* will represent so much Pleasantness, so much Activation and so much Control. Now, if the distribution of the points representing labels were homogeneous, there would be no clusters and hence no defendable "types" of expressions; if, on the other hand, the labels did fall into clusters — and the space were thus unevenly populated — then "types" could be identified and confirmed.

It appears that early students of this problem, like Allport (1924) and Woodworth (1938), were correct in fundamentals if not in details. The primary types of emotional expressions they suggested have been reaffirmed as well as extended by Tomkins & McCarter (1964). The cluster analyses reported in this paper generally confirm, but also may extend, those reported by Tomkins & McCarter — but we must drop the distinction between a Disgust type and a Contempt type proposed by Woodworth (cf. also Thompson & Meltzer, 1964). How do the clusters identified by $\overline{D}$ analysis and Varimax rotations in this paper distribute themselves in the "megaphone"? The clusters defined similarly by all three analyses (cf. Table 5) are shown in their approximate locations in Fig. 2. The high Activation corners yield definite clusters, but not the low Activation corners — as might be expected from the relative distances involved. One might have expected a Distress cluster (*physical pain, anxiety, acute sorrow, dismay*) to appear between Clusters F and E, and perhaps a series analogous to Clusters E, C and J on the Control side (e.g., a Loathing cluster (G) to a Determination cluster to an Irritation cluster) — but they are not evident in our data.

What determines such densities and rarifications in the population of the emotional expression space? It could be *either* structurally determined (a species-specific organization of the neurophysiology of emotions) *or* psycholinguistically determined (a culture-specific, and rather arbitrary, matter of the way continuous psychological variables are mapped into discrete linguistic categories — much in the way different languages differently carve up the color spectrum). I lean toward the latter position — which leads to the next point.

Generality of the Dimensions and Types of Expressions of Emotion

Triandis & Lambert (1958) made one of the first (to our knowledge) cross-cultural studies of expression of the emotions. They found that, while the Schlosberg dimensions seemed to be usable in another culture (Greek), the apparent shape of the emotional solid was somewhat different. We badly need systematic cross-language and cross-culture studies of communication via facial expressions — for their practical as well as their theoretical interest. When such studies are made, we predict the following general findings: (a) the major dimensions and shape of the space within which emotions are expressed and interpreted will prove to be common to all humans, regardless of language or culture; (b) the clusters or "types" discovered within this common space will vary markedly with both language and culture. In other words, we are suggesting that the *affective* meanings of facial expressions are relatively stable across languages and cultures (dependent upon how we are constructed as human beings), whereas the *referential* (or denotative) meanings of facial expressions are more subject to cultural variation (dependent upon what emotions are appropriate, permissible or anomalous in various social situations, these situations serving to confer similarity upon the language labels used).

Facial Expressions as a Communication System

If facial expressions communicate affective meaning primarily and denotative or referential meaning only secondarily, then one would expect to find a close relation between the dimensions operating here and those repeatedly found with the semantic differential technique (cf. Osgood, 1962, 1964) applied to linguistic signs. Pleasantness and Activation appear to be semantically identical with Evaluation and Activity, two of the three major factors in the general semantic space; what we have called the Control dimension is similar in semantic tone to the Potency factor — *scorn, sullen anger* and the like seem to imply strength and *bewilderment, surprise* and the like weakness — but the relation is not as compelling.

What about dimensionality when emotion *labels* are studied, apart from facial expressions? G. Ekman (1955) obtained global similarity judgments for all possible pairs of 23 Swedish words for emotional states; an oblique factoring of the matrix of similarity scores yielded nine interpretable unipolar factors that seem similar in part to our clusters — Pleasure, Discomfort, Agitation, Longing, Animation, Fear, Affection, Disgust, and Anger. Nummenmaa (1964) had one set of subjects give names to a series of 27 posed expressions, found the most characteristic label for each, and then had another set of subjects judge the similarities among all pairs of 27 labels; three of their five factors match ours very well — II (*furious, terrified, surprised* vs. *contented, mild*) looks like Activation, III (*contemptuous, moping, angry* vs. *amazed, frightened*) looks like Control, and IV (*contented, happy, glad* vs. *moping, sad, detesting*) looks very much like Pleasantness. Nummenmaa concludes that there is isomorphy between verbal and facial expressions of emotion. Our data support this conclusion.

However, despite this isomorphy, there is obviously a rather loose coupling between names and things in this semantic domain. What we have referred to as quasi-synonyms (within-cluster labels) appear to be denotative differentiations within constant affective cores. Why should the words (labels) be more finely differentiated than the things (emotional states)? Word usage, as etymologists well know, is peculiarly subject to "contamination" by situational context. Thus *surprise* may come to be *used* in situations featured by abruptness of onset and termination of the state, *amazement* in situations featured by more persistence of the state and striving by the victim, and *awe* in situations featured by slow onset, persistence and relative subordinateness of the individual − all with much the same affective state in dimensional terms and much the same facial expression. Variations in intensity of feeling, as inferred from context, may produce a graded series of quasi-synonyms such as *annoyance, disgust, scorn*, and *loathing*.

The only attempt to deal explicitly with the denotative aspect of emotion labels of which I am aware is to be found in a doctoral dissertation by de Rivera (1961). Analyzing how emotion terms are used in relation to the total context of behavior, de Rivera derives six denotative features of emotions (which he terms "decisions"): (1) *subject-object* (reference to external object or self as object, e.g., *afraid* vs. *ashamed*); (2) *attraction-repulsion* (expressing associative or dissociative tendencies, e.g., *envious* vs. *horrified*); (3) *extensor-contractor* (apparently a distinction between alter (outward) and ego (inward) orientation, e.g., *pity* vs. *shame*); (4) *presence-likeness-meaning* (apparently distinctions between contacting, comparing and empathizing, e.g., *anger* vs. *scorn* vs. *rejection*); (5) *involved-detached* (this appears to function as a kind of intensity distinguisher, e.g., *loathing* vs. *disapproving*); and (6) *express-inhibit* (a decision based on the availability of appropriate actions, e.g., *anger* vs. *hatred*). Although these criteria proved difficult to communicate to others, an experiment comparing classification on this basis with the usual semantic differential (Evaluation, Potency, and Activity factors) indicated that closer synonyms were obtained when sorting according to denotative features. De Rivera comments (p. 106b) that "evidently the names of emotions are not an exception and the three factors are concerned with the connotative meaning of emotion names, whereas the denotative meaning of the names may be governed by the six end-decisions". Whether or not one agrees with these particular denotative features — arrived at on an admittedly *a priori* basis — the importance of exploring the denotative side of emotional communication is clear. (Techniques presently being developed by the author and Dr. Kenneth Forster of the University of Melbourne for the assignment of semantic features to words in one form-class on the basis of their permissibility of usage with words of another form-class — e.g., to *repel angrily* vs. to *console angrily* — may be applicable to this problem.)

Pursuing the analogy with linguistics still further, we may inquire into the structure of the gestural code, in which facial features play a significant part. Temporal sequences of facial, gestural and postural movements seem analogous to *sentences*, momentary patterning of the whole (as might be caught in a still photograph) to *phrases*, the configuration of significant parts (e.g., the eyebrows, the mouth, the shoulders) to *words*, and the patterns of movement of the components of these significant parts (e.g., lips curled, mouth partly open) as the *phonemes*. The familiar Piderit face, with its substitutable parts, was an early step in this direction of analysis (Boring & Titchener, 1923). More recently, Frijda & Philipszoon (1963) returned to this aspect of the problem, reporting correlations between various facial cues of affective factors as does Nummenmaa (1964). P. Ekman (1965) offers evidence that body posture provides clearer cues for Activation than the face, whereas the reverse is true for Pleasantness. The application of linguistic as compared with experimental methods has been made by Birdwhistell (1960) and his associates.

In an as yet unpublished paper, Harrison & MacLean (1965) report an experimental analysis of the meaning of facial features which harks back to the Piderit faces. Caricature faces in circles were used as stimuli and ratings of them against 70 adjectives were the responses. Although factor analysis of the labels is confounded by inclusion of many non-emotion terms (like *male, female, young, old, robust, intelligent, supportive, attractive*, and the like), factor analysis of 60 "faces" obtained by combining various features (like medially downturned eye-brows with half-closed eyes with upturned mouth, etc.) and the adjectives associated with them were interesting in the present connection: I. Up-turned mouth (*satisfied, controlled, approving* and *happy*); II. Down-turned mouth and/or medially up-turned brows (*worried, perplexed, confused* and *unhappy*); III. Medially down brows (*menacing, disagreeing, angry* and *domineering*); IV. Droopy lids (*unhurried, remote, relaxed* and *disinterested*). Particularly interesting were the suggestions made by Harrison & MacLean that: (1) synchronically, features may be redundant (better, congruent, e.g., medially up-turned eye-brows with down-turned mouth), independent (better, *combinable*, e.g., down-turned mouth with half-closed eyes) or conflicting (better, *incongruent*, e.g., medially up-turned brows with up-turned mouth — where the adjectives elicited are opposed in meaning); (2) sequentially, in shifting from a neutral face to any face in which all features are modified in some fashion, one may follow N "pathways" depending on the order of feature changes. In other words, just as we may use different sentences to convey different shades of meaning, so there may be six different ways to "get mad"!

Confusability and Reliability

Our findings are consistent with those of others in showing that there is low reliability in naming and high reliability in scaling for affect. The low reliability of naming is due to confusability among labels. If such confusions were random, confusability would be identical with unreliability — but they are not. Rather, they are reasonably systematic, reflecting the loose mapping of names onto things and the existence of contextually determined quasi-synonyms.

The difference between naming and scaling can be understood in terms of constraints: The greater the *constraints on the stimulus*, the more accurate the labeling. Situational context is one constraint, and it helps to differentiate denotatively among labels that are quasi-synonyms affectively. Live and particularly moving expressions provide more constraints than photographs; for example, Thompson & Meltzer (1964), using live student actors as we had done in Experiment I — but *movement* being permitted — report much higher accuracies of naming than we did (Osgood, in Quastler, 1955). The greater the *constraints on the response*, the more accurate the labeling. The fact that Thompson & Meltzer gave only 10 alternatives to their judges, as compared with our 40, also presumably raised their accuracy scores. The same holds for the higher accuracies obtained by Tomkins & McCarter (1964). The ultimate in response restriction is scaling along a single dimension at a time, e.g., Schlosberg. When the scales are deliberately selected to represent affective factors, then, as Hastorf, Osgood & Ono (1966) find, reliability becomes extremely high.

The James-Lange Theory

Finally, we return to the purpose which originally motivated this experiment. In our comparison of mimicking conditions with ordinary passive observing, a positive result would have supported the James-Lange theory — augmented feedback serving to refine awareness of emotion and hence judgment. The results were ambiguous: With loose, within-cluster scoring, passive observing was better, at approximately the 5 per cent level of confidence. With tight, exact scoring, mimicking was better but not significantly — yet significantly more expressions improved under mimicking with the shift from loose to tight scoring, and the interpretations of some expressions (e.g., Physical Pain) were clearly aided by mimicking. It may be that passive observing serves best to get the judge into the right affective region, with mimicking and resultant feedback helping to make finer differentiations. The James-Lange theory also should predict that people who are themselves more expressive (the best actors) should be more sensitive to the expressions of others (when functioning as judges); we found no relation whatsoever between accuracy of judging and being judged. Thus this experiment provides little support for the James-Lange theory, without being able to disprove it.

Chapter 4

SEMANTIC INTERACTION TECHNIQUE

SPECULATION ON THE STRUCTURE OF INTERPERSONAL INTENTIONS[1]

In order to make comparisons across languages and cultures in any domain, it is necessary that these have something in common. Thus, in the domain of affective meaning, it is only because people can be shown to share certain gross dimensions of qualification — Evaluation, Potency, and Activity — that we have been able to determine how they differ in their allocation of concepts within this common factor space (see Osgood, 1964). If items of subjective culture (values, attitudes, meanings) were in fact completely unique, they would be completely incomparable.

What might we expect to be shared across human groups in the domain of interpersonal behavior? Certainly not the *overt expression* of interpersonal intentions — overt expressions of the intent *to help*, for example, should vary as much across cultures and across situations within cultures as modes of dress or items on a menu. Certainly not the *appropriateness of intentions* for particular role-pairs — the intent to *obey* may be quite appropriate for a mature son toward his father in one place but quite inappropriate in another. The only likely constant in this domain would seem to be *the dimensional structure of intentions* themselves. Thus, we might expect all human groups to distinguish between Associative and Dissociative intentions (for example, between *helping* vs. *hindering*), between Supraordinate and Subordinate intentions (for example, between *dominating* and *submitting*), and so on. If such a common system or structure of inter-

[1] This research was supported in part by the Institute of Communications Research, University of Illinois, and in part by the Advanced Research Projects Agency, ARPA Order No. 454, under Office of Naval Research Contract NR 177-472, Nonr 1834 (36), titled "Communication, Cooperation, and Negotiation in Culturally Heterogeneous Groups" (F. E. Fiedler, L. M. Stolurow, and H. C. Triandis Principal Investigators). Excerpted from *Behavioral Science*, 1970, *15*, 237-254.

personal intentions could be demonstrated, then comparisons across groups could be made in a reasonably rigorous and meaningful way. One could ask whether intentions involving a given dimension or feature (such as Ego- vs. Alter-orientation) are more appropriate for one role-pair than another (for example for SON toward FATHER, but not vice versa) and more appropriate within one culture than another for that role-pair.

There are several ways of approaching the problem of the dimensionality of intentions. One empirical approach is to have members of a given culture list appropriate overt behaviors for a sample of role-pairs, factor analyse the correlations of behaviors across roles, and then look for the underlying intentions behind the factors. This approach has been taken by Triandis and is described in a recently published report (Triandis, Vassiliou, and Nassiakou, 1968). Another empirical approach is through content analysis of interpersonal behaviors among role-pairs as described in the literature of various culture groups. This approach has been taken by Katz (1964a, b). Yet another approach is through a rational analysis of the language of interpersonal behavior in terms of a set of a priori dimensions. This was the approach taken here in search of a short cut into the essential semantic features that differentiate interpersonal verbs (IPVs). It is hoped that these diverse approaches will complement and support each other.

Theoretical Model for Interpersonal Behavior and Perception

Figure 1 describes a generalized mediation model for interpersonal perception and behavior. Any mature and participating member of any culture is assumed to have developed a set of symbolic processes $(r \text{ - - - - } s)$ for which the antecedents are the perceived interpersonal behaviors of others (B's) in certain situational contexts (S's), and for which the subsequents are interpersonal behaviors of the individual himself, also dependent upon situational contexts. As dependent events (that is, in decoding or perceiving), these symbolic processes will be termed *significances* (r's); as antecedent events (that is, in encoding or behaving), these symbolic processes will be termed *intentions* (s's). Thus, the perceived significance of someone else's behavior

Fig. 1.   A Significance-Intention Model for Interpersonal Behavior

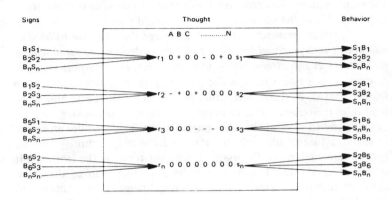

is an inference about that other's intention.

Like other semantic processes or meanings, it is assumed that each significance/intention (r - - - - s) can be characterized as a simultaneous bundle of distinctive features (A, B, C ... N). Behaviorally, these may be a simultaneous set of reactions in N component reaction systems, but they can be represented, as in Figure 1, as a code-strip. For convenience in exposition and preliminary analysis, it is assumed that possible coding on a feature is discretely bipolar and all-or-nothing — thus, plus, minus or zero; in fact, however, it seems likely that codings on many features will eventually prove to be continuously variable. *It is assumed that human groups will employ the same kinds of features despite differences in language or culture.*

Although the number of distinctive features (A, B, C ... N) should be relatively small, the number of significance/intention processes (r - - - - s) can be large and the number of interpersonal behaviors mediated may be very large indeed. The mediation processes in interpersonal perception and behavior serve to render many diverse overt behaviors functionally equivalent; depending on situational context, the ways in which the intention HUSBAND *to help* WIFE can be expressed are practically infinite. Since, in theory, the entire set of intentions can be described in terms of a relatively small number of semantic features, this represents a further reduction in complexity — or an increase in the economy of description, if you will.

It is further assumed that in any language the word forms used to talk about interpersonal intentions will be coded on the same semantic features as the intentions themselves. Thus, the interpersonal verb *to console* as a linguistic sign should evoke (in part, at least) the same feature pattern as those perceptual signs which give rise to this significance in the observer (for example, seeing a mother stroking the face of a frightened child). The assumption, if justified, provides an entrée to the structure of interpersonal intentions in any culture — through appropriate analysis of the usage of relevant terms in the language. It is not assumed that language provides a perfect map of the interpersonal intention system, that is, that "language is a mirror of thought." There are undoubtedly many subtle intentions for which a given language provides no adequate expression. However, the over-all extensiveness of the mapping of intentions into words should make it possible to determine the underlying feature system, and it is this which is assumed to be fundamental for cross-cultural comparisons in this domain.

In any analysis of this sort it is necessary to maintain a careful distinction between abstract IPVs (referring to generalized intention *types*) and concrete IPVs (referring to specific expression *tokens*). Thus one cannot "see" A *helping* B; what is seen is something like A *holding* B *by the arm and walking with him across the street.* One cannot "see" A *ridiculing* B; what is seen is A *alternately mimicking and laughing at* B. In her content analysis of interpersonal behaviors in short stories, Katz (1964a) utilized this distinction as a fundamental part of her method. It is also necessary to distinguish between verbs expressing interpersonal behavior intentions and verbs expressing interpersonal attitudes (see Vendler's, 1967, "state" verbs). Thus A *admires* B refers to a mental state of A but not to any type of behavioral intentions with respect to B.

A Priori Feature Analysis of a Sample of Interpersonal Verbs

As a first step in exploring the implications of the theoretical model described above, it was decided to work on an intuitive basis with language materials already available in Roget's *Thesaurus*. The author would use himself as an informant — native speaker as well as native "interpersonal-behaver." A small set of features that clearly seemed to differentiate among the meanings of interpersonal verbs would be selected. A large sample of IPVs would be coded on these features, according to the author's judgments but with the criteria for judgment made as explicit as possible. Then various checks would be made, for example, on the sufficiency of the a priori features for discriminating among IPVs, on the redundancy or independence of features, and so on. The main purpose of this analysis was to test the intuitive validity of the notion that a relatively large number of interpersonal intentions, as represented by IPVs in English, can be satisfactorily represented by a relatively small number of distinctive semantic features.

Selection of trial features. In the course of discussions with Triandis and Katz about the construction of a "Behavioral Differential," and particularly in helping Katz develop her coding system for the content analysis of short stories, many different dimensions along which interpersonal behaviors might be distinguished were considered. For the present purpose, six features were selected which it was felt might carry a heavy load in differentiating among interpersonal behaviors and which could be characterized with sufficient clarity to permit reasonably reliable judgments. Two of these features failed to pass certain statistical tests — to be described momentarily. The four surviving features, along with their definitions and certain test frames, are given below. Since in English, intentions take the infinitive form when isolated in metalanguage, such as, *to deprive*, this form is used in examples and tables.

In the definitions, *intent* is always referred to the actor or, in other words, to the subject of a *Subject-Interpersonal Verb-Object* sentence. Thus, in the sentence A *soothes* B, it is A's intent not B's, with which we are concerned. It must be kept in mind that intentions are complex feature-wise; A may intend to both dominate B and gratify himself when he *manipulates* B. Furthermore, whether the implied outcome of the concrete behavior conforms to the intention of A is here considered irrelevent.

For most features, certain test frames could be devised as aids in coding IPVs on them. In some cases distinguishing Subject/Object nouns could be found (for example, PEOPLE *usually* IPV (*help/*hinder*) *their* COLLEAGUES vs. PEOPLE usually IPV (hinder/*help) *their* OPPONENTS for the Associative/Dissociative feature); in other cases distinguishing adverbial modifiers were found (for example, A IPVs (*exploits/*corrupts*) B *selfishly* vs. A IPVs (**corrupts/*exploits*) B *considerately* for the Ego-Alter Orientation feature); and certain more complex test frames could be applied in some cases. But such frames are not infallible. Although *to corrupt* is Alter-oriented by my definition of the feature, one cannot ordinarily say *he corrupted her considerately* as indicated by the asterisk above — because *considerately* is also coded + on a Moral feature for which *corrupt* is minus. Although a MASTER IPVs SERVANT vs. SERVANT IPVs MASTER test distinguishes most Supraordinate/Subordinate verbs, it fails for certain IPVs like to *provide for* which seem intuitively Supraordinate.[2]

Associative/Dissociative. If the intent of PERSON A is to generate and/or maintain positive affective relations with PERSON B, it is Associative; if the intent of PERSON A is to generate and/or maintain negative affective relations with PERSON B, it is Dissociative.

Examples: *to help/to hinder; to inspire/to shame to guide/to corrupt; to hire/to exploit.*

Sample Test Frame: PEOPLE *usually* IPV *their* COLLEAGUES/OPPONENTS.

Initiating/Reacting. If the intent of PERSON A is to elicit some response from PERSON B, it is Initiating; if the intent of PERSON A is to respond to some prior behavior of PERSON B, it is Reacting.

Examples: *to cheer up/to congratulate; to persuade/to dissuade; to provoke/to frustrate.*

Sample Test Frame: none found.

---

[2] Different senses of interpersonal verbs are often revealed by such tests. For example, when the MASTER *praises* his SERVANT it becomes nearly synonymous with *reassures*, but when the SERVANT *praises* his MASTER it becomes nearly synonymous with *pays homage to.* Thus *to praise* flips senses with respect to the Supraordinate/Subordinate feature and must be coded 0 on it.

Ego-oriented/Alter-oriented. If the intent of PERSON A is to change his own state of affairs, it is Ego-oriented; if the intent of PERSON A is to change PERSON B's state of affairs, it is Alter-oriented. (Note: in either case the change could be deleterious as well as beneficial).

Examples: *to confide to/to cheer up; to impress/to inform; to exploit/to corrupt.*

Sample Test Frame: A IPVs B *selfishly/considerately.*

Supraordinate/Subordinate If the intent of PERSON A is to express his superior status with respect to PERSON B, it is Supraordinate; if the intent of PERSON A is to express his inferior status with respect to PERSON B, it is Subordinate.

Examples: *to supervise/to assist; to help/to serve; to indulge/to appease.*

Sample Test Frame: MASTERS *usually* IPV *their* SERVANTS; SERVANTS *usually* IPV *their* MASTERS.

The two features which were tried and later discarded because of their performance were *Directive/Non-directive* (an intent to selectively restrict another's alternatives vs. an intent to leave open another's alternatives) and *Tension-increasing/Tension-decreasing* (an intent to raise another's motivation level vs. an intent to lower another's motivation level). The reasons for discarding these features will be given later.

Selection of interpersonal verbs. One way of relating a priori features to particular IPVs would be to select patterns of codings on the features by some random method and then use the *Thesaurus* as an aid to one's knowledge as a native speaker in trying to find verbs which satisfy the codings. This *encoding* approach was tried at the beginning, but it proved to be an extraordinarily difficult task. Try, for example, to think of an IPV which is 0-Associative, Initiating, Ego-oriented, Supraordinate, Directive and Tension-decreasing (0++++−), or of one which is Associative, Alter-oriented and Subordinate but żero on all others (+0−−00). After much effort with these and a few others, this author could only come up with *to seduce* for the first codestrip and *to nag* for the second! It is apparently *not* part of the competence of native speakers to match words to abstractly defined features.

Another way of relating features to IPVs is to search the *Thesaurus* for verbs that are clearly interpersonal in nature and then assign them codings on the features. This is essentially, a *decoding* approach − reacting meaningfully to each word and introspecting on the semantic quality of the reaction. This proved to be an easier task. However, some features proved much easier than others, in the sense of feeling confident about assigning codings; Associative/Dissociative, Ego-oriented/Alter-oriented and Supraordinate/Subordinate features seemed much clearer than Initiating/Reacting, Directive/Non-directive and Tension-increasing/Tension-decreasing.[3]

All of the categories in a pocketbook version of Roget's *Thesaurus* were searched for verbs which could be considered interpersonal intentions. The broadest criterion was that such a verb should generate an acceptable English sentence when placed in the frame, ·PN$_1$————PN$_2$ (appropriate personal pronouns were used, such as, HE *courted* HER for testing *to court*). A second criterion was that the verb should refer to an abstract intention rather than a specific overt behavior (for example, *to court* but not *to kiss*) and a third was that the verb should refer to behavioral intentions rather than mental states (*to court* but not *to admire*). Where more than one acceptable interpersonal verb occurred in the same *Thesaurus* category, that one having the greatest (judged) familiarity was selected. In this manner a sample of 210 interpersonal verbs was obtained.

Coding of interpersonal verbs. Each word was assigned a coding on each feature according to the following system: plus (+), the verb has the feature in its positive form but not negative (Associative but not Dissociative); minus (−), the verb has the feature in its negative form but not positive (Dissociative but not Associative); zero (0), the verb is not distinguished by the feature (is neither Associative nor Dissociative or can be either). In many cases judgments were immediate and clear. In unclear cases, appropriate test frames, like those given as illustrations for the features earlier, were applied. Each of the IPVs was first coded globally on all six preliminary features (that is, absolute rather than comparative judgments); then the codings for each feature were re-checked one at a time across all IPVs for consistency (that is, comparative judgments), and some changes were made. The verbs were then put in an ordered list according to their codings, for example, ++++++, +++++0, +++++−, ++++0+, ++++00 and so forth

---

[3]   As will be seen in subsequent reports, these same features prove to be the most readily identifiable and reproducible by other methods as well.

throughout all possible combinations (not all of which represented IPVs in the sample, of course).

Redundancies among the initial six features and their distribution across intentions. Although the definitions of features are distinctive, it is possible that, as applied to the sample of 210 interpersonal verbs, certain features will turn out to be highly correlated with others. It is also possible that the distribution of codings on certain features may be very uneven — biased toward one pole or the other or non-different-iating (too many zero codings). To check on these possibilities, con-tingency tables for the codings of each feature against every other feature across the 210 verbs were plotted. Table 1A gives some illus-trations. If a large proportion of entries fall along one diagonal or the other, then the features are correlated, either positively or negatively. The marginals of these matrices show the distribution of codings for each feature, and these are summarized as Table 1B.

Looking first at the distributions of codings, the ratio of ± vs. 0 codings provides an index of the richness or sparseness of distinctive coding of intentions on features. In order of proportion of ± codings, we have Associative/Dissociative (70%), Ego-oriented/Alter-oriented (69%), Initiating/Reacting (67%), Directive/Non-directive (66%), Supraordinate/Subordinate (62%), and Tension-increasing/Tension-decreasing (38%). The Tension feature stands out as being definitely under-coded. Directional bias in coding can be indexed by the ratio of + to − codings. Associative/Dissociative (70/86) and Initiating/Reac-ting (68/73) are well balanced in this respect; Directive/Non-directive (84/55) and Tension-increasing/Decreasing (45/35) are less so; and Ego/Alter Oriented (46/99) and Supraordinate/Subordinate (99/30) are the most biased. Roughly twice as many intentions were coded Alter-oriented as were Ego-oriented and roughly three times as many were coded Supraordinate as were coded Subordinate. It should be noted that these distributional characteristics of features, unless extremely biased, are not necessarily evidence against their validity. As empirical data to be given in subsequent reports indicate, Associa-tive/Dissociative and Supraordinate/Subordinate features do appear to carry much more weight than other features in discriminating among interpersonal verbs, and it may well be that the English language (or Western culture?) has a richer vocabulary for Alter-oriented as well as Supraordinate intentions.

TABLE 1. *Illustrative Feature Contingency Tables (A), Coding Distributions On Features (B), and Coding Contingencies Among Features (C)*

A: Illustrative Contingency Tables

TENSION-INCREASING/DECREASING

ASSOCIATIVE/DISSO- CIATIVE C = .52 (.001)	+	0	-	
+	1	37	32	70
0	11	40	3	54
-	33	53	0	86
	45	130	35	210

SUPRAORDINATE/SUBORDINATE

EGO/ALTER ORIENTED C = .17 (ns)	+	0	-	
+	19	17	10	46
0	26	31	8	65
-	54	33	12	99
	99	81	30	210

B: Coding Distributions (Six Features)

	+	0	-
ASSOCIATIVE/DISSOCIATIVE	70	54	86
INITIATING/REACTING	68	69	73
EGO-ORIENTED/ALTER-ORIENTED	46	65	99
SUPRAORDINATE/SUBORDINATE	99	81	30
DIRECTIVE/NON-DIRECTIVE	84	71	55
TENSION-INCREASING/DECREASING	45	130	35

C: Coding Contingencies (Six Features)

	A/D	I/R	E/B	S/S	D/N	T/D
ASSOCIATIVE/DISSOCIATIVE	-	.30*	.30*	.34**	.35**	.53**
INITIATING/REACTING		-	.17	.26	.37**	.28*
EGO-ORIENTED/ALTER-ORIENTED			-	.17	.19	.33**
SUPRAORDINATE/SUBORDINATE				-	.40**	.27*
DIRECTIVE/NON-DIRECTIVE					-	.29*
TENSION-INCREASING/DECREASING						-

Contingencies among the features, given in Table 1C, were determined from the following formula.[4]

$$C = \frac{X^2}{N + X^2}$$

where the maximum C = .81. We note first that Tension-increasing/Tension-decreasing is highly contingent upon Associative/Dissociative (C = .53), and negatively; of the 45 verbs coded + on the Tension feature, 33 are − on Associativeness and only one is +, whereas of the 35 verbs coded − on Tension, 32 are + on Associativeness and none are − (see Table 1A). If the author's codings have any validity, and if this sample of interpersonal verbs is reasonably representative, then it would appear that most Tension-increasing interactions tend to be Dissociative in nature and vice versa. Directive/Non-directive displays moderate but significant (at the .001 level) contingencies upon all remaining features except Ego/Alter (C's = .35, .37, and .40); in other words, the more Directive and interpersonal verb was judged, the more it also tended to be judged Dissociative, Initiating and Supraordinate − which makes intuitive sense. This evidence suggests that the Directive/Non-directive feature, at least as used by this informant, is some compound of several other, more independent, features. Of the remaining features, Associative/Dissociative is somewhat related to the others, particularly Supraordinate/Subordinate, but Initiating/Reacting, Ego/Alter Orientation and Supraordinate/Subordinate are independent of each other.

On the basis of this evidence, it was decided to eliminate the Directive/Non-directive and Tension-increasing/Tension-decreasing features; they were also the most difficult to apply in coding. Also, at this point in the analysis, 12 more verbs thought to really refer more to specific, overt behaviors than to abstract intentions were eliminated (for example, *to give a present to, to marry, to bow to*). The remaining 198 verbs were then recategorized according to the reduced four-feature system.

[4] The author thanks Dr. Marilyn Wilkins for her assistance on these computations.

Insufficiency of a four-feature system. It had been anticipated that the a priori six-feature system would provide an insufficient character-ization of the distinctions among some 200 interpersonal verbs. Insuf-ficiency shows up most clearly in sets of quasi-synonyms which have the same codings and yet obviously can be further differentiated se-mantically. When the system is further reduced to four features, cate-gories collapse together, and the sets of quasi-synonyms become larger, and it becomes obvious that additional features are required. Table 2 illustrates this situation with a sample of some of the sets of quasi-synonyms drawn from the total categorization based on the four remaining features, Associative/Dissociative, Initiating/Reacting, Ego-oriented/Alter-oriented and Supraordinate/Subordinate.

These sets of quasi-synonyms served as the basis for a guided search for additional features. One looks for features that will do a maximum of work, that is, that will resolve discordances within as many sets as possible simultaneously, and at the same time have a definable semantic character. Contrasts within a considerable number of sets suggested three additional features: Terminal/Interminal, Fu-ture-oriented/Past-oriented, and Deliberate/Impulsive. Finally, the three affective features regularly found in semantic differential re-search and now demonstrably universal in human groups (see Osgood, 1964) — Evaluation (here, Moral/Immoral), Potency and Activity — were included. Although they do not do as much "work" in the domain of IPVs as elsewhere,[5] they are part of the total semantic system and do make some clear distinctions here as well. The added six features were characterized as follows:

Terminal/Interminal. If the intent of PERSON A with respect to PERSON B is toward behavior having relatively short duration and clear beginning-and-end boundaries, it is Terminal; if the intent of PERSON A with respect to PER-SON B is toward behavior that is relatively prolonged and has indefinite begin-ning-and-end boundaries, it is Interminal.
    Examples: *to unite with/to associate with; to command/to dominate; to inform/to supervise.*
    Sample Test Frame: *At what time did/For how long did* PERSON A IPV PERSON B? (These frames are borrowed from Vendler, 1967.)

---

[5] Unpublished research by Dr. Wilkins and the author indicates that, in the domain of Emotion Nouns, as much as 50 per cent of the total variance in semantic distinctions is accounted for by these affective features.

TABLE 2. Codings of some Interpersonal Verbs on four Semantic Features (Associative/Dissociative, Initiating/Reacting, Ego-oriented/Alter-oriented, Supraordinate/Subordinate)

++-+ to inspire, to guide, to strengthen

++-- to flatter, to entertain, to exalt

+000 to make a bargain with, to share with, to unite with, to joke with, to participate with, to associate with, to cooperate with, to accompany

+00- to apologize, to promise

+0-+ to be responsible for, to provide for, to support, to nurse, to heal, to help, to protect

+0-- to assist, to serve, to show respect for, to pay homage to

+--+ to lend to, to forgive, to pardon, to excuse, to reward, to indulge, to reassure

+--0 to praise, to pacify, to congratulate, to soothe, to comfort, to sympathize with, to agree with, to console, to thank

0+++ to reason with, to impress, to seduce

0+0+ to question, to dominate, to lead, to command, to tame

to preach to, to mold, to advise, to supervise, to reform, to teach, to convert, to modify, to stimulate, to arouse to exhort, to train

00+0 to profit from, to sell to, to compete with

00-+ to mystify, to bewilder, to explain to, to confuse

-+++ to bewitch, to exploit, to manipulate, to molest, to impose upon

-+0+ to bully, to persecute, to compel, to prohibit, to torture, to challenge

-+-+ to shame, to drive mad, to corrupt, to embarrass, to threaten, to humble, to weaken, to insult, to humiliate

+0-- to retaliate, to resist

+-+- to defy, to evade

0+-- to refuse, to spurn, to show no mercy for, to contradict, to refuse, to believe

---+ to punish, to condemn, to criticize, to rebuke, to scold, to ridicule, to restrain, to refute, to accuse, to blame

---0 to frustrate, to discourage, to disappoint

Future-oriented/Past-oriented. if the intent of ꞌPERSON A with respect to PERSON B is relevant to some anticipated situation, it is Future-oriented; if the intent of PERSON A with respect to PERSON B is relevant to some recalled situation, it is Past-oriented.

Examples: *to promise/to apologize; to enlist the support of/to confide to; to discourage/to disappoint.*

Sample Test Frame: A IPVs B *to (into, from) doing it* / for *(about,* by*) doing it.*[6]

Deliberate/Impulsive. If the intent of PERSON A toward PERSON B is voluntary and calculating ("cognitive") in nature, it is Deliberate; if the intent of PERSON A toward PERSON B is involuntary and uncalculating ("emotive") in nature, it is Impulsive.

Examples: *to pay attention to/to believe without question; to congratulate/ to praise; to guide/to inspire.*

Sample Test Frame: PERSON A IPVs PERSON B *deliberately/impulsively.*

Moral/Immoral (E). If the intent of PERSON A with respect to PERSON B includes socially ethical considerations, it is Moral; if the intent of PERSON A with respect to PERSON B includes socially unethical considerations, it is Immoral.

Examples: *to exalt/to flatter; to reason with/to seduce; to challenge/to bully.*

Sample Test Frame: *It was decent (fair, honorable,* etc.)/*indecent (unfair, dishonorable,* etc.) *of* A to IPV B.

Potent/Impotent. If the intent of PERSON A with respect to PERSON B has high intensity of feeling or motivation, it is Potent; if the intent of PERSON A with respect to PERSON B has low intensity of feeling or motivation, it is Impotent.

Examples: *to stand up for/to assist; to rob/to cheat; to defy/to evade.*

Sample Test Frame: None found.

Active/Passive. If the intent of PERSON A with respect to PERSON B is toward behavior having a high rate of overt activity, it is Active; if the intent of PERSON A with respect to PERSON B is toward behavior having a low rate of overt activity (or lack of activity), it is Passive.

Examples: *To nurse/to be responsible for; to reciprocate/to concur with; to retaliate/to resist.*

Sample Test Frame: A IPVs B *actively/passively.*

Following these general definitions and, when in doubt, using test frames if available, the 198 interpersonal verbs were coded on these

---

[6] Note that with the negatively coded IPVs, *discourage/disappoint,* these test frames have to be modified to A IPVs B *from doing it* vs. A IPVs B *by (not) doing it.* This further illustrates the difficulty one has in discovering universally applicable test frames for features of this sort.

additional six features, first absolutely (each IPV on all features) and then comparatively (all verbs on each feature).[7]

Evaluation of the ten-feature system. We may now ask of the 10-feature system the same questions asked of the original a priori 6-feature system, concerning redundancies in usage and coding distributions of features, as well as certain questions concerning the intuitive validity of the system. With regard to the former, Table 3 presents the coding distributions (A) and the coding contingencies (B)[8] The distributions of +, 0 and − codings for the original four features (D, E, F, G) are similar to those reported in Table 1, as would be expected. The affective features are the least differentiating in this domain, that is, have the most zero codings (percent ± codings being 25 per cent, 40 per cent and 46 per cent for A, B, and C respectively). The three new features differentiate nearly as well as the original four (per cent ± codings being 69 per cent, 56 per cent and 59 per cent for H, I, and J respectively). As far as coding bias (+/− ratios) is concerned, the affective features are reasonably unbiased within their limited usage (although there are about twice as many Active as compared with Passive IPVs); the three new features are as well balanced as the four which survived the original analysis, Terminal/Interminal actually being less biased than Ego/Alter or Supraordinate/Subordinate. Again, it must be pointed out that such bias toward Supraordinate and Alter-oriented as well as Terminal (short-term) intentions may well be part of the human condition.

Inspection of Table 3B indicates that, with the three affective features (A, B and C) excluded, there is only one significant contingency between the three new features and the original four − Feature I (Future/Past) being significantly contingent upon Feature E (Initiating/Reacting). Feature I (Future/Past) is also significantly contingent upon Feature H (Terminal/Interminal). The fact that future-oriented intentions tend to be initiating (rather than reacting) and

---

[7]   Table 3 in the original article, giving a priori codings of all 198 IPVs on all 10 final features, has been omitted here. It provided readers an opportunity to check the author's semantic intuitions and also served as a source of coded materials for future research (footnote added in 1973).

[8]   In other words, Table 3 summarizes the information from X^2 matrices like those shown in Table 1A.

TABLE 3. *Coding Distributions (A) and Inter-feature Coding Contingencies (B) for 10-Feature System*

	A — Coding Distributions for Features			B — Coding Contingencies within 10-Feature System									
	+	0	−	A^a	B	C	D	E	F	G	H	I	J
A	17	149	32	—	.20	.17	.42**	.18	.20	.09	.12	.11	.23
B	46	118	34		—	.36**	.15	.28*	.11	.46**	.08	.19	.34**
C	61	106	31			—	.19	.27*	.14	.16	.30	.23	.20
D	66	52	80				—	.30*	.30*	.34**	.18	.20	.13
E	75	57	66					—	.17	.26	.20	.45**	.19
F	45	51	102						—	.17	.20	.21	.09
G	95	75	28							—	.19	.18	.15
H	96	62	40								—	.40**	.25
I	58	87	53									—	.23
J	76	81	41										—

a. The feature identifications have been reordered as follows: A (Moral/Immoral), B (Potent/Impotent), C (Active/Passive), D (Associative/Dissociative), E (Initiating/Reacting), F (Ego/Alter), G (Supraordinate/Subordinate), H (Terminal/Interminal), I (Future-oriented/Past-oriented), J (Deliberate/Impulsive).

* Corresponds to a X² significant at the .01 level.

** Corresponds to a X² significant at the .001 level.

interminal (rather than terminal) seems to be eminently reasonable. The contingencies of the dominant Feature D (Associative/Dissociative) with E, F, and G remain as previously analysed, and the tendency for dissociative intentions to be more initiating (than reacting), more ego-oriented (than alter-oriented) and more supraordinate (than subordinate) remains reasonable.

The three affective features appear to operate on a somewhat different level from the others. They seem to be "nested" within the other features more specific to interpersonal verbs, providing an added feeling-tone to words already differentiated primarily on other bases. For example, with very few exceptions (four verbs), IPVs that have been coded as Associative (D+) will be coded only Moral or neutral in this respect; conversely, IPVs that have been coded Dissociative (D−) will be coded only Immoral or neutral. It is as if the affective features provide a finer branching within already established denotative distinctions. Feature B (Potent/Impotent) is significantly contingent upon C (Active/Passive) and both of these are contingent upon E — initiating intentions thus tending to be more potent and active, as might be expected. Potency has a highly significant contingency with Supraordinateness as well as Deliberateness, while Activity is somewhat contingent upon the Terminalness of intentions — all again as could be expected.

Turning now to the intuitive validity of the 10-feature semantic system, we may ask several questions of the final list of codings:[9] (1) *Synonymity*. Are the sets of interpersonal verbs which remain with identical semantic codings synonymous in meaning? (2) *Quasi-synonymity*. When IPVs are distinguished only by one or two non-contrastive feature codings (that is, ± vs. 0), do the shadings in meaning fit the intuitions of the native speaker? (3) *Contrast*. When two IPVs contrast (+ vs. − coding) on only one feature and are otherwise synonymous or quasi-synonymous in terms of their total code-strips, does the intuited basis of contrast agree with the feature having opposed signs? (4) *Opposition*. Do IPVs which are felt to be common opposites have opposed signs and are these on features which are felt to be intuitively appropriate? It should be noted that these tests of the "face validity" of the feature system are reasonably independent of

[9] As given in the original Table 3, deleted here (footnote added in 1973).

the process of coding; this is because the codings were made either absolutely or comparatively across the entire sample of verbs, not in terms of organized sets of synonyms or antonyms.

Synonymity. Inspection indicated that only 10 sets of IPVs have identical code-strips in the 10-feature system. These are: *to participate with/to accompany; to soothe/to comfort; to concede to/to acquiesce; to stimulate/to arouse; to mold/to teach/to train; to confuse/to mystify; to shame/to embarrass; to injure/to hurt; to condemn/to accuse/ to blame; to rebuke/to refute.* Although some further fine distinctions could be made, such as, to distinguish between *participate with* and *accompany*, between *mold* and *teach*, between *rebuke* and *refute*, this is generally an intuitively satisfying solution. The converse question — are there verbs distinguished which ought to be considered synonymous, at least as much so as the above? — can best be answered by inspecting the next set of terms.

Quasi-synonymity. Table 4 lists all pairs of IPVs which (A) differ by only a half step (± to 0) on a single feature or (B) differ by half steps on only two features. Looking first at the single-feature distinctions: *to forgive* is slightly more Moral than *to pardon*, and *to ridicule* is slightly more Immoral than *to criticize; to bewilder* is slightly more Active than *to mystify*, and *to concur with* is slightly more Passive than *to compromise with; to make a proposal to* is slightly more Ego-oriented than *to persuade*, and *to congratulate* is slightly more Alter-oriented than *to reciprocate with; to make a bargain with* is slightly more Terminal than *to cooperate with*, and *to associate with* is slightly more Interminal than *to participate with; to train* is slightly more Future-oriented than *to supervise*, and *to console* is slightly more Past-oriented than *to comfort.* It is worth noting than even a single half-step difference on the dominant Associative/Dissociative feature creates a sense of rather gross distinction, for example, *to help* (+) vs. *to bewilder* (0) and *to provoke* (−) vs. *to persuade* (0).

Looking second at the double-feature distinctions: *to hire* differs from *to reason with* by being less Moral but more Associative; *to be firm with* differs from *to tolerate* by being both more Potent and more Alter-oriented; *to praise* is distinguished from *to reassure* by being more Active but less Supraordinate; *to dissuade* differs from *to warn* by being both more Reactive and more Deliberate ("cognitive"); and *to greet* is distinguished from *to charm* by being more Terminal but less Future-oriented. Few of these pairs seem to be as closely synonymous as those having identical codings and the distinctions made are, again, intuitively satisfying. The reader may explore Table 4 further for himself.

Contrast. Pairs of IPVs that have opposed signs on a single feature should differ more in meaning than pairs differing in a single half-step and at least as much as pairs differing by half-steps on two features. Only four such pairs could be located, however: *to persuade* differs from *to dissuade* only on Feature E (Initiating/Reacting); *to promise* vs. *to apologize, to lend to* vs. *to pardon* and *to advise* vs. *to explain to* all differ in terms of Feature I (Future vs. Past Orientation). If we allow a single half-step difference along with the single contrast, then we have 14 additional pairs: *to reason with/to seduce* on Morality (which makes sense!); *to defy/to evade* on Potency; *to irritate/to retard* and *to reciprocate/to concur with* on Activity; *to reciprocate/ to disagree with* and *to be responsible for/to confine* on Associativeness; *to shame/to blame* on Initiating; *to hire/to guide* on Ego-Alter Orientation; *to excuse/to concede to* on Supraordinateness; *to command/to dominate* on Terminality; *to enlist the support of/to confide to* and *to persuade/to remind* on Future-Past Orientation; and *to congratulate/to praise* and *to annoy/to distress* on Deliberateness.

The direction of the contrast in listing these items was not indicated because they should be intuitively obvious — if the codings are valid. With the possible exception of Feature J (Deliberate/Impulsive), these distinctions based on opposed signs for a single feature "feel" more extreme than those based on either single- or double-feature half-step comparisons (the sets of quasi-synonyms above).

Opposition. The basis for psychologically-experienced opposition has always been a puzzle, and it remains so in the present a priori analysis of interpersonal verbs. One possibility would be that words felt to be opposites would contrast on only one feature and be identically coded on all others. Some of the minimal contrasts given above (*persuade/dissuade, promise/apologize*) do seem to fit this notion, but others do not (*lend to/pardon, advise/explain*). Another possibility would be that psychological opposites are opposed on all non-zero features (that is, wherever one word is signed, the other has the opposed sign). Unfortunately, given as many as 10 features (and despite several hours of inspection) I have been unable to locate any pure

TABLE 4.   *Pairs of IPVs Differing by Only a Half-step on a Single Feature (A) or by Half-steps on Only Two Features (B)*

A :   Quasi-synonyms Differing by only a Half Step (±/0) on a Single Feature

    A: MORAL/IMMORAL
        to forgive (+)/to pardon (0); to reform (+)/to modify (0); to shame (0)/to humiliate (−); to weaken (0)/to corrupt (−); to confine (0)/to deprive (−); to criticize (0)/to ridicule (−)

    B: POTENT/IMPOTENT
        to support (+)/to provide for (0); to pardon (0)/to excuse (−)

    C: ACTIVE/PASSIVE
        to bewilder (+)/to mystify (0); to torture (+)/to bully (0); to scold (+)/to condemn (0); to provide for (0)/to be responsible for (−); to compromise with (0)/to concur with (−)

    D: ASSOCIATIVE/DISSOCIATIVE
        to help (+)/to bewilder (0); to mold (0)/to weaken (−); to persuade (0)/to provoke (−); to answer (0)/to disagree with (−)

    E: INITIATING/REACTING (none)

    F: EGO-ORIENTED/ALTER-ORIENTED
        to make a proposal to (+)/to persuade (0); to repudiate (+)/to contradict (0); to compromise with (0)/to agree with (−); to reciprocate with (0)/to congratulate (−)

    G: SUPRAORDINATE/SUBORDINATE
        to contradict (+)/to disagree with (0)

    H: TERMINAL/INTERMINAL
        to make a bargain with (+)/to cooperate with (0); to participate with (0)/to associate with (−)

    I: FUTURE-ORIENTED/PAST-ORIENTED
        to train (+)/to supervise (0); to bribe (+)/to ambush (0); to comfort (0)/to console (−)

"mirror-image" IPVs. If we limit ourselves to the four originally proposed, and presumably most relevant, IPV features (Associative/Dissociative, Initiating/Reacting, Ego-oriented/Alter-oriented and Supraordinate/Subordinate), we find the following "mirror-image" verbs: *to guide* vs. *to evade; to flatter* vs. *to repudiate; to inspire* vs. *to defy; to court* vs. *to restrain; to appease* vs. *to molest*; and *to concede to* vs. *to manipulate*. There is certainly the feeling of complete, all-faceted opposition about these pairs (examples: *he evaded the person trying to guide him; he repudiated the person trying to flatter him*; and so on), but these are also certainly *not* familiar opposites in English.

Another possible way of getting at this question is to take sets of IPVs which would be accepted as familiar opposites and see how they are in fact coded within this 10-feature system. Table 5 gives 15 such

TABLE 4. *(continued)*

J:	DELIBERATE/IMPULSIVE
	to answer (+)/to repay (0); to annoy (+)/to irritate (0); to pay no attention to (+)/to disregard (0); to criticize (+)/to scold (0); to rebuke (+)/to blame (0)
B:	Quasi-synonyms Differing by Half Steps (+/0) on Two Features
A and *D:*	to hire (0+)/to reason with (+0)
A and *I:*	to protect (++)/to support (00)
A and *G:*	to soothe (+0)/to indulge (0+)
B and *F:*	to tolerate (00)/to be firm with (+−)
B and *H:*	to injure (++)/to harm (00)
B and *J:*	to argue with (00)/to quarrel with (+−)
C and *G:*	to praise (+0)/to reassure (0+)
C and *I:*	to agree with (00)/to congratulate (+−)
D and *H:*	to impress (00)/to impose upon (−−)
D and *I:*	to agree with (+0)/to dissuade (0+)
E and *J:*	to warn (00)/to dissuade (−+)
F and *J:*	to follow (00)/to be submissive to (−−)
G and *H:*	to question (++)/to consult with (00)
G and *I:*	to protect (++)/to defend (00); to assist (0+)/to serve (−0)
G and *J:*	to advise (++)/to warn (00)
H and *I:*	to make a proposal to (++)/to consult with (00); to greet (+0)/ to charm (0+)
H and *J:*	to command (++)/to lead (00); to convert (+0)/to reform (0+)
I and *J:*	to exhort (+−)/to preach to (00)

---

pairs. From the sums of the feature *columns*, it can be seen that the original four a priori features (D, E, F, G) contribute most to the production of psychological opposites. From the sums of the opposite-pair *rows*, it can be seen that there is great variation in the coding relations that can result in psychological opposition — from seven shared signs as against only one contrast (*to reward/to punish*) to one shared sign as against four contrasts (*to command/to obey*). If we omit that one case with zero opposed signs (*to cooperate with* vs. *to compete with*, where I probably should have coded *compete* as Dissociative) and the one case with zero shared signs (*to lead* vs. *to follow*, where *lead* probably should have been coded as Interminal along with *follow*), then the only general condition for psychological opposition would seem to be "contrast on at least one feature and

TABLE 5. *Semantic Feature Codings for a Sample of Familiar Opposites*

	A	B	C	D	E	F	G	H	I	J	N SAME	N OP-POSED	N ZERO
to defend	+	+	0	+	0	−	0	−	0	0	1	3	6
to attack	0	+	+	−	0	+	0	+	0	−			
to praise	0	+	+	+	−	−	0	+	−	−	4	1	5
to blame	0	0	0	−	−	−	+	+	−	0			
to reward	0	+	+	+	−	−	+	+	−	0	7	1	2
to punish	0	+	+	−	−	−	+	+	−	0			
to accept	0	−	−	+	−	0	0	+	0	0	2	2	6
to reject	0	+	0	−	−	+	+	+	0	−			
to pay attention to	0	0	0	+	−	0	−	0	0	+	2	1	7
to pay no attention to	0	0	−	−	−	0	0	−	0	+			
to lend to	0	0	0	+	−	−	+	+	+	+	3	3	4
to borrow from	0	0	0	0	+	+	−	+	+	+			
to lead	0	+	+	0	+	0	+	0	0	0	0	4	6
to follow	0	−	−	0	−	0	−	−	0	0			
to cooperate with	0	0	0	+	0	0	0	0	+	+	1	0	9
to compete with	0	+	0	0	0	+	0	0	+	0			

TABLE 5. (continued)

to question	0	0	0	0	+	0	0	+	0	0	2	1	7
to answer	0	0	0	0	−	0	0	+	−	+			
to agree with	0	0	+	+	−	−	0	+	0	+	3	1	6
to disagree with	0	0	−	−	0	0	0	+	−	+			
to persuade	0	0	0	+	0	0	+	+	+	+	4	1	5
to dissuade	0	0	0	−	0	0	+	+	+	+			
to promise	+	−	0	+	0	0	−	0	+	+	6	1	3
to apologize	+	−	0	+	0	0	−	−	−	+			
to strengthen	0	+	0	+	+	+	+	0	+	0	4	1	5
to weaken	0	0	0	−	+	+	−	−	−	+			
to command	0	+	0	+	+	+	+	+	0	−	1	4	5
to obey	+	−	+	−	−	−	+	−	−	−			
to teach	0	0	0	+	+	−	+	−	+	+	3	3	4
to learn from	0	0	0	+	−	+	+	−	+	+			
N SAME	1	3	1	1	6	4	3	10	7	7			
N OPPOSED	0	3	1	7	6	3	4	1	1	1			
N ZERO	14	9	13	7	3	8	8	4	7	7			

sharing of at least one other feature." But this, of course, would not explain why the many other pairs of IPVs which meet this condition are *not* felt to be opposites. Probably some non-semantic factors are also operating in the determination of "felt" opposition. That the features on which the opposite IPVs contrast generally make intuitive sense can be seen by inspecting Table 5; examples: *to praise* and *to blame* contrast only on Associativeness; *to question* and *to answer* contrast only on Initiating/Reacting; *to promise* and *to apologize* contrast only on Future/Past Orientation.

Conclusions

In many respects, the intuitive approach employed in this study is similar to that employed by the lexicographer — reliance upon oneself as a native speaker and native "behaver," the use of minimal contrasts in meaning as a discovery procedure, and the notion of hierarches of markers and distinguishers, for example. It differs possibly in the source of distinctions (its behavioral science orientation) and certainly in its validation procedures — the use of statistical tests of contingency and distribution in the present analysis and the use of empirical validity tests in experiments to be reported subsequently.

What are the limitations on such an a priori investigation of a semantic domain? One obvious limitation is that, up to this point, at least, it depends entirely upon the semantics of one informant, the writer, and hence is liable to scholarly schizophrenia. At any point where he deviates from other American English speakers, the features assigned and the distinctions made will be uncharacteristic of the speech community. No doubt each reader had picked up certain examples in this paper where he would disagree with the writer's decisions. Along with the subjectivity of this a priori analysis, there was considerable difficulty in making many of the judgments. Although no formal test of within-individual reliability of the coding has been made, informal evidence on between-individual reliability has been obtained from working with my colleagues. [10] Within a pattern of over-all agreement on the nature of the features involved and their use in coding, numerous points of divergence were also evident — giving

[10]   Particularly Kenneth Forster and Marilyn Wilkins.

rise to many spirited arguments about the meanings of words! If there is no corroboration of these features in future research, of course, the entire endeavor can be put down as a most elaborate and time-consuming *tour de force*.

On the more positive side, most of the features isolated in this a priori analysis do seem to make sense in relation to interpersonal behavior and its perception. Certainly, there are Associative and Dissociative relations, Initiating and Reacting behaviors, Ego-oriented and Alter-oriented behaviors and Supraordinate and Subordinate relations; although the affective features and the three new ones — Terminal/Interminal, Future-oriented/Past-oriented and Deliberate/Impulsive — are perhaps not so obviously relevant to interpersonal behavior, in practice they seem to be effective in producing the refinements required by the usage of interpersonal verbs in English. Furthermore, the sample of interpersonal verbs against which these a priori features were tested was reasonably large and designed to be maximally representative.

Successful differentiation among some 200 interpersonal verbs with only 10 features does, if valid, represent a considerable economy of description. It supports the underlying thesis — namely, that the meanings of word-forms can be conceived as simultaneous bundles of distinctive semantic features. This thesis is not an original conception by the author, of course. To the extent that such features can be shown to characterize the discriminations people make about interpersonal behaviors, then the feasibility of determining the structure of a behavior domain via semantic analysis of the language referring to that domain is enhanced. To the extent that such features can be shown to be universal, despite differences in both language and culture, then a more precise way of contrasting norms of interpersonal behavior in different communities around the world becomes feasible.

INTERPERSONAL VERBS AND INTERPERSONAL BEHAVIOR [11]

This paper is my attempt to summarize and interpret some four years of research on the semantics of interpersonal verbs in relation to the

[11] Excerpted from Chapter 6, by same title, in J. L. Cowan (Ed.), *Studies in thought and language*. Tucson, Arizona: The University of Arizona Press, 1970.

norms of interpersonal behavior. Quite a number of colleagues and graduate students in the Center for Comparative Psycholinguistics at the University of Illinois have contributed to this research. [12] Some of their studies, and mine, have already been published, some others will be in the near future, and some will never be published because we were thoroughly dissatisfied with them. Nor are we at this point satisfied that we have solved the central problem of specifying a theoretically principled and empirically rigorous procedure for discovering the semantic features of word forms. Nevertheless, in the patterning of failures and partial successes we are beginning to see some sense and some relationships to the approaches of others.

Intentions, Behaviors, and Perceptions

If A and B are members of different cultures, we might (in theory) expect them to use the same distinguishing features, to vary somewhat in the set of intentions they employ, to differ considerably in codings and weights given to translation-equivalent intentions, to differ considerably in the exact overt behaviors by which they express these translation-equivalent intentions, and to differ markedly in the rules governing the appropriateness of having and expressing certain intentions in certain role relations. Assume that **American business man** *slaps on the back* **Japanese business man** when *meeting by surprise on a street corner in Tokyo*. If the nearest equivalent of the intent *To Express Friendship* in the Japanese system includes a negative coding on the Supraordinate-Subordinate feature, the Japanese may correctly interpret the American's behavior, yet respond in a deferential manner that surprises the American. Or, if the intent *To Express Friendship* is inappropriate between businessmen role-pairs, the Japanese may correctly interpret the action but privately think the American is a fool. Or, if *slapping on the back* between adult males signifies the intent *To*

---

[12]   Contributors to particular studies will be cited in course, but I want to express special gratitude to Dr. Kenneth Forster, with whom I first explored some new directions in semantic feature analysis while on sabbatical in 1964-65 at the University of Hawaii, and to Dr. Marilyn Wilkins, with whom I have worked closely since returning to the University of Illinois. Both have served as intellectual goads and sophisticated critics throughout.

Insult, our Japanese friend is most likely to *turn away abruptly* and the American might conclude that Japanese are unfriendly! Needless to say, this illustration is thoroughly hypothetical.

In order for a person to assimilate the norms of another culture, he presumably must experience a sample of interpersonal behaviors in that culture involving various roles and overt expressions, and gradually establish a set of inferences about the significance-intention mediators that are operating. The test of his assimilation is the success with which he can project this knowledge into novel interpersonal situations. The term "knowledge" is used here in much the same sense that one may be said to have "knowledge" of the rules of his grammar — by following the rules but not necessarily being able to verbalize them. There is probably more than just an analogy between "knowing" the rules of a grammar and "knowing" the norms of a system of interpersonal behavior. In both cases, a sure intuitive feeling is a better guarantee of fluency than an ability to verbalize the abstract rules. And in both cases induction of the semantic features operating and their "deep structure" is essential if one is to make successful projections into new instances.

The Problem of Characterizing Meaning

There appears to be fairly general agreement among psycholinguists, regardless of their disciplinary origins, that meanings can be characterized as "simultaneous bundles of distinctive semantic features," in much the same way that Jakobson and Halle (1956) and others after them have characterized phonemes as simultaneous bundles of distinctive phonetic features. There is disagreement about whether all, most or only some of the features known to be operating are properly called "semantic" rather than "syntactic," but this issue will not concern us at the moment. The efficiency with which a relatively small number of features can generate an extraordinarily large number of distinctive meanings makes such a componential system very appealing. The problem, of course, is to devise a principled basis for discovering these features. An ideal discovery procedure would meet the usual scientific criteria of objectivity (comparability of features discovered across observers), reliability (yielding the same features in repeated, independent observations), validity (yielding features that correspond to those discovered by other methods) and generality (applicability of the procedures to the discovery of features of all types). This is a large order, and no ideal discovery procedure may be attainable.

It is possible to distinguish two grossly different discovery procedures at the outset, and these do reflect the disciplinary backgrounds of those who use them. The first involves intuitive methods. Here the investigator utilizes his intimate knowledge of (usually) his own language as a native speaker. Semantic features are discovered by the same strategies of substitution and contrast that have proven so successful at the phonemic level. The criteria of objectivity, reliability and validity are sought, typically, by the use of compelling demonstrations that appeal to the intuitions of other (scholarly) native speakers. As a classic example, it might be shown that in the sentence *John is eager to please*, *John* is obviously coded for subject whereas in the superficially similar sentence *John is easy to please*, *John* is obviously coded for object (appropriately chosen paraphrases reinforce the appeal). Generality of application is not a problem.

The second type of discovery procedure uses empirical methods. Here the investigator may also employ his own intuition as a native speaker (indeed, he should), but his intuition is used in devising appropriate linguistic measures to be applied to *other* native speakers and for interpreting the results. Here the strategies of substitution and contrast take the form of quantitative similarities and differences which appear in the judgments about, or usages of, selected language items by these other native speakers. Objectivity (across investigators) and reliability (across repetitions) are tested statistically; validity is sought by checking features against those obtained by other methods (where available) or against the linguistic intuitions of other investigators. But here generality becomes a significant problem: a method that works for certain types of features or for certain form classes may not work for others.

Intuitive or rational methods are typically used by linguists, semanticists, lexicographers and philosophers; they are part of their tradition. Empirical methods are typically used by psychologists; these are part of *their* tradition. Intuitive methods have the advantages of obvious generality and full utilization of the competence of sophisticated native speakers, but they also have certain disadvantages - what may be compelling demonstrations to one native speaker may not appeal at all to another, as the many delightful bickerings at linguistic symposia testify, and what may be easy to intuit in one's own language may be difficult if not impossible to intuit in a foreign language, particularly an "exotic" one.

Empirical methods have the advantages of scientific objectivity and quantification, as well as the potential for application to languages of which the investigator is not a native speaker; they also have certain disadvantages — beyond the problem of generality, there are questions about the fruitfulness of using ordinary native speakers, about the appropriateness of statistical determinations in an area like this, and about the sensitivity of such procedures in discovering the subtle distinctions made in semantics. The semantic differential is one empirical method.

From Rules to Features

In 1964-65, with a sabbatical in Hawaii, time to do some much needed reading, and a young colleague, Kenneth Forster, to debate with more or less continuously, a quite different approach to the discovery of semantic features began to take form. The general notion that motivated our thinking was that the rules which govern usage of words in sentences and phrases are themselves based upon semantic distinctions. [13] This meant, in the first place, that we should study the meanings of words in combination rather than in isolation. It also implied a return to the linguistic notion that similarity of meaning varies with the extent to which speakers use forms in the same or different contexts or frames (e.g., Harris, 1954). If acceptability of utterances depends on both grammatical and semantic congruence among their parts — and if purely grammatical congruences are assured — then differences in acceptability should become direct func-

---

[13] This notion was not new then (cf., Jakobson's paper in memory of Franz Boaz, 1959) and is even more familiar today after the publication of Chomsky's *Aspects of a Theory of Syntax* (1965), in which he indicates that "selectional rules" may well belong in the lexicon. It was, however, still a rather novel notion to us in 1964.

tions of semantic congruences. But what syntactical frames are appropriate, and can the task be adapted to ordinary speakers?

An assist from Gilbert Ryle. In reading and discussing some of Ryle's papers on philosophy and ordinary language, we came across the following illustration: Ryle claimed that one could not say significantly in ordinary English *he hit the target unsuccessfully*. Why? Although he does not put it exactly this way, it is because the verb phrase *hit the target* is coded for what might be called "goal achievement" whereas the modifying adverb is explicitly coded for "goal non-achievement"; therefore the sentence is, in Ryle's terms, "absurd." It occurred to us that, rather than merely using such examples as compelling arguments in philosophical debate, one might systematically explore the compatabilities of verb/adverb phrases as a discovery procedure in experimental semantics. In other words, our purposes were a bit different from those of philosophers identified with the Oxford School.

There was also a difference in stress. Whereas the Oxford philosophers repeatedly emphasize that sentences have meanings and words only uses (the analogy of words with the moves of pieces in a chess game is offered), it seemed to us that there were two sides to this coin. If certain sentence frames can be said to accept certain words and reject others as creating absurdity, then the words so accepted or rejected can be said to share certain features which are either compatible or incompatible with the remainder of the sentence.

It was interesting to discover that, in one of his earlier papers (1938), Ryle seems to accept the two-sidedness of this coin: [14] "So *Saturday is in bed* breaks no rule of grammar. Yet the sentence is absurd. Consequently the possible complements must not only be of certain grammatical types, they must also express proposition-factors of certain logical types. The several factors in a non-absurd sentence are typically suited to each other; those in an absurd sentence or some of them are typically unsuitable to each other. (Ryle, 1938, p. 194)"

Compare the following:

* (1) sleep ideas green furiously colorless
* (2) colorless green ideas sleep furiously

[14]   I am grateful to John Limber for bringing this article to my attention.

? (3) colorless grey misery weeps ponderously
  (4) colorful green lanterns burn brightly

String 1 breaks both grammatical and semantic rules and must be read as a word list. String 2, Chomsky's classic, is not agrammatical but "asemantical," clashing semantically at every joint and for different reasons. [15] String 3 breaks many of the same rules as string 2, but by maintaining congruence of certain semantic features it creates a quasi-poetic meaning. String 4 is an entirely acceptable sentence, even if less interesting than 3.

Returning to the early Ryle paper, we find him saying, quite appropriately: "We say that (a sentence) is absurd because at least one ingredient expression in it is not of the right type to be coupled or to be coupled in that way with the other ingredient expression or expressions in it. Such sentences, we may say, commit type-trespasses or break type-rules (1938, p. 200)."

It was our own insight, [16] and I hope a felicitous one, that if indeed this is a two-sided coin, then it should be possible to infer the semantic features of word forms from their rules of usage in combination with other words in appropriate syntactical frames. Let us take some verbs and try them in some frames: Using the frame *It verbed.* vs. the frame *I verbed.*, one can make an acceptable sentence by inserting *fastened* in the first but not in the second and by inserting *prayed* in the second but not the first; thus we may infer that *it* and *pray* contrast on some feature(s) as do *I* and *fasten*. (Although we need not worry about naming features at this point, it would appear that Human/Non-Human and Transitive/Intransitive features are involved.) Or take the alternative frames *He verbed her successfully* vs. *He verbed her unsuccessfully*. The interpersonal verbs *Plead With* and *Courted* will go in either frame (implying that on whatever features distinguish *successfully* from *unsuccessfully*, here presumably Goal-achievement, *Plead With* and *Courted* are not coded). On the other

---

[15] Many would call some of these clashes grammatical, in the sense of breaking selectional rules (*green ideas*), and others really semantic, in the sense of breaking lexical rules (*sleep furiously*). It seems to me that we have a continuum rather than a dichotomy here. I shall return to this matter.

[16] I realize that the word *insight* is also coded for goal-achievement, and we are far from it!

hand, the verbs *Confided In* and *Reminded* fit easily in neither frame (implying that they contrast on some feature which *successfully* and *unsuccessfully* share, perhaps a Striving feature). Examples like these make it seem reasonable that regularities in the acceptability vs. absurdity judgments of speakers about sets of interpersonal verbs in sets of adverbial frames could be used to infer the semantic features of both sets. But some theory about how semantic features interact in the production of such judgments is required, both for asking native speakers the right questions and for interpreting their responses.

Fragment of a theory of semantic interaction. I start from the notion that the meaning of a word can be characterized as a simultaneous bundle of distinctive semantic features. I assume that each of these features represents the momentary state of a single, reciprocally antagonistic representational system; this means that a word cannot be simultaneously coded in opposed directions on the same feature — it must be *either* "positive", *or* "negative" *or* neither. Whether or not these features are independent of each other, with the coding of a word on one feature not restricting the coding of the same word on any other feature, is left open at this point. The simultaneous bundle of features characterizing the meaning of a word form can be represented by a code-strip without anything being implied as yet about the form of the coding or, for that matter, about the psychological nature of the features. I do assume that the features would be ordered according to some psycholinguistic principle.

The meaning of a grammatical string of words (phrase, acceptable sentence, absurd or anomalous sentence) is assumed to be the momentary resolution of the codings on shared features when words are forced into interaction within syntactic frames. This is required by the previous assumption that the system of any single feature can only be in one state, can only assume one "posture," at a given time. Thus if one is to understand the meaning of *He's a lazy athlete*, the simultaneous pattern of semantic features generated cannot be only that associated with *athlete* or only that associated with *lazy*, but must be some compromise. This semantic interaction can be represented as the fusion of two or more word code-strips, according to some set of rules. Going back to Ryle's example, and assuming the simplest kind of rules, the phrase *hit the target unsuccessfully* might be represented

	A	B	C	D	E	F	.	.	.	. features
hit the target	0	–	0	+	0	+	.	.	.	.
unsuccessfully	+	0	0	–	0	+	.	.	.	.
	+	–	0	X	0	+	.	.	.	. fusion

by, A, B, etc. representing features, X representing antagonism on a goal-achievement feature (signal for absurdity judgment) and the +, 0 or – representing simple coding directions.

When we come to the nature of the coding on features, the kind of interaction within features and the mode of combining influences across features, we must simply admit to alternative models and seek empirical answers. Coding on features could be *discrete* (+, 0, or –) or *continuous* (e.g., +3 through 0 to –3, as in semantic differential scaling); interactions within features could be *all-or-nothing* (the fusion must be antagonistic, represent the dominant sign, or be zero) or *algebraic* (same signs summate and opposed signs cancel); relations between features could be *segregate* (numbers of shared or antagonistic codings being irrelevant) or *aggregate* (final resolution depending upon, for example, the ratio of shared to antagonistic codings across the entire strip). Almost any combination of these possibilities is at least conceivable, and it is even conceivable that different levels of features operate according to different types of rules. [17] The kinds of rules assumed will influence both the kinds of judgments required from speakers and the kinds of statistical treatments that are appropriate.

We were already familiar with a general cognitive interaction model which assumed continuous coding on features (factors), segregation between features and a special type of weighted interaction within features. This was the Congruity Hypothesis. Applied to semantic differential type data and hence affective features, it was used to predict attitude change (Osgood and Tannenbaum, 1955) and semantic fusion under conditions of combining adjective-noun pairs, like *shy*

[17]   For example, "grammatical" features might be discretely coded, all-or-nothing in fusion, and segregate in combination across features, whereas "semantic" features might be continuously coded, algebraic in fusion, and aggregate in combination across features.

secretary, breezy husband, sincere prostitute (as reported in Osgood, Suci and Tannenbaum 1957, pp. 275-284). Using the geometric model discussed earlier, the projections of the vectors representing the two words to be combined (e.g., *shy* and *secretary* as components) onto each factor were independently entered into a formula which, in effect, predicted a resolution point which was inversely proportional to the semantic intensities of the words combined (e.g., +3 with 0 on a factor yields +3, +2 with −2 yields 0, +2 with −1 yields +1, etc.). It was noted at the time that opposed codings (directions) on the same factor yielded what was termed "incredulity" (e.g., for *sincere prostitute* on the E-factor). However, the model yields compromise rather than intensification when words having codings of the same sign but different magnitude are combined, and this has been a matter of experimental debate in recent years.

On the ground that denotative features, as compared with affective E-P-A features, might well be discretely coded, Forster and I devised a model which assumed discrete (+, 0, −) coding on features, all-or-nothing rather than algebraic interaction within features and, like the Congruity Model, segregation across features. We assumed an ordered set of rules and tried to relate them to potential judgments of combinations by speakers:

Rule I. If the strip-codes for words to be combined in a syntactic frame have opposed signs on any shared feature, then the combination will be judged semantically anomalous (e.g., *happy boulder, the brakes shouted, plead with tolerantly*). In cognitive dynamics more generally, this is the condition for "cognitive dissonance" or "incongruity."

Rule II. If Rule I does not apply (if there are no features with opposed signs) and there are the same signs on any features (either ++ or −−), then the combination will be judged semantically apposite or fitting (e.g., *hopeful sign, the brakes shrieked, plead with humbly*). This is the condition for intensification of meaning.

Rule III. If neither Rule I (opposed signs) nor Rule II (same signs) apply and either code-strip contains unsigned (zero) features where the other is signed, then the combination will be judged simply permissible (e.g., *sad face, the brakes worked, plead with sincerely*). This is the condition for ordinary modification of meaning.

Several things should be noted about this model. First, it requires three types of judgment from subjects: anomaly, appositeness and permissiveness criteria. Second, anomaly criteria take precedence over appositeness criteria in determining judgment, and these both take precedence over mere permissiveness. Third, there is no summation or compromise within or across features; several opposed features do not make a combination more anomalous than one opposed feature, and several same features do not override a single opposition.

In a most intriguing paper titled "The Case for Case" [18] Charles Fillmore proposes what he calls a Case Grammar which

.. is a return, as it were, to the "conceptual framework" interpretation of case systems, but this time with a clear understanding of the difference between deep and surface structure. The sentence in its basic structure consists of a verb and one or more noun phrases, each associated with the verb in a particular case relationship. ... The arrays of cases defining the sentence types have the effect of imposing a classification on the verbs in the language (according to the sentence types into which they may be inserted), and it is very likely that many aspects of this classification will be of universal validity. (1967, pp. 29-30)

The case relationships which Fillmore assigns to noun phrases (subjects or objects) and verb phrases, and the uses to which he puts them, are clearly semantic in nature and generally similar to the approach we have been taking. The Agentive (A) Case is "the case of the animate responsible source of the action identified by the verb; Instrumental (I), the case of the inanimate force or object which contributes to the action or state identified by the verb; Dative (D), the case of the animate being affected by the action or state identified by the verb ..." (1967, p. 32), and so forth.

There is one significant difference between Fillmore's approach and ours: whereas he assigns what he calls "frame features" to verbs, which represent case relations between verbs and noun phrases which he believes simplify the lexicon, we assign codings to common features in each of the form classes, in the belief that this is a more generally applicable procedure. Thus, he expresses the frame feature for the verb *cook* as + [_____(O) (A)], where either O (Objective Case) or A (Agentive Case), or both, may occur. If both occur, we

---

[18]   As of the time of this writing, to the best of my knowledge, this paper had not been published. I borrowed a dittoed version from Professor Robert Lees; it was dated April 13, 1967, from Austin, Texas.

have sentences like *Mother is cooking the potatoes*; if only O, then we have sentences like *The potatoes are cooking*; and if only A, then we have sentences like *Mother is cooking* — and he notes that the last is potentially ambiguous only because we are familiar with the diversity of customs in human societies.

Our procedure would probably break "case" down into semantic features like ± H (Human), ± C (Concrete) and assign them to nouns and verbs separately, letting the interactions within features thus assigned determine acceptability. But, admittedly, in this case we would have to include "semantic" features specifying subjects versus objects as well as form-classes more generally.

It might be noted that all *interpersonal* verbs must be marked +A (Agentive) in relation to subject noun phrases and +D (Dative) in relation to object noun phrases, or perhaps better, they cannot be marked —A or —D in relation to these noun phrases. This means that features associated with case relations will *not* be discoverable in the rules of combination of IPVs (interpersonal verbs) with AVs (adverbs) — case features being, in effect, held constant — but rather features "further down the line" in generality, so to speak, will have a chance of appearing. This relationship between type of linguistic sampling and level of features discoverable will become clearer in the next section.

Our Search for Empirical Discovery Procedures

A theory about meanings of word forms as componential patterns of features, about how codings on shared features interact to yield the meanings of words in combination — and so on — is all very fine, but there is very little one can do with it until he can specify what the significant semantic features are. In the domain of interpersonal behavior, for example, there is little one can do about predicting similarities and differences across cultures from their usage of interpersonal verbs until one can code such verbs on a sufficient set of valid features. As already noted, intuitive discovery procedures are pretty much limited to the language of which one is a native speaker and are of debatable validity even then. The trouble is that one's theory about semantic features is in continuous interaction with the empirical procedures one uses for discovering them. So our search of necessity has been something of a bootstrap operation — and it still is.

Problems of sampling linguistic data. Sampling problems appear in many forms in an endeavor like this. First there is the question of what semantic domain to investigate (in our case this was largely decided by our interest in interpersonal behavior, although we have also worked with emotion nouns [19]) and how openly or restrictively to define this domain. There is the question of what syntactic frames to use as complements for the items in the domain under investigation and what lexical content to give them. Once decisions have been made on these matters there rises the question of what size sample of linguistic data is necessary, whether it is to be drawn from natural sources or experimentally induced, whether it is to be random or systematic, and so on. And, of course, there is the usual question of what subjects (speakers) to use.

Early in our explorations at the University of Hawaii, in an attempt to clarify such problems, we took a reasonably random sample of 100 verbs-in-general (the first verbs appearing on the second 100 pages in James Michener's *Hawaii*, appropriately enough!) and subjected them to various tests in comparison with a smaller sample of interpersonal verbs drawn from my own a priori analysis as previously described.

Our general procedure was to make what we termed "intersections" of the verb class under study with various other form classes or combinations of form classes, the latter being either sentences or phrases. Figure 2 illustrates some of the intersections we tried. The whole circles represent the entire (hypothetical) sets of the classes in question and the shaded regions of intersection represent those subsets of each class which are actually brought into syntactical relation. Within these intersections, *all possible combinations of the two subsets* (e.g., all PN frames with all Vs in intersection I) *are created and judged for acceptability or anomaly in ordinary English.* Kenneth Forster and myself were the only native speakers involved in these

---

[19]   A report on semantic interactions of emotion nouns and modifying adjectives was in preparation at the time of this writing by Dr. Marilyn Wilkins and myself.

Fig. 2.   Sample intercepts of verbs and frames

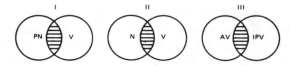

preliminary tests and by no means did we always agree. The linguistic data generated by this means were sometimes submitted to a computer program which categorized elements of either sub-set into hierarchical "trees" in terms of similarity of usage over the other sub-set. [20]

Before making some general observations about sampling let me note briefly what happens in some of the intersections illustrated in Figure 2. Intersection I related the sample of 100 verbs-in-general (V) to simple sentence frames of three types, all composed of pronouns (PN): Type I, *intransitive: I, We, It,* or *They* ____(V)____ ; Type II, *transitive: They* ____(V)____ *me, us, it* or *them*; Type III, *reflexive: I, We, It* or *They* ____(V)____ PN-*self*. Beyond the gross transitive and reflexive relations for verbs, there are finer distinctions in terms of which pronouns in these frames, as subjects or objects, will accept which verbs. Figure 3 displays the pronoun categorizations based upon this intersection — nine sentence frames in all. As expected, we find Subject vs. Object, Personal vs. Impersonal, and Singular vs. Plural categories. Perhaps less expected is the fact that *they* (subject) is more Personal than *them* (object), where both should be coded zero on this feature, and the fact that reflexive seems more Personal than

[20]   This program creates similarity trees "from the ground up", so to speak. All elements are searched for the ones most similar in usage, and these are linked under a node; then the mean of these plus all remaining elements are searched and another node is established. When a previously linked set becomes most similar to another element or set, a higher node connects them, and so on. This program seems very much like a categorizing procedure developed by S.C. Johnson of the Bell Telephone Laboratories and used by G. A. Miller and his associates for similar purposes (Johnson, 1967).

Fig. 3. Pronoun categorizations based on verb intersection

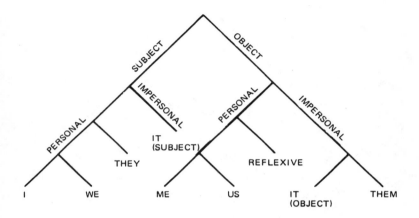

Impersonal — this latter situation perhaps indicating a tendency for reflexive verbs to require Animate subjects.

Figure 4 presents the categorization of verbs resulting from the intersection with pronouns, or the inverse of the pronoun categorization. Not only is this "tree" much more complex, but it must be kept in mind that it is based on the (to some degree) fallible judgments of one English speaker (myself). As to the major categories: verbs under node 1 are characterized by taking personal subjects (*I, we, they*) but not personal objects (*me* or *us*); verbs under node 2 are marked in common as being necessarily transitive, i.e., they are not acceptable in frames of Type I above; verbs under node 3 have in common only the fact that they will take both *they* as a subject and *them* as an object, but what this signifies, if anything, is obscure. Finer distinctions are made beneath these major nodes. Nodes 4 and 5 are distinguished by the fact that the latter will accept both *them* and *it* as objects while the former will accept only *it*, if any object. Within node 4, nodes 6 and 7 are completely intransitive, the former taking *it* as a subject and the latter not (*Reply, Insist, Hope*, etc.: can these be called Human coded?); whereas node 8 verbs will take *it* as object. Even finer dis-

Fig. 4.   Verb categorizations based on pronoun intersection

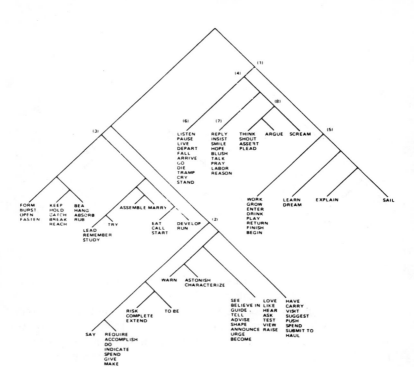

tinctions appear among the "twigs": Personal/Impersonal (*Marry me* but not *Assemble me, Assemble it* but not *Marry it*), Reflexive/Non-reflexive (*Study themselves* but not *Try themselves*), for example.

In the sense of revealing features previously undiscovered, of course, these results are trivial. But in the sense of testing the adequacy of a procedure, they are not. If, under appropriate sampling conditions for an intersection, such basic grammatical distinctions as Transitive/Intransitive, Personal/Impersonal, Subject/Object and the like can be obtained, then it implies both generality for the method and its potential validity in less familiar (or perhaps better, less open) semantic domains. The categories of verbs established by Fillmore via his case frames appear similar to our PN/V intersection results, but I have not been able to make a successful analysis in his terms. The use of an appropriate set of subject nouns and object nouns, drawn from his examples, might yield a closer relationship between his intuitive and our empirical methods. But this remains to be done systematically.

We did try an intersection of 14 plural nouns with the set of 100 random verbs, using the nouns in both a subject frame (N _____(V)_____ PN (or *zero*), e.g., *Dogs* _____(V)_____ *them*) and an object frame (PN (*I, they, it*) _____(V)_____ (PP) N, e.g., *They* _____(V)_____ *doctors*). Because at that time we considered the noun set too small for such a large category, we did not submit the data to the "tree" categorizing analysis — which I realize, after reading Fillmore, may have been a mistake. Informal inspection of the data, however, indicates expected noun categories (in terms of Concrete/ Abstract, Animate/Inanimate, Human/Non-human). With *women* and *doctors* in the subject frame, every verb is accepted, and for these nouns in the object frame the largest numbers of verbs are accepted (76/100 and 74/100) — suggesting that human languages were designed primarily to enable humans to talk about humans! What verbs will not accept *women* and *doctors* as objects? One set includes verbs like *form, complete, accomplish, finish* and *begin* (verbs requiring non-animate objects?); another includes *say, learn, explain, indicate* and *reason* (verbs requiring abstract objects?); another includes *die, arrive, fall,* and *live* (intransitive verbs?). What verbs fall out when *dogs* rather than humans are subjects? Exclusively human-coded cognitive processes (*say, reply, insist, advise, explain,* etc.), emotive processes (*smile, blush, hope, pray*) and activities (*sail, hang, spend,* and *marry*). Abstract nouns linke *anger* and *respect* as subjects, accept relatively few verbs (mostly spatio-temporal generalizations like *develop, grow, hold, start, begin, return,* but also reference to an observer like *astonish* and *urge*). Let me now return to problems of sampling.

The first general observation I have concerns the effect of restricting the domain of forms analysed: When we compare the types of features obtained from open classes (randomly selected verbs) with those obtained from more restricted classes (interpersonal verbs),[21]

---

[21] Compare the types of features yielded by the PN/V intersection and by the IPV/AV intersections displayed in Figures 5-8.

the more open domains yield more general, "grammatical" features and the more restricted domains yield more specific, "semantic" features. The primary reason for this is that restricting the semantic domain, in effect, holds features shared by items in that domain constant and hence "undiscoverable." If we assume that the semantic component is an ordered system, with those features doing the most "work" (e.g., Abstract/Concrete) being in some way prior to those doing the least (e.g., Moral/Immoral), then this makes sense – an efficient algorithm would look first for the distinctions that are most likely to make a difference.

My second observation concerns the nature of the syntactic frames to be used in empirical analyses. Within sentences there are what might be called "intimate" syntactic relations and more "remote" syntactic relations. In the sentence, *The tall boy leaped eagerly to the side of the fainting woman*, it is obvious intuitively (as well as from immediate constituent analysis) that *tall* is more intimately interactive with *boy* than with *side*, that *eagerly* is more intimately interactive with *leaped* than with *woman*, that *boy* is more intimately related to *leaped* than to *fainting*, and so forth. The more remote the syntactic relation, the weaker should be the syntactical constraints upon semantic interaction. Therefore, it would seem that semantic features would be most clearly revealed in intersections of intimate form classes. It is also the case that the greater the complexity of syntactic frames, the greater the number of interactions that must be involved, if we change the last two words of the sentence above to *decadent dictatorship*, whole sets of semantic relations fall into confusion. Of course, one may deliberately vary several elements of sentences simultaneously, but this complicates matters. [22]

The effect of size of sample upon discovery of semantic features seems to be relatively straight-forward. Given that one is working within a particular syntactic frame (or specifiable set of frames) there should be a negatively accelerated increase in the number of features discovered as the number of items in the sample increase – that is, the

---

[22]   For example, in his dissertation John Limber simultaneously varied 10 nouns, 10 sentence frames, and 50 adjectives (e.g., N is A *about it*, *it is* A of N *to do it*, etc.) in an attempt to determine the interactions among these sources of variance in sentence interpretation.

features found to determine judgments of earlier items should serve to determine later items as well, and the new features required should become progressively fewer. Of course, there is always the possibility of some new distinction being required — such as X being closer or further from Paris than Y — but such distinctions will not be very productive and should not inhibit one's search "in principle". [23]

Finally, as to the source of data: should they come from natural texts or experimentally devised samples, from random or systematic arrays? I think that here we come back to the basic nature of methods. At one extreme we have the purely distributional study of forms-in-contexts, as proposed hypothetically by Harris (1954); although in principle it might be possible to categorize interpersonal verbs in terms of the sharing of linguistic frames in natural texts, it would require miles and miles of text and a very heavy computer to assemble a sufficient sample of shared frames. At the other extreme we have the "compelling examples" of linguists and philosophers; here the "heaviest" computers of all rapidly search their memories and use their projection rules to create apposite examples, but the N is one, or a few, and compulsion is liable to lead to obsession. A middle road is one which decides upon a domain and a type of frame, selects as representative as possible a sample of each, and then literally (experimentally) forces all possible combinations to be evaluated.

As a result of our explorations and debates, we decided upon the following criteria for sampling with respect to the domain of interpersonal verbs: (1) we would use the syntactic frame which most intimately relates interpersonal verbs and some other single form class, that is, intersections of such verbs with modifying adverbs; (2) we would begin with a manageable set of interpersonal verbs and adverbs (30 x 20), try to determine by our methods their distinguishing features, and then expand the sample in subsequent experiments; (3) we would use our a priori analyses of interpersonal verb features as a basis for selecting representative samples of verbs and modifying adverbs (coded on the same features), forcing all possible combinations within the verb/adverb syntactic frame; and (4) we would use first ourselves, as reasonably sophisticated (and undoubtedly biased) English speak-

---

[23] This is a delayed response to a criticism posed "in principle" by Jerry Fodor several years ago in informal discussions.

ers, and then samples of ordinary English speakers (college sophomores) as subjects in judging the linguistic materials created in these procedures.

The trouble with trees.   George Miller, assisted by Virginia Teller and Herbert Rubenstein, has been carrying on studies designed to test the potential of empirical categorizing methods for determining similarities and differences in the meaning of words. [24] The verbal items to be classified are sorted into piles by judges, as many piles as are felt required. These sorting data are analysed by a computer program [25] that joins items under nodes progressively — first groups of items that are placed in the same piles by the most subjects and finally those placed in the same piles by the fewest subjects. Application of this procedure to 48 word-forms which could function either as nouns or as verbs in English (e.g., *kill, aid, inch, mother*), but with a "set" for nouns, yielded the tree shown here as Figure 5. Labelings of the major categories are inferential, of course, but they are similar to what I have referred to as Abstract/Concrete, with Animate/Inanimate categories under Concrete and Human/Non-human under Animate. The distinctions within the Abstract category are less familiar (Social/Personal/Quantitative). One advantage of this procedure is that the hierarchical ordering of features in terms of generality and clarity of usage comes out directly in terms of the numbers of native speakers agreeing on co-assigning items. A disadvantage, as I see it, is that the use of words in isolation rather than in syntactic frames allows this powerful syntactic factor to vary randomly. It is interesting that "when the 48 words ... were presented *as verbs* in another study, neither the object-concept distinctions appeared nor did anything else that was recognizable (Miller, 1967, p. 23)." I think that this was precisely because the semantic features of verbs depend heavily upon the syntactic frames in which they participate, and this factor does not enter into the Miller, *et al* discovery procedure.

Our own initial approach to the differentiation of interpersonal

---

[24]   I have not seen this work reported in detail as yet, but it is summarized in the Seventh Annual Report (1966-67) of the Center for Cognitive Studies at Harvard University and in Miller (1967).

[25]   See footnote 20.

Fig. 5. Results of a Cluster Analysis of 48 Nouns (Miller, Teller, and Rubenstein)

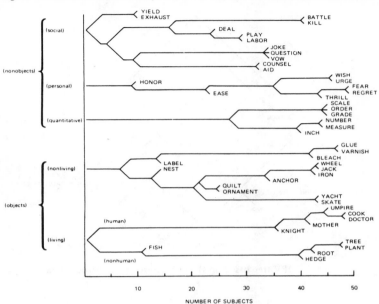

NUMBER OF SUBJECTS

verbs was also through a categorizing procedure — that described in the preceding section of this paper. It differs from Miller's in that (a) similarities among one set of items (IPVs) depend upon similarities of usage across syntactic frames involving another set of items (AVs) and (b) inter-subject agreement does not enter directly into the process — indeed, single-subject analyses are feasible and are employed. The linguistic data determining the "trees" to be reported in this section were derived from the intersection of 30 IPVs (drawn from my earlier a priori analysis) with 20 AVs (selected to give some representation to the same ten a priori features used for the IPVs). The frame was simply *IPV AV*, in all 600 possible combinations, e.g., *humiliate firmly, plead with hopefully, corrupt excitedly,* and so forth.

Figures 6 and 7 compare the IPV trees generated from the judgments of Kenneth Forster (Figure 6) and myself (Figure 7). The overall similarities in structure are apparent — for example, in the basic division into Associative (right branch) and Dissociative (left branch) behaviors and the subdivision of the latter into Immoral (*Disable,*

Fig. 6. IPV tree based on IPV/AV intersection (Forster data)

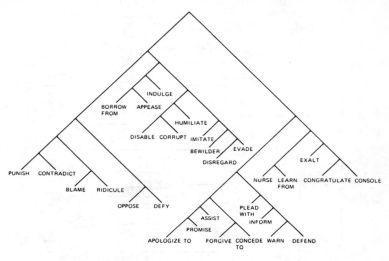

Fig. 7. IPV tree based on IPV/AV intersection (Osgood data)

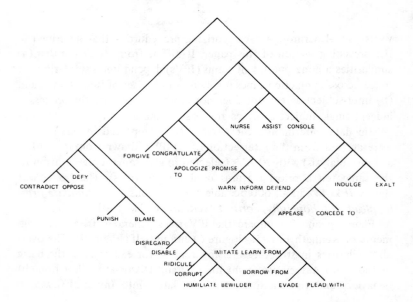

Corrupt, Humiliate, Bewilder) and Not-immoral (*Contradict, Punish, Blame, Oppose, Defy*) — but there are many fine differences. Osgood considers *Ridicule* Immoral, while Forster does not; Forster links *Borrow from, Appease, Indulge, Imitate* and *Evade* with clearly Dissociative behaviors — Osgood links them all with Associative behaviors. In discussion between us, it became apparent that some of our differences reflected either errors in our judgments or inadequacies in the method — e.g., KF's *Ridicule* not being Immoral and CO's *Evade* not being Dissociative. On the other hand, there were some real differences in our semantics, in how we thought certain verbs ought to be coded — as when for KF *Indulge, Appease, Imitate* and *Borrow from* were clearly Dissociative and somewhat Immoral interpersonal intentions, whereas for me they were clearly Associative intentions, albeit a bit tinged with immorality. Our differences on parent *Indulging* child were sharp — clearly immoral for him, clearly not for me. Perhaps it should be in the record that Forster speaks Australian English and I speak American!

What would a sample of "ordinary" English speakers tell us? We asked the graduate students in my seminar in psycholinguistics at the University of Hawaii (about 20 people) to perform the same task on the same materials. Although they were by no means "ordinary" English speakers (they included Chinese, Filipinos, Canadians and residents of Hawaii as well as students from the U.S. mainland), they produced a tree more consistent over-all than either Forster or I produced, at least in my opinion. In Figure 8, we may note some of the more interesting items: *Evade* is still Associative as it was for me, for some reason I do not fathom; the students agree with me about *Indulge* being Associative, but also with both KF and CO about *Disregard* and *Bewilder* being Immoral, which seems strange; the fact that the students use *Learn from* in a fashion similar to *Exalt* (rather than like *Nurse* by KF and like *Imitate* by CO) may simply reflect their student status. By checking the limbs, branches and twigs of the student tree against my a priori features for these verbs, it is possible to make some feature assignments: An Alter-oriented/Ego-oriented feature and an Initiating/Reacting feature appear within the Associative set, and a Moral/Immoral feature divides the Dissociative set. A careful inspection of the terminal twigs suggests that a kind of Dynamism feature (Potent and Active/Weak and Passive) is making common dis-

Fig. 8.   IPV tree based on IPV/AV intersection (subject data)

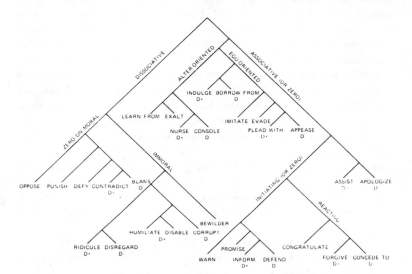

tinctions at this level, indicated in Figure 8 by the assignments of D +
and D −. This illustrates one of the troubles with trees; the lower the
order or significance of a feature, the more dispersed will be its operation over the tree and hence the more difficult it will be to identify.

As an internal check on tree categories as discovery procedures, we
decided to create an IPV tree directly from a priori feature codings.
The 20 adverbs were carefully coded on the same 10 features (e.g.,
firmly was + Potent, + Supraordinate, + Deliberate and 0 on all other
features). Then the code-strips of IPV/AV pairs were used to generate
the "judgments" of anomalous (one or more opposed codings), apposite (no opposed and one or more same codings) and permissible (no
opposed and no same codings) combinations for all 600 items. In a
sense, we were testing a "native speaker" whose semantics we knew
absolutely. Figure 9 presents the resulting tree. Here we can do a
better job of identifying features, as would be expected: the Associ-
ative/Dissociative limbs are nearly perfectly consistent with the a priori codings of the IPVs, with the single misplacement of *Evade* again.
A major subdivision of both the Associative and Dissociative limbs is

Fig. 9.   IPV tree based on a priori IPV features (Osgood)

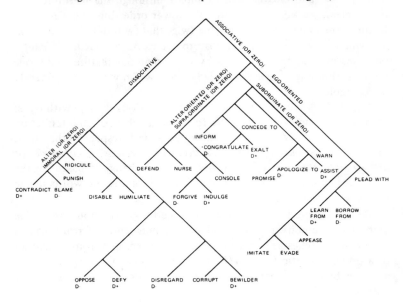

into Alter-oriented/Ego-oriented branches, and all verbs are perfectly allocated, with the single exception of *Corrupt* (which is coded as Ego-oriented as contrasted with *Seduce*, for example), but we notice that an Immoral/Not Immoral feature overlaps with Alter/Ego on the Dissociative side. The Associative Alter-oriented set is further subdivided into Supraordinate/Subordinate, and without errors. Again, inspecting the terminal twigs, we find the same dispersed Dynamism feature, indicated in the figure by D + vs. D —. However, we find no clear evidence for an Initiating/Reacting feature, for a Future-oriented/Past-oriented feature, for a Terminal/Interminal feature or for a Deliberate/Impulsive feature. Of course, these latter a priori features may well be Osgoodian fictions.

What is the trouble with trees? For one thing, it seems that very slight distinctions, if they are on a higher order feature, can override many similarities. A strictly hierarchical system may not be appropriate for finer semantic features. For another, as the a priori analysis shows, the methodology of treemaking is capable of mis-assigning items (*Evade* and *Corrupt*, for example), although the reason for this is not clear. As yet another trouble, lower order but still significant features are so dispersed among the twigs that (without already knowing what they are) they get lost to view. As a fourth difficulty, branches may be co-determined by more than one feature, and if one does not know the features already, they will not be independently discoverable.

But there is a quite different and more serious trouble with trees: even though one can derive trees for both members of an intersection (here, IPVs and AVs), each based on usage with respect to the other, *there is no rigorous way we could discover to relate the categories of one to the categories of the other*. Yet our theory is based on the notion of interaction within shared features among the words in the two sets.

Before leaving them I should say something nice about trees. The fact that an empirical tree based on the judgments of real speakers (Figure 8) matches as well as it does a tree generated from a small set of a priori semantic features (Figure 9) is very encouraging. It encourages me to believe that an empirical discovery procedure is at least possible.

Factor and feature analysis methods. Since factor analytic methods are generally familiar, they need not be detailed here. Either discrete (+1 = Apposite, 0 = Permissible, or − = Anomalous) or continuous (scaled) judgments are entered into a rectangular matrix, with columns defined, in our case, by IPVs and rows by AVs. Correlations among the columns indicate similarity of usage of the verbs (across the adverbs) and correlations among the rows indicate similarity of usage of the adverbs (across the verbs). Factor analysis serves to cluster together those verbs (or adverbs) which, as indicated by large factor loadings, share certain dominant characteristics of usage but not necessarily the same single semantic feature. By assigning the adverbs factor scores on the verb factors (or vice versa), verb and adverb usages can be directly (mathematically) related. The factor analytic measurement model assumes that codings on features are continuous, that the interactions of verb and adverb meanings on the features are algebraic, and that the weights on different features are cumulative or aggregate in determining each judgment. This method will be appropriate to the degree that the semantic system actually has these characteristics.

What kind of a measurement model is appropriate for the semantic theory Forster and I postulated as one possibility? It will be recalled that this theory assumed discrete coding on features, all-or-nothing resolutions within features for word combinations, and independence or segregation of effects across features. There appeared to be no familiar quantitative measurement model that would both satisfy these requirements and serve to relate IPV and AV features directly. So we tried to devise such a procedure from scratch. Since we never quite succeeded, even to our own satisfaction, my description will be appropriately brief.

The verb x adverb matrix of judgments of all combinations as being anomalous (−1), permissible (0) or apposite (+1) is what we call the "Target Matrix" — i.e., the pattern we wish to predict from the features "discovered" by our empirical procedure. This information is also the input to the Feature Analysis Program. The same program that generates "trees from the bottom up" is used to isolate a small number of IPVs that are maximally similar in usage (e.g., *Promise, Apologize to* and *Appease*), and these are automatically assigned + on the first Trial Feature; AVs judged apposite or anomalous with all of these verbs are assigned + or − respectively on this Trial Feature, and all others are assigned zero. Applying the same similarity procedure to the AVs, with the restriction that the AV sub-sets all have the same + or − coding as the IPV subset, all remaining IPVs are coded on the same hypothetical feature. [26]

The computer now uses this first Trial Feature to generate a Predicted IPV/AV Matrix, i.e., those judgments of each combination which, in theory, would have to be made if only this feature were involved. Obviously many errors are made, some being "patchable" (e.g., Predicted +, Target −) by subsequent features and others "unpatchable" (e.g., Predicted −, Target +, since the theory says that a single opposition is sufficient for anomaly). The computer "decides"

---

[26] We now believe selection of IPV and AV "pivots" in this manner to be a weakness in the method; not only may the verb and adverb subsets have more than one feature in common, but one of these shared features may determine the verb assignments and another the adverb assignments.

on the minimum number of changes in coding which will eliminate
the "unpatchable" errors. This series of linked programs now reiter-
ates, generating a second Trial Feature and both features are now used
simultaneously to produce another Predicted Matrix. This procedure
is continued until some criterion (e.g., less than five per cent "unpatchable" errors) is reached.

Intuitive vs. empirical features.   Throughout these studies I have used
myself as a preliminary guinea pig, executing exactly the same tasks
that the subjects would face (but not always with the prescribed
methods), and I have used my own processed data as a kind of criterion for the group results.[27] I am certainly a dedicated and, I hope,
sensitive native speaker, and, being aware of a wider variety of potential semantic features than the "ordinary" speaker, it seemed that my
own computed results could serve as a guide for interpreting and
evaluating the group results.

   If one reads a list of those IPVs loading high and low on a given
factor or feature in a computer print-out without "having a particular
feature in mind," it is usually very confusing (eg.: + *Oppose, Defy,
Corrupt, Warn, Promise, Nurse, Borrow from, Plead with; − Punish,
Blame, Ridicule, Apologize, Congratulate, Console, Concede to*). The
reason is that each word form is simultaneously coded on many features, only one of which is presumably being consistently contrasted
in the factor or feature array. If, on the other hand, one does have a
specific semantic feature in mind, the array may be sharply meaningful. (Try the feature Future-oriented/Past-oriented on the above example.) The intuitively derived solutions also serve another purpose:
they provide data against which to evaluate the empirical methodology itself. I will come back to this point.

   I am sure that some linguists and philosophers will ask: "Why
bother with empirical tests at all? Isn't your own competence as a
native speaker, coupled with your training as a scientist, a more valid
instrument for making fine discriminations among the meanings of
words than a casual (if nor bored) college sophomore?" This *may* be

---

[27]   I am not in this case referring to the a priori analysis of the semantic
features of interpersonal verbs; the latter was done explicitly as an intuitive
approach.

true, but it is also the garden path to "scholarly schizophrenia." We already have evidence in the IPV trees for Forster and Osgood that two native speakers of the same language can have honest differences in their semantic codings of words: can this not also hold for inferred features? Furthermore, as noted earlier, the intuitions of even the most sophisticated native speaker of Language A are likely to be misleading when he wades into Language B. [28] What we would prefer would be rigorous empirical discovery procedure that could be applied "blindly" to appropriate samples of linguistic data from any language and yield semantic features.

Some results to date. To obtain really ordinary native speakers of English we turned to the usual source: college sophomores taking Introductory Psychology at the University of Illinois and required to put in so many hours as subjects for experiments. (Nothing derogatory is intended here!) A somewhat modified set of 30 IPVs and an expanded set of 30 AVs were presented in all 900 possible combinations to 40 subjects, [29] along with careful instructions and examples. For each item we obtain a distribution of +, 0 and − judgments (apposite, permissible, anomalous), e.g., *Nurse rashly* (2, 15, 23), *Criticize unceasingly* (29, 11, 0), *Manipulate considerately* (5, 21, 14); although in general the modal subject judgments agreed with mine, there were some exceptions. For example, our subjects considered *Cooperate reluctantly* to be apposite (merely permissible, I would say), *Contradict unceasingly* to be apposite (I would say anomalous), *Help appreciatively* to be apposite (anomalous, I would say), and so on. A single value for each item was obtained by the following formula:

$$\frac{\text{Apposite} - \text{Anomalous}}{\text{Apposite} + \text{Permissible} + \text{Anomalous}}$$

---

[28] Within any given language, there could be a fruitful "mix" of judgments of sophisticated native speakers and empirical checks − a kind of computerized lexicography.

[29] I wish to thank Dr. Earle Davis for his help in administering this test and arranging for the data summations. Because of the length of the task, 4 groups of 40 subjects each judged 225 items. Particular appreciation is due Dr. Kenneth Forster, who made all of the computer analyses of these early IPV/AV matrices after returning to Melbourne, Australia, from Hawaii.

It was treated as a continuous variable (in factor analyses) or assigned to one of three categories (in feature analyses).

Table 6 presents the results of a Varimax rotation of the Illinois subject data; factor scores for the verbs high and low on each adverb factor are related to their a priori feature codings. Factor I is the dominant Associative/Dissociative feature; differentiated adverbs on this factor are *considerately, kindly* and *sincerely* versus *despicably* and *unfairly*. The second factor is hard to interpret on the basis of the Verb Factor Scores, but the adverb loadings make it look like a Dynamism feature (combination of Potency and Activity) — *emphatically, firmly, angrily* and *rashly* are opposed to *appreciately* and *warmly*. Factor III appears to tap the Alter vs. Ego-orientation feature: verbs *Congratulate, Concede to, Show Respect for* and *Forgive* and adverbs *appropriately, generously, sincerely* and *unwillingly* versus verbs *Compete with, Manipulate, Repel* and *Plead with* and adverbs *efficiently, desperately, successfully* and *hopefully*. Factor IV does not yield to any obvious interpretation in terms of a priori features. Factor V is probably best identified as a version of Supraordinate/Subordinate, and the unipolar adverb factor, defined by *unwillingly, submissively, reluctantly* and *timidly*, fits this interpretation. The Verb Factor Scores for VI suggest the a priori Future/Past Orientation feature (*Oppose, Defy, Hinder* vs. *Congratulate, Forgive, Show Respect*), and the adverbs of Factor VII also carry this feeling (*hopefully, resolutely, excitedly* vs. *contemptuously* and *guiltily*). The verbs on Factor VII suggest our Deliberate/Impulsive feature, but there is no confirmation in the Adverb Factor Loadings.

How did the discrete feature analysis method fare with data from ordinary native speakers? The answer, in a nutshell, is *miserably*. Not only did no identifiable features appear, but is was obvious that the program was not working. For some reason, it was the adverbs which were being assigned values while nearly all of the verbs on each feature were being turned back to zero. Various adjustments were made — in the cut-off points for assigning +1, 0 and −1 to combinations in the target matrix, in the number of unpatchable errors tolerated, and so on — but nothing came of it.

It was also at about this time we were becoming disenchanted, for other reasons, with the discrete theoretical model and measurement procedure. In our work at Illinois with the intersection of emotion

TABLE 6.   *Illinois Subject and Osgood Features Compared; Varimax Solution of 30 IPV/30 Matrix*

	Factor Scores	A Moral Immoral	B Potent Impotent	C Active Passive	D Associative Dissociative	E Initiating Reacting	F Ego- Alter	G Supra Sub	H Terminal Interminal	I Future Past	J Deliberate Impulsive
Factor I											
Congratulate	1.34	?	0	0	*		–	0	+	–	+
Help	1.31	0	0	+	+	0	–	+	0	0	0
Apologize	1.30	+	–	0	+	–	0	–	+	–	+
Forgive	1.30	+	–	0	+	–	–	+	+	–	0
Nurse	1.24	0	0	+	+	0	–	+	–	+	0
Ridicule	–1.61	–	0	+	–	–	–	+	+	–	–
Defy	–1.51	0	+	+	–	0	+	0	0	0	–
Deceive	–1.34	–	–	–	–	+	0	0	0	–	+
Corrupt	–1.31	–	0	0	–	+	–	+	–	+	+
Repel	–1.29	0	+	+	–	–	+	0	+	0	0
Factor II											
Learn from	2.17	0	0	0	0	0	+	–	0	+	+
Console	1.44	+	0	0	+	+	–	0	0	–	–
Corrupt	1.39	–	0	0	–	–	–	+	–	+	+
Show Respect for	1.22	0	0	–	+	0	–	–	0	–	–
Nurse	1.09	0	0	+	+	0	–	+	+	+	0
Forgive	1.00	+	0	0	+	–	+	0	–	+	0
Oppose	–1.86	0	+	0	–	0	+	0	–	+	0
Criticize	–1.55	0	0	+	+	–	–	+	+	–	+
Cooperate	–1.43	0	0	0	+	0	0	0	–	0	+
Disregard	–1.17	0	0	–	0	–	0	0	–	0	+
Warn	–1.16	0	0	0	–	0	–	0	–	+	0
Repel	–1.07	0	+	+	–	–	+	0	+	+	0

TABLE 6. *(continued)*

	Factor Scores	A Moral Immoral	B Potent Impotent	C Active Passive	D Associative Dissociative	E Initiating Reacting	F Ego Alter	G Supra Sub	H Terminal Interminal	I Future Past	J Deliberate Impulsive
Factor III											
Congratulate	2.20	0	0	?	+	-	*	0	+	?	+
Concede to	2.07	0	-	-	+		-	-	+	-	+
Show Respect for	2.05	0	0	0	+	0	-	-	0	-	0
Forgive	1.83	+	0	0	+	-	-	+	+	-	-
Compete with	-1.47	0	+	0	0	0	+	0	-	+	0
Manipulate	-1.32	0	0	+	0	+	+	+	0	+	0
Repel	-1.23	0	+	+	-	-	+	0	+	0	+
Plead with	-1.05	0	0	0	0	+	+	-	0	+	0
Factor IV											
Show Respect for	2.01	0	0	-	+	0	-	-	0	-	-
Learn from	1.82	0	0	0	0	0	+	0	0	+	+
Congratulate	1.47	0	0	0	+	-	-	+	+	-	+
Console	1.35	+	0	0	+	0	-	0	0	-	0
Nurse	1.26	0	0	+	+	0	+	+	-	+	-
Plead with	-1.77	0	0	0	0	+	+	-	0	+	0
Seduce	-1.60	-	+	0	0	+	+	+	-	+	+
Defy	-1.53	0	+	0	-	-	+	0	0	+	-
Apologize	-1.08	+	-	0	+	-	0	-	+	-	+
Factor V											
Apologize	1.91	+	-	0	+	-	0	*	+		+
Cooperate	1.48	0	0	0	+	0	0	-	+	0	+
Inform	1.41	0	0	0	0	+	-	0	+	0	0
Concede to	1.25	0	-	-	+	-	-	-	+	-	+

TABLE 6. *(continued)*

	Factor Scores	A Moral Immoral	B Potent Impotent	C Active Passive	D Associative Dissociative	E Initiating Reacting	F Ego Alter	G Supra Sub	H Terminal Interminal	I Future Past	J Deliberate Impulsive
Corrupt	-1.72	-	0	0	-	+	-	+		+	+
Ridicule	-1.63	-	0	+	!	!	!	+	+	.	-
Seduce	-1.62	-	0	0	0	+	+	+	-	+	+
Deceive	-1.37	-	-	-	-	0	0	0	0	0	+
Factor VI											
Oppose	1.64	0	+	0	-	0	+	0		*	0
Deceive	1.42	-	-	-	!	0	0	0	0	+	+
Defy	1.26	0	+	+	!	-	+	0	0	0	-
Hinder	1.13	0	0	0	!	+	-	0	+	+	0
Congratulate	-2.28	0	0	0	+	-	-	0	+	-	+
Forgive	-1.72	+	0	0	+	!	-	+	+	-	0
Show Respect for	-1.47	0	0	-	+	0	-	-	0		-
Factor VII											
Concede to	1.96	0	?	-	+	-		-	+	-	*
Learn from	1.51	0	0	0	0	0	+	-	0	+	+
Seduce	1.44	-	0	0	0	+	+	+	-	+	+
Oppose	-1.61	0	+	0	-	0	+	0	-	+	0
Compete	-1.61	0	+	0	0	0	+	0	-	+	0
Plead with	-1.54	0	0	0	0	+	+	-	0	+	0

nouns and modifying adjectives, it was becoming clear that factor analysis, with its continuous theoretical assumptions, did a consistently better job than feature analysis. And a colleague in mathematics demonstrated conclusively that, given the number of features we were working with and their possible combinations, the number of alternative solutions of the *same* Target Matrix was — if not infinite — very large. [30]

The *coup de grace*, empirically, for the feature analysis method was delivered by Dr. Marilyn Wilkins. Using my own a priori code-strips for 40 emotion nouns and 30 adjectives, she generated that specific Target Matrix which *had* to be consistent with these specific features and their codings, following the discrete theory described earlier. In other words, we knew that here a unique and "correct" solution was possible. A feature analysis run through 11 iterations, to equal the number of hypothesized features, accounted for 81 per cent of the Target Matrix, but the features themselves clearly did not match the a priori ones. The basic affective features (dominant in this domain) were there along with a couple of our other features and a couple of novel but interpretable ones, but the remainder were meaningless. It appears that our friend in mathematics was right.

We are left with something of a paradox. How are we to explain the fact that when applied to my own Target Matrix (but made up of judged combinations, not generated from a priori features) for the 30 IPV/20 AV intersection, the feature analysis method did just as well as, and perhaps a bit better than, the factor analysis method? [31] This may have just been coincidence, of course, the feature program yielding one of many alternative solutions that happened to match the a priori one. Or the difficulty may lie in the looseness of the procedure whereby the program determines the IPV and AV pivots to be used in assigning codings for Trial Features. We have noted that the verbs assigned to a given computed feature sometimes may reflect a different a priori feature than the adverbs assigned to it.

---

[30] We wish to thank Dr. Klaus Witz for the interest he has shown in our work and for the time he has put into trying to help us solve this problem.

[31] A number of other factor and feature analyses that were made have been omitted from this version; see original article for details (footnote added in 1973).

By way of summarizing the results obtained with these empirical discovery procedures, we may note, first, that there is reasonable consistency across testings in terms of which a priori features are "discovered" and which are not. Omitting the feature analysis of the Illinois subject data, which yielded nothing interpretable, we find that Associative/Dissociative, Supraordinate/Subordinate and Ego-oriented/Alter-oriented features come through clearly in all tests — suggesting that these characteristics of interpersonal behavior are most sharply represented in the semantics of interpersonal verbs. Moral/Immoral, Future/Past, Deliberate/Impulsive and some fusion of Potent-Active/Impotent-Passive (which I have called Dynamism) appear occasionally and less clearly. Initiating/Reacting and Terminal/Interminal never appear clearly and independently. It looks as if ordinary native speakers, when presented with interpersonal verb/adverb combinations, react primarily in terms of those features which are most salient to them in the given semantic domain. From the point of view of a performance model, this is not surprising. If, however, one wishes to determine the semantic competence of speakers, these procedures leave much to be desired.

Finally, we might ask this question: if "ordinary" speakers are given the a priori features explicitly, can they use them to differentiate the meanings of interpersonal verbs consistently among themselves and in agreement with the "expert" codings? As part of a larger study, Judith Ayer gave her subjects a scaling task, using semantic differential format but with the ten seven-step scales defined by the a priori features themselves (e.g., Initiating/Reacting, Moral/Immoral, Deliberate/Impulsive, etc.), with each of 40 IPVs to be rated by each subject on each feature-scale. Very careful instructions, definitions and examples of each a priori feature were given. This is not a discovery procedure, of course, but rather a validity test.

Our first answer comes from a factor analysis of these scaling data. Several features appeared clearly and independently: Ego/Alter, Supraordinate/Subordinate, Future/Past and, interestingly enough, for the first time Initiating/Reacting. Potency and Activity again fused into what we have called Dynamism. The dominant Associative/Dissociative feature appeared as Factor I, but it was fused with Moral/Immoral, Impulsive/Deliberate, and, particularly, a version of Reacting/Initiating — in other words, in our subjects' semantics, Associative behaviors tend to be Moral, Impulsive and Reactive, and the converse qualities characterize Dissociative behaviors.

More impressive were contingency analyses of the relations between a priori and subject scalings. Where the distributions of subject mean judgments into plus 3 and plus 2 on the scale (coded +), plus 1, zero and minus 1 (coded 0), and minus 3 and minus 2 (coded –) were sufficiently balanced, these mean judgments were used for contingency analyses; where they were highly skewed, the subjects' ratings were divided into upper, middle and lower thirds. Table 7 summarizes these analyses, reporting numbers of words (N = 40) in corresponding cells (perfect agreements in direction of coding), numbers of words in diametrically opposed cells (a priori judgments coded one sign, subjects chose the opposed sign), and significance levels. The features on which we would expect agreement – Associative/Dissociative, Ego/Alter, and Supraordinate/Subordinate – show agreement at the .001 level (i.e., one chance in a thousand of such agreement occurring by chance); but now to this group are added Initiating/Reacting and Future/ Past. Two features reach only the .05 level of significance – Potent/ Impotent and Terminal/Interminal – and one feature clearly does not show a significant relationship between a priori and subject coding – Deliberate/Impulsive. It should be noted that, with the exception of

TABLE 7. *Significance Tests for Contingency Tables Relating A Priori Codings to Subject Feature Scaling*

FEATURE	WORDS IN ++ and –– CELLS	WORDS IN +– and –+ CELLS	SIGNIFICANCE LEVEL
Moral/Immoral	10	0	*
Potent/Impotent	10	0	.05
Active/Passive	11	0	*
Associative/Dissociative	24	0	.001
Initiating/Reacting	22	0	.001
Ego/Alter Orientation	21	0	.001
Supraordinate/Subordinate	22	1	.001
Terminal/Interminal	14	0	.05
Future/Past Orientation	16	0	.001
Deliberate/Impulsive	14	3	.30 (ns.)

* Coefficients have not been computed because a priori codings were too skewed for a legitimate test.

Deliberate/Impulsive, radical disagreements in a priori and subject codings almost never occur; there is only one exception, on Supraordinate/Subordinate *Defy* is considered Subordinate by the author but Supraordinate by the subjects, and I still think I'm right!

This highly significant correspondence between a priori codings and subject scalings may, at first blush, seem rather trivial since, after all, we told them what the features were and gave them good examples. If these semantic features were explicitly tagged in word-forms (like the singular vs. plural of nouns), then, of course, this *would* be trivial. But such is not the case. Something about the meaning of the interpersonal verbs must be operating. If these interpersonal verb word-forms produced no semantic reactions which differentiate them in ways corresponding to the a priori features, then no amount of instruction and example would enable native speakers to make such fine and agreed-upon distinctions — if, for example, we asked them to apply a feature such as "being closer to or further from Paris than Boston." As for Deliberate/Impulsive, either IPVs are not coded discriminatively in such terms or our instructions and examples were inadequate. We take these results in general, then, as strong evidence for the psycholinguistic reality of most of the a priori features or close correlates of them.

A Cross-cultural Test of a Role Differential

A practical purpose behind our studies of the semantics of interpersonal verbs was to develop instruments for comparing norms of interpersonal behavior across cultures and languages. It was expected that people in different language-culture communities would share the same underlying feature system, but would differ in the weights given to features, in the codings of translation-equivalent verbs and roles, and particularly in the prescribed appropriateness of certain intentions for certain role relations. Although we had not demonstrated the universality of the IPV semantic features at the time, Hawaii seemed an ideal location in which to initiate a comparative study of role differentiation. Japanese college students in Tokyo, English-speaking college students of Japanese ancestry in Hawaii, and English-speaking college students in Illinois would serve as subjects. All possible 800 combinations of 20 IPVs and 40 role-pairs (drawn from a set of 100 used by Triandis and his associates at Illinois) would be rated. The interpersonal verbs used are listed in Table 8 and the role-pairs in Table 9.

Since 800 items constituted too long a task, eight groups of 20 subjects each rated subsets of 100 items, role-pairs and verbs being rotated against each other through the entire 800 items so that repetitions of either were maximally separated. Each item appeared as follows:

father *to defy* son

never seldom sometimes depends often usually always

The subject was instructed to circle the appropriate quantifier. In the instructions, *never* was specified as "practically zero per cent of the time," *seldom* as "from 1 to 20 per cent of the time," *sometimes* as "from 20 to 40 per cent," *depends* as from "40 to 60 per cent." Quantifiers were valued equivalently on the other side of the scale. After some discussion, it was decided to use an "actual" (how people *actually* behave toward each other) rather than an "appropriate" (how people ought to behave) [32] criterion, in the thought that ideal cultures might be overly polarized and obscure differences.

With the exception of two IPVs (*Keep at a Distance* and *Attract the Attention of*), all verbs were among those translated by Agnes Niyekawa and tested in the previously described study. [33] In the present instance we would expect translation difficulties to show up in consistent differences between Illinois-Hawaiian means (same language) and Japanese means. The greatest apparent offender is *Show Respect for*, with Japanese subjects attributing less of it to 30 of the 40 role relations; since this verb was successfully translated, we assume this is characteristic of Japanese (college student) culture — and

[32]   A subsequent comparison of the two types of instructions by Marilyn Wilkins, using Illinois subjects and only Form A (first one hundred items), suggests that this was a wise decision. The "appropriate" criterion produced greater, not lesser, item variance than the "actual" criterion, and the item means were pushed outward toward *never* or *always*, depending on the Social Desirability of the interpersonal behaviors involved.

[33]   Not reported in this shortened version; see original article (footnote added in 1973).

it is consistent with Berrien's (1966) observations. For verbs which were considered to be translation failures (*Defy* better translated as *Oppose, Criticize* better as *Blame* or *Accuse, Confide in* perhaps better as *Disclose to,* and *Concede to* perhaps better as *Compromise* or *Yield*), only *Confide in* yields consistent Illinois-Hawaiian versus Japanese differences (12/40 role-pairs) and should be considered a translation failure for present purposes. It would appear that the semantic shifts involved in *Defy* to *Oppose, Criticize* to *Blame,* and *Concede to* to *Yield* have little effect upon appropriateness judgments in role relations, even though they may influence acceptability judgments of IPV/AV combinations.

Factor analyses. To obtain an overview of the role differential data, factor analyses for both behaviors-across-roles and roles-across-behaviors were run separately for each language/culture community. Factor-matching of the first four rotated factors across cultures proved to be simple in both cases, testifying to the underlying similarities. Table 8 gives the results for interpersonal behaviors. Those IPVs having large and consistent loadings for all three cultures may be used as identifiers of the factors, and inspection of those role relations having the most extreme ratings on these IPVs — again consistently across cultures — helps to clarify the semantic quality of the factors.

Verb Factor I has its highest negative loadings on *Cooperate with*, and *Show Respect for* and its highest positive loadings on *Defy, Ridicule, Criticize* and *Hinder*; it would thus appear to be some variant of Associative/Dissociative. Factor II has its highest positive loadings on *Display Affection for, Console, Protect* and *Help*, with its only negative loading on *Keep at a Distance*; it would thus appear to be some other variant of Associative/Dissociative. However, the verbs in Factor I suggest Formal Associative relations, and the extremely rated role-pairs confirm this inference. **Patient *to* doctor, sales person *to* customer, host *to* guest, guest *to* host** and **teacher *to* student** are Formally Associative while **stranger *to* local person, old person *to* young person** and, interestingly enough, **man *to* woman** are Formally Dissociative. The verbs in Factor II suggest Intimate Associative vs. Remote Dissociative, and again the extremely rated roles confirm the inference. **Husband *to* wife, wife *to* husband** and **girl friend *to* girl friend** are distinctively Intimate while **local person *to* stranger, citizen**

TABLE 8. Rotated Factors and Variances for Interpersonal Verbs for Illinois (I), Hawaiian (H) and Japanese (J) Subjects

	I			II			III			IV		
	I (17%)	H (28%)	J (25%)	I (27%)	H (21%)	J (25%)	I (14%)	H (14%)	J (20%)	I (19%)	H (10%)	J (7%)
1. Defy	74	86	90	-06	-15	-13	08	14	-12	-49	-10	03
2. Imitate	-08	27	03	-09	-12	-18	46	59	83	-59	02	-36
3. Display Affection for	13	13	-03	88	73	83	21	18	16	-02	-28	09
4. Ridicule	72	87	72	-17	-10	-47	-05	07	02	-51	22	-16
5. Console	04	04	08	90	91	82	-25	-20	-11	-08	-11	-25
6. Corrupt	20	67	79	08	-01	07	-26	07	02	-80	-52	-23
7. Cooperate with	-60	-48	-11	48	30	75	35	51	46	14	-23	11
8. Deceive	35	55	64	-19	-38	15	41	24	02	-70	-56	-39
9. Plead with	40	26	02	53	44	-05	65	62	90	08	28	02
10. Criticize	82	76	80	-04	10	-34	-10	-15	03	-04	04	08
11. Confide in	-17	04	07	61	49	34	56	71	66	-31	-34	-52
12. Protect	-11	-29	-11	86	85	89	-11	01	-12	23	22	08
13. Hinder	50	78	68	-28	-29	-35	-12	-07	-21	-64	-20	-38
14. Show Respect for	-37	-54	-11	66	41	14	44	55	92	14	-07	06
15. Concede	-12	-20	-05	-01	-27	07	92	80	87	01	-20	19
16. Keep at a Distance	51	52	55	-77	-65	-63	-06	-11	-15	-13	17	-02
17. Compete with	17	76	51	05	-01	-17	-04	11	00	-92	-31	-70
18. Help	-46	-51	-05	79	72	89	-19	-01	01	19	07	04
19. Manipulate	21	40	66	37	26	52	-48	-43	-12	-39	-31	-08
20. Attract Attention of	-17	01	61	46	20	39	22	10	25	-29	-83	04

to **political leader** and, interestingly, **boy friend** *to* **boy friend** are consistently Remote. Most parental relations (**father** *to* **daughter** and vice versa, **mother** *to* **son** and vice versa, but not **father** *to* **son**) are rated high on both Formal and Intimate Associativeness, whereas **person** *to* **his opponent** is rated extremely negative on both factors. Appropriately enough, **employee** *to* **employer** is simultaneously Formally Associative but Remote.

Verb Factor III is clearly Supraordinate/Subordinate across all groups, although it is unipolar. *Plead with* and *Concede to* have the highest positive loadings (Subordinate) and, except for the Japanese, *Manipulate* represents the other direction. The extremely rated role-pairs confirm this identification: **father** *to* **son** and *to* **daughter, employer** to **employee, doctor** to **patient, teacher** to **student** and **political leader** *to* **citizen** are all highly Supraordinate while all of their opposite role relations (e.g., **son** *to* **father, student** *to* **teacher**) are highly Subordinate. The fourth verb factor shows the least scale consistency. The only common theme seems to be Immorality: *Corrupt, Deceive, Hinder* and *Compete with* for Illinois; *Corrupt, Deceive* and *Attract the Attention of* for Hawaii; *Compete with, Confide in* (translated as *Disclose to*), *Deceive* and *Imitate* for Japan. The role-pairs consistently differentiated by these verbs are interesting, cross-sex parental and nurturent professional being what might be called Morally Alter-oriented (**mother** *to* **son, father** *to* **daughter, son** *to* **mother, daughter** *to* **father, doctor** *to* **patient, patient** *to* **doctor,** and **teacher** *to* **student,** but *not* **student** *to* **teacher**) and various remote relations (permitting immoral behavior?) being what might be called Immorally Ego-oriented (**person** *to* **opponent, light-skinned person** *to* **light-skinned person** and **light-skinned person** *to* **dark-skinned person** — but *not* **dark-skinned person** *to* **dark-skinned person**).

Some sharp differences in verb loadings are worth noting: *Corrupt* is less Dissociative but more Immoral for Illinoians; *Cooperate with* is less Formally Associative and more Intimately Associative for Japanese; *Hinder* is more Immoral for Americans; *Show Respect for* is less Intimately Associative for Japanese but much more Subordinate; *Compete with* is more Dissociative and much less Immoral for Hawaiians, but *Attract Attention of* is distinctly Immoral for the Hawaiians as compared with the others; *Help* is less Formally Associative for the Japanese than the other groups. If one assumes that the four verb

TABLE 9.   *Rotated Factors and Variances for Interpersonal Role-pairs for Illinois (I), Hawaiian (H), and Japanese (J) Subjects*

	I			II		
	I (28%)	H (39%)	J (36%)	I (18%)	H (20%)	J (27%)
1. Father-Son	.91	.89	.94	.03	.15	.11
2. Employee-Employer	.11	.36	.20	.88	.84	.90
3. Old-Young	.85	.88	.40	-.18	-.16	.04
4. Light Skinned-Another	.11	.40	.62	-.04	-.04	.22
5. Patient-Doctor	.19	.21	-.05	.72	.84	.90
6. Host-Guest	.55	.73	.72	.30	.43	.61
7. Wife-Husband	.64	.74	.66	.22	.27	.56
8. Person-Opponent	-.28	-.36	-.38	-.00	.02	-.31
9. Mother-Son	.87	.90	.85	.11	.19	.31
10. Citizen-Policeman	.01	.17	.17	.87	.83	.78
11. Man-Woman	.75	.78	.90	-.05	-.01	.10
12. One Sister-Another	.46	.72	.89	.04	.19	.14
13. Student-Teacher	.04	.26	-.09	.95	.85	.94
14. Brother-Sister	.70	.78	.76	.02	.31	.38
15. Stranger-Local	-.32	-.23	-.10	.77	.52	.51
16. One Neighbor-Another	.41	.61	.44	.28	.39	.46
17. Sales Person-Customer	.35	.50	.46	.44	.55	.67
18. Daughter-Father	.62	.65	.50	.37	.55	.76
19. Dark Skinned-Light Skinned	-.14	.00	-.17	.36	.55	.47
20. Girl-Girl Friend	.26	.57	.32	.01	.20	.19
21. Son-Father	.33	.46	.40	.53	.56	.72
22. Employer-Employee	.72	.76	.85	.35	.39	-.13
23. Young-Old	.39	.57	.73	.54	.58	.44
24. One Dark Skinned-Another	.37	.59	.66	.02	.20	.48
25. Doctor-Patient	.77	.90	.94	.10	.18	.18
26. Guest-Host	.46	.57	.10	.53	.57	.83
27. Husband-Wife	.65	.77	.83	.07	.19	.28
28. Boy-Boy Friend	.16	.48	.45	.15	.42	.30
29. Son-Mother	.70	.76	.65	.39	.47	.65
30. Policeman-Citizen	.74	.80	.84	.20	.30	.31
31. Woman-Man	.42	.37	.32	.08	.14	.57
32. Worker-Co-Worker	.43	.54	.57	.09	.19	.73
33. Teacher-Student	.78	.85	.90	.32	.31	.06
34. Sister-Brother	.67	.81	.55	.28	.33	.66
35. Local-Stranger	.25	.32	.12	.36	.34	.17
36. One Brother-Another	.30	.59	.87	.11	.32	.03
37. Customer-Sales Person	.21	-.02	.15	.76	.72	-.23
38. Father-Daughter	.88	.93	.95	.14	.22	.18
39. Light Skinned-Dark Skinned	.06	.18	-.18	.20	.06	-.38
40. Citizen-His Political Leader	.27	.54	.19	.65	.74	.77

TABLE 9. *(continued)*

	III			IV		
	I (11%)	J (8%)	H (10%)	I (27%)	J (17%)	H (9%)
1. Father-Son	.03	-.07	-.04	.33	.24	.13
2. Employee-Employer	-.15	.00	.17	.31	.31	.05
3. Old-Young	-.10	-.15	-.58	.08	.19	-.16
4. Light Skinned-Another	.14	.14	.26	.83	.82	.53
5. Patient-Doctor	.31	.30	.25	.38	.25	.10
6. Host-Guest	.14	.12	.08	.63	.42	.00
7. Wife-Husband	.44	.22	.33	.53	.46	.32
8. Person-Opponent	-.71	-.71	-.78	-.32	-.06	-.12
9. Mother-Son	.25	.09	.19	.31	.25	.23
10. Citizen-Policeman	-.10	-.30	.10	-.06	-.12	.08
11. Man-Woman	.19	-.00	.05	.47	.47	.00
12. One Sister-Another	.23	.26	.03	.78	.48	.33
13. Student-Teacher	-.06	.02	-.11	-.05	.27	.07
14. Brother-Sister	.00	.02	-.04	.51	.10	.30
15. Stranger-Local	-.23	-.16	-.36	.05	.70	-.45
16. One Neighbor-Another	-.14	.12	.42	.82	.57	.50
17. Sales Person-Customer	-.01	-.14	.13	.42	.28	.09
18. Daughter-Father	.51	.34	.06	.31	.30	.21
19. Dark Skinned-Light Skinned	-.78	-.19	-.63	.11	.61	.10
20. Girl-Girl Friend	.06	.18	-.12	.93	.62	.83
21. Son-Father	.30	.39	.12	.60	.39	.29
22. Employer-Employee	-.42	-.26	-.14	.09	.04	-.14
23. Young-Old	.33	.30	-.14	.52	.33	.29
24. One Dark Skinned-Another	.33	.23	-.06	.80	.70	.40
25. Doctor-Patient	.12	.02	-.00	.46	.28	.16
26. Guest-Host	.09	.05	.26	.63	.49	.24
27. Husband-Wife	.30	.17	.20	.64	.47	.30
28. Boy-Boy Friend	-.09	.13	.04	.84	.43	.62
29. Son-Mother	.38	.25	.15	.31	.20	.15
30. Policeman-Citizen	-.30	-.09	-.17	.38	.18	.01
31. Woman-Man	.26	-.05	.10	.50	.58	.17
32. Worker-Co-Worker	-.12	-.06	.16	.83	.73	.19
33. Teacher-Student	-.28	-.26	-.25	-.28	.07	.17
34. Sister-Brother	.11	.08	.00	.54	.30	.42
35. Local-Stranger	-.80	-.72	-.80	.15	.23	.05
36. One Brother-Another	.03	-.24	-.09	.90	.52	.38
37. Customer-Sales Person	-.28	-.37	-.80	-.07	.06	.28
38. Father-Daughter	.17	.06	-.01	.29	.11	.13
39. Light Skinned-Dark Skinned	-.81	-.91	-.68	-.41	-.16	-.42
40. Citizen-His Political Leader	-.23	-.05	-.19	.14	.07	-.15

factors are shared (based on the sets of verbs with consistent loadings), then these differences can be interpreted as differences in semantic coding for the three cultures involved.

Commonness of interpersonal verb factors was expected and, indeed, hoped for; what was *not* expected, and not exactly hoped for in
the interest of cross-cultural comparisons, was the extraordinarily high
correspondence of role-pair factors taken across the IPVs, as evident
in Table 9. Since these factors tend to be unipolar, I will report
only the highest loading role-pairs in each case. Role Factor I identifies itself as what might be called Nurturence (Supraordinate Associativeness); culture-common role relations loading high are **father** *to*
son, mother *to* **son, employer** *to* **employee, doctor** *to* **patient, policeman** *to* **citizen, teacher** *to* **student** and **father** *to* **daughter,** and the
lowest loading roles are **stranger** *to* **local person** and **person** *to* **opponent.** Role Factor II identifies itself as what might be called Dependence (Subordinate Associativeness); culture-common role relations
are **employee** *to* **employer, patient** *to* **doctor, citizen** *to* **policeman,**
and **student** *to* **teacher.** It is notable that the **children** *to* **parents**
relations are *not* highly loaded, Factor II thus not being a mirror
image of Factor I. Factor III identifies itself neatly as an Intimacy/Re-
moteness dimension, and it is more bipolar; relatively Intimate relations for all cultures are **patient** *to* **doctor, wife** *to* **husband, husband**
to **wife, son** *to* **mother** and (excepting Japanese) **daughter** *to* **father,**
but *not* **father** *to* **daughter** or **son** nor **mother** *to* **son.** The very Remote relations are **person** *to* **opponent, local person** *to* **stranger** (but not
reverse) and **light-skinned person** *to* **dark-skinned person.** Role Factor
IV identifies itself with equal clarity as what I shall call Egalitarianism,
the high loading relations are **light-skinned person** *to* **another, one
neighbor** to **another, girl** to **girl friend, boy** to **boy friend** and **one
dark-skinned person** *to* **another** while the lowest loading relations are,
most interestingly, **light-skinned person** *to* **dark-skinned person** and
person *to* **opponent,** the former being more extreme than the latter.

Within this overall pattern of similarity, there are differences that
are both consistent and intriguing. On Nurturence (Factor I) the Japanese students see **old** *to* **young** relations as less so and **young** *to* **old** as
more so. **Man** *to* **woman, husband** *to* **wife** and **brother** *to* **another** are
also seen as more Nurturent (protective?) by the Japanese. The Illinois
subjects attribute much less Nurturence to **sister, brother** and **boy**

friend relations than the other groups, as well as to young toward old and light-skinned toward dark; only in sister to brother and citizen toward political leader do Hawaiians see more Nurturence. As to Dependence (II) differences are all on the Japanese side — wives more on husbands, women more on men, dark-skinned more on each other, hosts more on guests and workers more on co-workers; for both daughter *to* father and son *to* father relations, a trend of increasing Dependence is noticeable from Illinoians through Hawaiians to Japanese; and whereas customers are highly dependent upon sales persons for both groups of Americans, they are decidely not so for Japanese. On the Itimacy/Remoteness dimension (III), customers are extremely Remote from sales persons for Japanese, as are old from young and vice versa, as compared with the American groups. Illinoians see employers as more Remote from employees while Hawaiians, appropriately enough, see much less Remoteness between dark-skinned and light-skinned persons. The daughter toward father (but *not* son toward father) relations are progressively less Intimate from Illinoians through Hawaiians of Japanese ancestry to native Japanese.

Finally, on Egalitarianism (Factor IV) we observe a remarkably consistent trend on many role relations for Illinoians to be most Egalitarian, Hawaiians to be in the middle and Japanese to be least Egalitarian — in family relations (wife *to* husband and reverse, one sister *to* another, son *to* father) as well as social and professional relations (guest *to* host and reverse, young *to* old, sales person *to* customer, policeman *to* citizen, worker *to* co-worker and doctor *to* patient and reverse). The Hawaiian students stand out in seeing light-skinned *to* dark-skinned and the reverse as relatively *more* Egalitarian and brother at opposite poles from the Japanese in this respect regarding relations between strangers and local persons. The Japanese differ sharply from both American groups in attributing less Egalitarianism to the relation between man and woman — in both directions.
between man and woman — in both directions.

Semantics of role relations.   Do the a priori semantic features of interpersonal verbs display any consistent relations to the norms of interpersonal behavior, as inferred from the role differential? Several severe limitations of the present data must be emphasized as cautions against over-interpretation. First, the a priori features apply to American English at best, the hypothesis of universality remaining to be demonstrated. The IPV factor analyses given in Table 8 provide evidence for two types of Associativeness (Formal and Intimate), for a common Supraordinate/Subordinate feature, and perhaps for some combination of Moral and Ego/Alter features, but there is no evidence for other features. Second, the over-all similarities in the patterning of judgments about role relations across these cultures, evident in Table 9, will certainly reduce the likelihood of discovering fine differences in semantic feature assignments. And there remain, of course, questions as to the validity of some of the a priori features and the coding of IPVs on all of them.

One must also question the notion of "semantic anomaly" when applied to assertions relating role-pairs and interpersonal verbs. Since all IPVs by definition, so to speak, share higher-order codings on Transitiveness, Concreteness, Animateness and Humanness, any role subject or any role object should be semantically acceptable with any IPV. Thus **fathers** *imitate* **successful people** but not ***Pebbles** *imitate* **successful people** and sons *often defy* **fathers** but not ***Sons** *often defy* **pebbles**. Therefore it is not semantically anomalous for any role-pair to accept any IPV, and one can certainly imagine some human societies in which the assertion **fathers** *imitate* **sons** would be entirely appropriate. Nevertheless, in most human societies it is culturally "anomalous" for **fathers** *to imitate* **Sons**, and so it would appear that "cultural features" corresponding to the semantic features of interpersonal verbs have been assigned or attributed to Actor-Object role-pairs. If such is the case, then one should be able to infer the cultural features of role-pairs from the shared semantic features of the IPVs that are considered appropriate or inappropriate in association with them.

As a first step in inferring such "cultural features," all role-pairs for each culture having mean appropriateness values on verbs greater than 5.0 (i.e., judged "usually" or "always") were assigned the feature code-strips for those IPVs. They were then assigned the inverse code-strips (signs reversed) for those IPVs on which they had appropriateness values less than 3.0 (i.e., judged "seldom" or "never"). In the summation over all IPVs meeting these criteria, a ratio of 4-to-1 plus-over-minus, or the reverse, was required for assigning that coding to the role-pair on a given feature.

As could have been predicted from the factor analyses of roles, the "cultural features" of role-pairs proved to be very similar for Illinoians, Hawaiians and Japanese. A few marked differences do appear, however: **employee** *to* **employer** is + Moral For H (Hawaiian) and J̄ (Japanese), but zero for I (Illinois); **old** *to* **young** is Alter-oriented for I and J but zero for H, for whom, however, it is Impulsive; **person** *to* **opponent** is + Potent for I and H, but zero for J; **citizen** *to* **policeman** is Passive for H and J but zero for I. **Student** *to* **teacher** is Impotent, Passive and Past-oriented for J, but zero on these features for H and I; **stranger** *to* **local person** is Dissociative for I, but zero for H and J; **neighbor** *to* **neighbor** is coded Moral, Associative and Subordinate for H, but zero on these features for I and J; **daughter** *to* **father** is Initiating for I and not for H and J, but Subordinate for H and J and not for I; both **daughter** *to* **father** and **son** *to* **father** are coded Past-oriented by J, but zero by H and I; and, finally, **worker** *to* **co-worker** is not Active and Future-oriented for J, as it is for I and H, but it is Subordinate for J.

General culture differences between Illinoians, Hawaiians of Japanese ancestry and native Japanese have already been noted in connection with the verb and role factor analyses. If we think of the Hawaiians as a group in transition between two cultures, Japanese and American, we may now ask in terms of particular role-behavior norms about some of the details of this process of culture change. All 800 tri-culture sets of role pair/verb appropriateness means were inspected; any item displaying a difference equal to or larger than 0.9 scale units for any pair of cultures was assigned to one of four categories:

(I)   I = H > J Hawaiians and Illinoians more alike and differing from Japanese

(II) I > H = J Hawaiians and Japanese more alike and differing from Illinoians

(III) I > H > J progression from Illinoians to Hawaiians to Japanese

(IV) H > I = J Hawaiians differing from both American and Japanese cultures

Items in Category I presumably reflect American norms which have been largely adopted by Hawaiians of Japanese ancestry, and this constitutes the largest group of differences (150 of 800 items, or 19 per cent). Items in Category II presumably reflect Japanese norms which have tended to be preserved (42 items, or 5 per cent) and those in Category III reflect retardation in culture change (17 items, or 2 per cent). Items in Category IV presumably reflect either "overshooting" of the American norms or norms unique to the multi-racial Hawaiian situation (35 items, 4 per cent).

Clearly, the over-all picture is one of adaptation to American norms, but can we identify the regions of relatively complete and relatively retarded adaptation as well as those which appear to be uniquely Hawaiian? The differences for particular role-pairs are worthy of inspection. [34] For example: Hawaiians of Japanese ancestry are like other Americans in seeing **daughters** as *Confiding in* and *Protecting* but also *as Conceding to, not Competing with* and *not Imitating* **fathers** (generally Associative, alter-oriented behaviors); Hawaiians are more like Japanese in seeing **daughters** as *not Defying, not Pleading with, not Manipulating* and *not Displaying Affection toward* **fathers** (generally negative on Initiating, Future-oriented and Ego-oriented behaviors). Another example: Hawaiians are more like Illinoians in seeing **students** as both *Cooperating with* and *Manipulating* **teachers**, but they are more like Japanese in *Protecting* and *not Ridiculing* **teachers** as well as tending toward the Japanese in *not Deceiving, not Criticizing*, and *not Attracting the Attention of* **teachers**. And a third example: Hawaiians are like Illinoians in seeing **neighbors** as *Cooperating with, Confiding in* and *Helping* each other; they are like the Japanese in seeing **neighbors** as *not Manipulating* and *not Competing with* **each other** the way most Americans do!

Can we generalize about IPV usage across roles and see what features seem to be operating? The verbs representing behaviors shared by Illinoians and Hawaiians as against Japanese are *Console, Cooperate with, Protect, Show Respect for* and *Help*; in terms of the a priori features, these verbs would be characterized as dominantly Moral, Associative, and Alter-oriented. Verbs having the reverse pattern of appearance (i.e., behaviors tending to be shared by the Hawaiians and Japanese as against the Illinoians) are *Ridicule, Criticize, Manipulate*

---

[34] The lengthy table (# 14), in the original article is omitted here (footnote added in 1973).

and *Attract Attention*; these verbs would be characterized as sharing Active, Deliberate, Terminal and Supraordinate features. In other words, these behaviors would seem to be aspects of American culture which the Hawaiians of Japanese ancestry have *resisted* taking over. Verbs which represent behaviors perhaps most uniquely characterizing the Hawaiian culture are *Console, not Imitate, not Corrupt, not Deceive, not Criticize* and *not Compete with*; the shared semantic features of this set are interesting – Morally Associative and Alter-oriented, like other behaviors Hawaiians share with Illinoians, more Passive like the Japanese, and distinctively Impulsive (rather than Deliberate).

The only role-pairs for which there are more differentiating verbs representing Hawaiian/Japanese affinites than Hawaiian/Illinoian affinities are **father *to* son, father *to* daughter, son *to* mother, student *to* teacher, employer *to* employee** and **dark-skinned person *to* light-skinned person**. In general, there are not enough differentiating verbs in the different categories for particular role-pairs to warrant interpretation. However, it is possible to collapse the role-relations into certain components: Sex, Age, Status and Egalitarianism. The feature codings of the IPVs associated with each role-pair displaying a given component (e.g., **man *to* woman**, + sex) under each category (e.g., I = H > J) were tabulated and inspected for points of gross cultural difference.

Sex component. The +Sex role-pairs consisted of **father *to* daughter, son *to* mother, brother *to* sister, husband *to* wife** and **man *to* woman**. Illinois (I) and Hawaiian (H) subjects agree, and differ from the Japanese (J), in the attribution of behaviors to males which are Supraordinate and Past-oriented; H and J agree, and differ from I, in having Males more often display Alter-oriented behaviors; I subjects depart from both H and J in having more Male behaviors that are simultaneously Ego and Future Oriented toward Females (*Pleading, Defying, Competing, Manipulating*). The –Sex role-pairs are the reverse of the above, of course (**daughter *to* father, mother *to* son** etc.). Americans (H and I) differ from Japanese in having Females behave more Associatively but also more Supraordinately and Deliberately toward Males; H and J differ from I in having Females behave more Passively and Reactively toward Males.

Age component. The +Age role-pairs are **father** *to* **son, father** *to* **daughter, mother** *to* **son, old** *to* **young** and **teacher** *to* **student**. Americans (I and H) differ from Japanese in seeing the Old as being more Potently and Supraordinately Alter-oriented toward the Young, whereas Illinoians differ from both H and J in the tendency to attribute behaviors to the Old which are more Actively Supraordinate (e.g., *Ridiculing, Criticizing, Corrupting*). Again, it should be kept in mind that these are all *relative* differences. For the —Age role-pairs (opposites of above), Americans see the Young as being more Initiating and Deliberate toward the Old, whereas H and J agree in seeing the Young as being more Impulsive and Interminal in their relations with the Old.

Status component. The +Status role-pairs include both professional and social relations: **teacher** *to* **student, doctor** *to* **patient, employer** *to* **employee, policeman** *to* **citizen, customer** *to* **sales person** and (things being as they are) **light-skinned person** *to* **dark-skinned person**. The only marked difference here is that Illinoians see High Status persons as being less Associative in their behaviors toward Low Status persons than the other cultures. This contrast is even more marked for the —Status role-pairs, with Illinoians tending to attribute behaviors to Low Status persons which are not only less Associative but also relatively more Active, Terminal and Supraordinate. Both American groups agree, and differ from the Japanese, in seeing Low Status people as behaving more Deliberately (calculatedly?) with respect to High Status people.

Egalitarianism. This is treated as a uni-polar component. The role-pairs considered logically Egalitarian are **sister** *to* **sister, brother** *to* **brother, girl** *to* **girl friend, boy** *to* **boy friend, neighbor** *to* **neighbor, worker** *to* **co-worker, light-skinned person** *to* **light-skinned person** and **dark-skinned person** *to* **dark-skinned person**. We have already noted in the role factor analysis that Americans generally tend to attribute the most Egalitarianism to these parallel roles and Japanese the least. What about differences in the (English) a priori features of the verbs whichs distinguish the cultures for these role relations? Americans (I and H) differ from Japanese in seeing these role relations as more Moral, Active, Initiating and Ego-oriented (a more competitive Egalitarianism?); H and J agree on behaviors which are more Passive and Alter-oriented (a more cooperative Egalitarianism?); and Hawaiians stand out in attributing Morality (even more than their agreement with Illinoians), Associativeness and particularly Impulsiveness to these Egalitarian relations (*not Deceive, not Criticize, not Compete with, not Manipulate,* but *Console*).

Conclusion. This exploratory study with a Role Differential was our first attempt to fuse semantic feature analysis with cross-cultural research on interpersonal norms. It was premature, in that we have still to validate and stabilize our analysis procedures and demonstrate generality of the features derived. It is probably best construed as a methodological demonstration of what *might* be done cross-culturally with better materials. Even within these limitations, I find the results very encouraging. The verb factors — including Formal Associative/ Dissociative, Intimate/Remote, Supraordinate/Subordinate and some fusion of Morality and Ego/Alter Orientation — are very similar to those reported in related research by Triandis and his associates with American, Indian and Japanese cultures (Triandis, Shanmugam and Tanaka, 1966) and with American and Greek cultures (Triandis, Vassiliou and Nassiakou, 1968). These investigators have developed what they call a Behavioral Differential; it differs from the Role Differential, as used here, in that (a) many of the IPVs refer to observable behaviors (e.g., *throw rocks at, go to movies with*) rather than more abstract intentions and (b) there is no explicit selection of IPVs in terms of previously analysed semantic features.

Does analysis in terms of differences in semantic and "cultural" feature coding contribute in any way? Within the limitations noted earlier, many of the distinctions drawn are consistent with my own observations during a year in Hawaii and several visits to Japan. To cite examples: the greater and more competitive Egalitarianism (Active, Initiating and Ego-oriented) of the American culture as compared with the Japanese, including the American perception of low status individuals as more Dissociatively and Actively Supraordinate in their behavior toward high status individuals; the uniquely Hawaiian stress on Impulsive and Moral Associativeness among people, among equals as well as among unequals; the more Actively Supraordinate behaviors of older Americans toward younger, along with general acceptance by

Americans (but not Hawaiians and Japanese) of more overtly aggressive behaviors toward others (e.g., *Criticizing, Ridiculing, Manipulating* and the like); the greater Ego-orientation, Deliberateness and Supraordinateness of the American female toward the male — this showing up particularly in **daughter** *to* **father** relations — coupled with the American male's greater competitiveness with the female (Ego and Future-oriented); the more Passive, Impotent and Subordinate role of the Japanese student with respect to his teacher as compared with the more competitive American student.

Of course, since casual observations on "national character" have an ink-blottish and projective nature, apparent consistency of these data with my own observations does not constitute very strong evidence. On the other hand, Triandis, Shanmugam and Tanaka (1966) also report on the relatively greater supraordinateness of the Japanese male and the American female, on the "greater importance of subordination and respect in the Japanese than in the American Behavioral Differential," and on the fact that "older people may not be liked, but they are respected" by the Japanese. The potential value of linking comparative studies of interpersonal norms to the (hopefully universal) semantics of interpersonal verbs is that this can provide a standardized, stable and reasonably rigorous basis for the comparisons.

Critical Summary

As I observed early in this paper (pp. 171, 187), the appropriate method of analysis of a semantic domain depends upon how that domain is "in truth" organized. One of the difficulties of research in this area is that we do not know on a priori grounds how particular domains are arranged — and worse, we have good reasons to suspect that different domains are quite differently and even inconsistently arranged. To get an idea of at least some of the possibilities, observe the five "types" of possible semantic systems described in Figure 10. Only three variables are treated here: *nested* vs. *replicated* features, *ordered* vs. *unordered* features, and *independent* vs. *dependent* (or *contingent*) features. Many other variables could have been considered: unipolar vs. bipolar feature systems (items being marked or unmarked rather than + or −), binary vs. trinary vs. continuous feature systems, and so forth.

The Type I system (nested, ordered, independent) is called a "taxonomic hierarchy," I believe. It is the only nested system given, for nesting presupposes both hierarchical ordering and independence of

Fig. 10. Some Types of Semantic Systems*

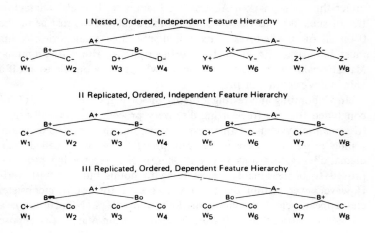

* All letters except W (word) and F (feature) refer to specific semantic features.

features (because either B+ or B− can only occur when A is +, B cannot be correlated with A). This is the most constrained system. Only when the higher-order feature has been determined does it make sense to ask about any lower-order feature; only when a term is marked as Concrete (rather than Abstract) does it make sense to ask if it is Animate or Inanimate, only when it has been marked Animate does it make sense to ask if it is Animal or Vegetable, and so forth down the nested hierarchy. Furthermore, each distinguishing feature appears only once in the system, e.g., Animal/Vegetable cannot appear anywhere under the nodes marked Abstract or Inanimate. It is also characteristics of such systems that all supraordinate categories must be marked 0 on all of the features of its nested subordinate categories; Animal must be marked 0 on Vertebrate/Invertebrate, Human/Non-human, Male/Female and so forth — which is why it is reasonable to ask if an animal is Vertebrate or Invertebrate, etc.

In elaborating and testing a theory of sorting, George Miller (1968) concluded that his free-sorting discovery procedure was ideally suited to semantic systems of this nesting type, but that multi-dimensional scaling procedures were more appropriate for what he called "paradigmatic" organizations (Type IV here). His free sorting procedure proved to be reasonably successful with nouns but not with verbs. However, even within the taxonomic system for nouns, inconsistencies appear below the node marked Human (vs. Non-Human): although a Married/Single feature is nested within Mature (as opposed to Immature), Mature/Immature can be asked sensibly about either Male or Female and vice versa, so both nesting and hierarchical ordering principles are violated.

In Type II systems (replicated, ordered, independent) each semantic feature is applicable to all terms (W_1 through W_8 in the diagrams), but the *order* in which decisions are made must be maintained. In the pure or ideal case, it would be absurd to ask if a word was B+ or B− before deciding whether it was A+ or A−. In a sensitive intuitive analysis, Vendler (1967, Ch. 4) derives a two-feature system of this type for English verbs with respect to the time dimension. The supraordinate feature is Action vs. State: one can say significantly *I am pushing it* (Action verb), but it is strange to say *I am knowing it* (State verb); conversely, one can answer the question *Do you know...?* sensibly by saying *I do*, but there seems to be no sensible answer to the question *Do you push...?* The subordinate feature is Terminal vs. Interminal (my terms, not Vendler's): one can reasonably ask *How long did it take to dress?* (Terminal Action verb) but not really *For how long did you dress?* The situation is the reverse for *push* (an Interminal Action verb). Similarly, one can ask *At what time did you meet the girl?* (Terminal State verb) but not really *For how long did you meet the girl?* The situation is likewise the reverse for *know* (an Interminal

State verb). Although there are some verbs with fuzzy edges (by virtue of having several senses), as Vendler acknowledges, these features seem necessary, if not sufficient, for the semantic characterization of verbs-in-general [35] Vendler refers to the four verb categories established by these features as "Activities" (Interminal Actions), "Accomplishments" (Terminal Actions), "Achievements" (Terminal States) and "States" (Interminal States). Note that one cannot decide on the appropriate Terminal/Interminal questions until he has answered the Action/State question — hence the ordered, hierarchical nature of the system.

In "pure" systems of Types I and II, the basis of ordering is logical inclusion. However, there may also be ordering on the basis of psychological salience, and the latter clearly plays some role in the semantics of interpersonal verbs. Throughout all the analyses reported in this chapter the Associative/Dissociative feature has been the dominant mode for characterizing interpersonal verbs, this typically being followed by Supraordinate/Subordinate and Ego-orientation/Alter-orientation. The other features, to the extent that they appear at all — Morality, Dynamism, Terminality, Time-orientation and the like — seem to merely refine the basic semantic categories already established. What is not clear is the performance implications of psychological salience as compared with logical inclusion. Whereas "inclusion" would definitely imply temporal ordering of decisions, "salience" could merely imply differences in the weights or generalities of features.

The Type III semantic system shown in Figure 10 (replicated, ordered, dependent) differs from Type II in that the features are not independent of each other. To illustrate the situation as diagrammed, an interpersonal verb must be Associative (+A) if it is to be Subordinate (−B) and Dissociative (−A) if it is to be Supraordinate (+B), and it must be both Associative and Subordinate (+A, −B) if it is to be Moral (+C) or both Dissociative and Supraordinate (−A, +B) if it is to be Immoral (−C). This situation is approximated by our data, but

---

[35]   In asking these questions of a sample of 40 of our interpersonal verbs, I find a nearly perfect correlation of Vendler's Action vs. State with our Active/Passive feature and of his Definite (*the* time stretch or instant) vs. Indefinite (*a* or *any* time stretch) with our Terminal/Interminal feature.

only approximated; for example, IPV *Seduce* is Supraordinate and Immoral but not Dissociative and IPV *Defy* is clearly Dissociative but neither Supraordinate nor Immoral. Note that this kind of system, in its extreme form, resembles the nested hierarchy, but the "limbs" of subordinate features are bifurcated, and separated within the tree. Any correlational discovery procedure will tend to fuse such dependent features into single factors — in the present case, an Associative-Subordinate-Moral vs. Dissociative-Supraordinate-Immoral factor. Yet, logically speaking, three distinct features are operating, the lower ones in the hierarchy serving to further distinguish terms already grossly distinguished by the higher features.

If a semantic system is unordered, then any "tree" diagram is both arbitrary and misleading. The unordered system instead must be represented by a Feature-By-Term Matrix or, equivalently, by an N-Dimensional Spatial Model, in which the features are dimensions and the terms are locations. In the Type IV semantic system (replicated, unordered, independent), the features are uncorrelated and the dimensions are orthogonal; in the Type V system (replicated, unordered, dependent), the features are correlated and the dimensions are oblique with respect to each other. For simplicity of exposition, in the diagrams in Figure 10 I have assumed discreteness in coding, although I am sure this is not the general situation in semantics. Such discreteness gives a simplistic system toward which behavioral principles may tend, but only occasionally reach. It should be noted that my own representational mediation theory of meaning (in which the meaning of a sign is that simultaneous "bundle" of distinctive mediating reaction components elicited by the sign, termed its r_M) implies an unordered system although it does not rule out differences in salience and does not make any assumptions about discrete vs. continuous coding.

Pure Type IV systems (features independent) seem to be rare in semantics — at least I cannot think of any. I believe the Turkish vowel phonemic system is of this type; three distinctive phonetic features (tongue high/tongue low, tongue front/tongue back, lips rounded/lips flat) generate a complete eight-phoneme system, neatly representable as the corners of a cube. Our affective E-P-A (Evaluation, Potency, Activity) system approximates this, but E has much more weight than P and A. Kinship systems ("paradigmatic" according to Miller, 1968) approximate Type IV, but again usually imperfectly. The American

English kinship system, for example, is unordered in the sense that questions about Sex (Male/Female) seem to have no logical priority over questions about Generation (+Ego, 0 Ego, −Ego) or Consanguinity (Blood-related/Blood-non-related). Furthermore, it is replicated, in the sense that one may ask about the Sex of any Generationally defined member (and vice versa), about the Generation of any Consanguinally defined member (and vica versa), and so on. But questions about Lineality ("Is X in my lineage or not? My *mother* is but my *aunt* is not.") only make sense when Consanguinity has already been determined to be positive. Therefore this kinship system is partially nested, and hence neither perfectly unordered nor perfectly replicated.

The Type V system (features to various degrees dependent or correlated) probably holds for many semantic systems, and it greatly complicates empirical discovery procedures. Features A and B, as distributed in Figure 10 (V), are highly correlated, as are features B and C; features A and C, on the other hand, are independent (zero correlation). Only an oblique factor analysis (or feature analysis) would "discover" the three underlying features, and oblique analyses are difficult to interpret in my experience. The results of all of our studies suggest this Type V system, with "fused" rather than independent features, but nothing readily interpretable has emerged from oblique factor analyses. However, the data also clearly imply a system partially ordered in terms of the psychological salience of the features.

In sum, it would appear that the semantic system for interpersonal verbs (1) is not nested, (2) is partially replicated (features applying to all terms only when zero codings are allowed), (3) is partially ordered (but in terms of psychological salience rather than logical inclusion), and (4) is partially dependent (with features correlated in usage to various degrees). This is obviously not the neatest kind of system to study.

Not only is a particular empirical discovery procedure appropriate to a semantic domain of a particular type, but when it is applied to a domain of a *different* type it will tend to force the data toward correspondence with the system for which it is appropriate. Fortunately, our intuitions as native speakers enable us to note the absurdities which must result. Thus when Miller's free sorting procedure was applied to verbs it necessarily yielded a "nested" system, but not apparently an intuitively satisfying one. Miller did not present these results because, as he said (1967), "I do not yet understand them." And thus when our factor and feature analytic procedures, which are most appropriate for a pure Type IV paradigmatic system, are applied, they do yield independent factors, but when these factors are compared with the a priori features it becomes clear that the semantic system of interpersonal verbs is not of this straightforward type either.

The resolution is at once obvious and complicated: *restrict the semantic domain under study to a pure type of system and then apply the appropriate discovery procedure.* If the domain is even partially ordered by logical inclusion (Types I, II, and III), then one must ask first questions first à la Vendler and thereby divide the domain into subdomains, all of which are at the same hierarchical level and each of which contains terms with the same supraordinate features. If these subdomains do include more than one term and they are not synonymous (which seems most likely for the major form classes), then multivariate procedures of the sort we have employed should be appropriate for the discovery of finer semantic feature distinctions. In part, this is what we did by restricting our domain to interpersonal verbs — a subdomain of verbs defined by the sharing of certain higher-order features.

Working in the domain of adjectives, and applying the three-mode factoring method developed by Ledyard Tucker (1966), John Limber [36] has made such a serial approach explicit. The three modes were sentence frames (N = 10), nouns (N = 10) and adjectives (N = 50). The sentence frames were deliberately selected to differentiate the major types of adjectives in terms of syntactic derivation, e.g.:

(1) The N that they did it was A.
(2) It was A of the N to do it.
(3) The N was A about something.

The nouns were deliberately selected to represent major semantic categories, e.g., *man, horse, team, tree, computer, pebble, fact.* Simple acceptability judgments of each of the 5,000 possible combinations *(The fact that they did it was obvious; The computer that they did it*

---

[36] *Semantic Categorization of English Adjectives in Terms of Usage.* Doctoral dissertation, University of Illinois, August, 1968.

was happy, and so forth) and their latencies were obtained. Three frame factors account for a large share of the variance, and these do seem to tap higher-order semantic features. Frames 2 and 3 above, for example, both load on a factor requiring Animate subjects; for most speakers, it was absurd to say *It was A of the (tree, fact, gravity* — but not *computer) to do it*, but frame 3 accepts mental state adjectives (like *happy*) whereas frame 2 does not. However, *within* frames which accept particular nouns (with certain adjectives) and particular adjectives (with certain nouns), it is apparent that semantic interactions *between* these nouns and adjectives serve to further differentiate them. *The horse was happy about something* and *The man was strict about something* are both acceptable, but *The horse was strict about something* is clearly absurd. By analysis of usage distributions within the sub-domains defined by such sentence frames it would seem possible to get at lower-level semantic features. The problem, of course, is to select those frames ("questions") which reliably differentiate higher-order features and have complete generality of application across the domain in question. Limber was guided in his selections by a great deal of prior linguistic spade-work.

Similar spade-work is required in the domain of interpersonal verbs. Much of it already has been done for verbs-in-general by linguists and philosophers or ordinary language, as exemplified by Vendler (1967) and Fillmore (1967). The features distinguished obviously relate to what is now referred to as the "deep" structure of the syntactic component, and I wonder how long it will be before the deep structure of the syntactic component and the semantic component become identified as the same thing. Fillmore seems to be thinking along similar lines when he includes among his closing words the following statement (p. 110): "If it is possible to discover a semantically justified universal syntactic theory along the lines I have been suggesting; if it is possible by rules, beginning, possibly, with those which assign sequential order to the underlying representations, to map these 'semantic deep structures' into the surface forms [37] of

---

[37] Precisely such a sequentially ordered scanning of a hierarchically ordered semantic system has been suggested by James E. Martin as an explanation of pre-nominal adjective ordering in the surface structure of English in his doctoral dissertation, *A Study of the Determinants of Preferred Adjective order in English*. University of Illinois, July, 1968.

sentences; then it is likely that the 'syntactic deep structure' of the type that has been made familiar from the work of Chomsky and others is going to go the way of the phoneme." There is also a question as to whether the universals we have been discovering — certainly in the domain of affect and apparently as well in the domain of interpersonal behavior as reflected in language — are properly to be considered a part of semantics or a part of pragmatics. But questions like these go far beyond the scope of this paper.

REFERENCES

Abelson, R. P., and Sermat, V.
1962   Multidimensional scaling of facial expressions. *Journal of Experimental Psychology, 63*, 546-554.

Allport, F. H.
1924   *Social psychology*. Cambridge, Massachusetts: Houghton-Mifflin.

Berrien, F. K.
1966   Japanese values and the democratic process. *Journal of Social Psychology, 68*, 129-138.

Birdwhistell, R. L.
1960   Kinesic analysis in the investigation of the emotions (paper presented to the American Association for the Advancement of Science).

Boring, E. G., and Titchener, E. E.
1923   A model for the demonstration of facial expression. *American Journal of Psychology, 34*, 471-486.

Burt, C.
1948   The factorial study of temperamental traits. *British Journal of Psychology, Statistical Section, 1*, 178-203.

Cantril, H.
1965   *The pattern of human concerns*. New Brunswick, New Jersey: Rutgers University Press.

Carroll, J. B.
1959   Book review of C. E. Osgood, G. J. Suci, and P. H. Tannenbaum, *The measurement of meaning. Language, 35*, 58-77.

Chomsky, N.
1959   Review of B. F. Skinner, *Verbal Behavior. Language, 35*, 26-58.
1965   *Aspects of the theory of syntax*. Cambridge, Massachusetts: The M.I.T. Press.

Darwin, C.
1872   *Expression of the emotions in man and animals*. London: Murray.

deRivera, J.
1961   A decision theory of the emotions. (doctoral dissertation, Stanford University).

Ekman, G.
1955   Dimensions of emotion. *Acta Psychologica, 11*, 279-288.

Ekman, P.
  1965   The differential communication of affect by head and body cues;
            a test of Schlosberg's theory of emotion. (mimeo draft, privately
            distributed).
Engen, T., Levy, N., and Schlosberg, H.
  1957   A new series of facial expressions. *American Psychologist, 12*,
            264-266.
  1958   The dimensional analysis of a new series of facial expressions.
            Journal of Experimental Psychology, 55, 454-458.
Festinger, L.
  1957   *A theory of cognitive dissonance*. Evanston, Illinois: Rowe, Peter-
            son.
Fillmore, C. J.
  1967   The case for case. Ohio State University (Austin, Texas), (mimeo).
  1968   The case for case. In *Universals in linguistic theory*, E. Bach and
            R. Harms (Eds). New York: Holt, Rinehart and Winston.
Fodor, J. A.
  1965   Could meaning be an r_m? *Journal of Verbal Learning and Verbal
            Behavior, 4*, 37-81.
  1966   More about mediators: a reply to Berlyne and Osgood. *Journal of
            Verbal Learning and Verbal Behavior, 5*, 412-415.
Frijda, N. H., and Philipszoon, E.
  1963   Dimensions of recognition of expression. *Journal of Abnormal and
            Social Psychology, 66*, 45-51.
Gladstones, W. H.
  1962   A multidimensional study of facial expression of emotion. *Austra-
            lian Journal of Psychology, 14*, 95-100.
Harris, Z. S.
  1954   Distributional structure. *Word, 10*, 146-162.
Harrison, R., and MacLean, M. S.
  1965   Facets of facial communication. (mimeo, Michigan State Univers-
            ity).
Hastorf, A. H., Osgood, C. E., and Ono, H.
  1966   The semantics of facial expression and the prediction of the mean-
            ings of stereoscopically fused facial expressions. *Scandinavian
            Journal of Psychology, 7*, 179-188.
Heider, F.
  1946   Attitudes and cognitive organization. *Journal of Psychology, 21*,
            107-112.
  1958   *The psychology of interpersonal relations*. New York: Wiley and
            Sons.
Howes, D., and Osgood, C. E.
  1954   On the combination of associative probabilities in linguistic con-
            texts. *American Journal of Psychology, 67*, 241-258.

Jakobson, R.
    1959   Boas' view of grammatical meaning. *American Anthropologist, 61*,
            139-145.
Jakobson, R., and Halle, M.
    1956   *Fundamentals of language.* 'sGravenhage (The Hague), Nether-
            lands: Mouton.
Johnson, S. C.
    1967   Hierarchical clustering schemes. *Psychometrika, 32*, 241-254.
Karwoski, T. F., Odbert, H. S., and Osgood, C. E.
    1942   Studies in synesthetic thinking: II. The roles of form in visual
            responses to music. *Journal of General Psychology, 26*, 199-222.
Katz, Evelyn W.
    1964a   A content-analytic method for studying interpersonal behavior.
            Technical Report No. 19, Urbana Illinois: Group Effectiveness Re-
            search Laboratory, University of Illinois.
    1964b   A study of verbal and nonverbal behaviors associated with social
            roles. Technical Report No. 20, Urbana, Illinois: Group Effective-
            ness Research Laboratory, University of Illinois.
Kumata, H., and Schramm, W.
    1956   A pilot study of cross-cultural methodology. *Public Opinion Quar-
            terly, 20*, 229-238.
Kuusinen, J.
    1969   Affective and denotative structures of personality ratings. *Journal
            of Personality and Social Psychology, 12*, 181-188.
Landis, C.
    1924   Studies of emotional reactions: II. General behavior and facial
            expression. *Journal of Comparative Psychology, 4*, 447-509.
Lees, R. B.
    1953   The basis of glottochronology. *Language, 29*, 113-127.
Limber, J.
    1968   Semantic categorization of English adjectives in terms of usage.
            (doctoral dissertation, University of Illinois).
Martin, J. E.
    1968   A study of the determinants of preferred adjective order in English.
            (doctoral dissertation, University of Illinois).
Miller, G. A.
    1967   Psycholinguistic approaches to the study of communication. In
            Journeys in science: small steps − giant strides, D. L. Arm (Ed.).
            Albuquerque, New Mexico: University of New Mexico Press.
    1968   A psychological method to investigate semantic relations. (prepub-
            lication draft, The Rockefeller University, pp. 39).
Mosier, C. I.
    1941   A psychometric study of meaning. *Journal of Social Psychology,
            13*, 123-140.

Moss, C. S.
1970   *Dreams, images, and fantasy.* University of Illinois Press.
Munn, N. L.
1940   The effect of knowledge of the situation upon judgment of emotion from facial expressions. *Journal of Abnormal and Social Psychology, 35,* 324-328.
Noble, C. E.
1952   An analysis of meaning. *Psychological Review, 59,* 421-430.
Nummenmaa, T.
1964   The language of the face. *Jyväskylä Studies in Education, Psychology and Social Research,* Jyväskylä: Jyväskylän Yliopistoyhdistys.
Nummenmaa, T., and Kauranne, U.
1958   Dimensions of facial expression. *Reports of the Department of Psychology,* University of Jyväskylä.
Osgood, C. E.
1946   Meaningful similarity and interference in learning. *Journal of Experimental Psychology, 36,* 277-301.
1952   The nature and measurement of meaning. *Psychological Bulletin, 49,* 197-237.
1955   Fidelity and reliability. In *Information theory in psychology,* H. Quastler, (Ed.). Glencoe, Illinois: The Free Press.
1960   Cognitive dynamics in human affairs. *Public Opinion Quarterly, 24,* 341-365.
1962   Studies on the generality of affective meaning systems. *American Psychologist, 17,* 10-28.
1964   Semantic differential technique in the comparative study of cultures. *American Anthropologist, 66,* 171-200.
1966a   Dimensionality of the semantic space for communication via facial expressions. *Scandinavian Journal of Psychology, 7,* 1-30.
1966b   Meaning cannot be an r_m?
        Journal of Verbal Learning and Verbal Behavior, 5, 402-407.
1969   On the whys and wherefores of E, P, and A. *Journal of Personality and Social Psychology, 12,* No. 3, 194-199.
1970a   Speculation on the structure of interpersonal intentions. *Behavioral Science, 15,* 3, 237-254.
1970b   Interpersonal verbs and interpersonal behavior. In *Studies in thought and language,* J. L. Cowan, (Ed.). Tucson, Arizona: The University of Arizona Press.
1971   Exploration in semantic space: a personal diary. *Journal of Social Issues, 27,* 4, 5-64.
1974   Exploration in semantic space: a personal diary. In *The Psychologists,* T. S. Krawiec, (Ed.). Oxford University Press, in press. (different version.)
1974   Probing subjective culture. *Journal of Communications, 24,* 1, 21-34; *24,* 2, 82-100.

Osgood, C. E., Allen, C. N., and Odbert, H. S.
  1939   Separation of appeal and brand-name in spot radio advertising. *Journal of Applied Psychology, 23*, 60-75.
Osgood, C. E., and Luria, Zella.
  1954   A blind analysis of a case of multiple personality using the semantic differential. *Journal of Abnormal and Social Psychology, 49*, 579-591.
Osgood, C. E., May, W. H., and Miron, M. S.
  1975   *Cross-cultural universals of affective meaning.* Urbana, Illinois: University of Illinois Press.
Osgood, C. E., and Suci, G. J.
  1952   A measure of relation determined by both mean difference and profile information. *Psychological Bulletin, 49*, 251-262.
Osgood, C. E., Suci, G. J., and Tannenbaum, P. H.
  1957   *The measurement of meaning.* Urbana, Illinois: University of Illinois Press.
Osgood, C. E., and Tannenbaum, P. H.
  1955   The principle of congruity in the prediction of attitude change. *Psychological Review, 62*, 42-55.
Osgood, C. E., Ware, E. E., and Morris, C.
  1961   Analysis of the connotative meanings of a variety of human values as expressed by American college students. *Journal of Abnormal and Social Psychology, 62*, 62-73.
Osgood, C. E., and Wilson, K. V.
  1961   Some terms and associated measures for talking about human communication. (mimeo, Institute of Communication Research Publication, University of Illinois).
Piderit, T.
  1859   *Mimik und Physiognomik.* Detmold: Meyers.
Roget, P. M.
  1941   *Roget's thesaurus,* 1941 Edition. New York.
  1963   *Roget's college thesaurus.* New York: New American Library.
Ryle, G.
  1938   Categories. *Proceedings of the Aristotelian Society, 38*, 189-206.
Schlosberg, H.
  1941   A scale for the judgment of facial expressions. *Journal of Experimental Psychology, 29*, 497-510.
  1952   The description of facial expressions in terms of two dimensions. *Journal of Experimental Psychology, 44*, 229-237.
  1954   Three dimensions of emotion. *Psychological Review, 61*, 81-88.
Sherman, M.
  1927   The differentiation of emotional responses in infants: I. Judgments of emotional responses from motion pictures views and from actual observation: II. The ability of observers to judge emotional characteristics of the crying infants and of the voice of an

adult. *Journal of Comparative Psychology, 7,* 265-284, 335-351.

Stagner, R., and Osgood, C. E.
1941　An experiment analysis of a nationalistic frame of reference. *Journal of Social Psychology, 14,* 403-418.
1946　Impact of war on a nationalistic frame of reference: I. Changes in general approval and qualitative patterning of certain sterotypes. *Journal of Social Psychology, 24,* 187-215.

Suci, G. J.
1960　A comparison of semantic structures in American Southwest culture groups. *Journal of Abnormal and Social Psychology, 61,* 25-30.

Swadesh, M.
1950　Salish internal relationships. *International Journal of American Linguistics, 16,* 157.

Thigpen, C. H., and Cleckley, H.
1954　A case of multiple personality. *Journal of Abnormal and Social Psychology, 49,* 135-151.

Thompson, D. F., and Meltzer, L.
1964　Communication of emotional intent by facial expression. *Journal of Abnormal and Social Psychology, 68,* 129-135.

Thurstone, L. L.
1947　*Multiple-factor analysis.* Chicago: University of Chicago Press.

Tomkins, S. S., and McCarter, R.
1964　What and where are the primary affects? Some evidence for a theory. *Perceptual Motor Skills, 18,* 119-158.

Torgerson, W. S.
1958　*Theory and methods of scaling.* New York: Wiley.

Triandis, H. C., and Lambert, W. W.
1958　A restatement and test of Schlosberg's theory of emotion with two kinds of subjects from Greece. *Journal of Abnormal and Social Psychology, 56,* 321-328.

Triandis, H. C., Shanmugam, A. V., and Tanaka, Y.
1966　Interpersonal attitudes among American, Indian and Japanese students. *International Journal of Psychology, 1,* 177-206.

Triandis, H. C., Vassiliou, Vasso, and Nassiakou, Maria.
1968　Three cross-cultural studies of subjective culture. *Journal of Personality and Social Psychology,* Monographed Supplement, *8,* No. 4, Part 2, p. 42.

Tucker, L. R.
1951　A method for synthesis of factor analysis studies. *Department of Army, Personnel Research Section Report,* No. 984, p. 43.
1966　Some mathematical notes on three-mode factor analysis. *Psychometrika, 31,* 279-311.

Tuomela, R.
1973　A psycholinguistic paradox and its solution. *Ajatus, 35,* 124-139.

Tzeng, O.
   1972   Differentiation of affective denotative meaning system in personal-
           ity rating via three mode factor analysis. (doctoral dissertation,
           University of Illinois).
Vendler, Z.
   1967   *Linguistics in philosophy*. Ithaca, New York: Cornell University
           Press.
Woodworth, R. S.
   1938   *Experimental psychology*. New York: Holt.
Woodworth, R. S., and Schlosberg, H.
   1954   *Experimental psychology*. New York: Holt.
Wrigley, C., and McQuitty, L. L.
   1953   The square root method of factor analysis. (mimeo, Department
           of Psychology, University of Illinois).

INDEX OF AUTHORS AND SUBJECTS